ENVISIC

Envisioning the Empress illuminates dynamic and powerful empresses who impacted not only women in their own time but whose influence extended to later generations of royalty, creating a greater role for imperial women and elevating the status of women's roles at a crucial juncture in Japanese history. The central focus of this book is visual monarchy, exploring how the empress' biographies were primarily expressed in visual culture and how their images worked in support of Japan's imperial policies in the late nineteenth and early twentieth centuries. The book begins with a brief overview of premodern and modern imperial women to orient the reader. In each chapter, different media, audiences, and distribution channels for constructing the narrative of feminine imperial power in Japan are addressed alongside biographical information. It is argued that the ultimate purpose of all of these images was to elevate the empress and promote her image as a conventional role model for modern women, but one with enough celebrity cache to maintain popularity. The images of the modern empresses, as distributed by the Imperial Household Agency, strike a balance between propaganda and popular media, noble philanthropist and upper-middle class role model, celebrity and mother of the nation. The modern empress image was crafted to be both exalted and approachable and worked to establish individual biographies while simultaneously establishing the position of the empress as timeless in the public eye. *Envisioning the Empress* introduces students of royal studies as well as modern Japanese history and art history to this fascinating element of the history of monarchy and women's history more broadly.

Alison J. Miller is Associate Professor of Art History at the University of the South (Sewanee). Her scholarship focuses on images of women across visual media in modern Japan. She is co-editor of *The Visual Culture of Meiji Japan: Negotiating the Transition to Modernity* (2021) and *Transposed Memory: Visual Sites of National Recollection in 20th and 21st Century East Asia* (2024).

Lives of Royal Women

Series Editors:- Elena Woodacre
Ellie.Woodacre@winchester.ac.uk
Louise Wilkinson
LWilkinson@lincoln.ac.uk

This series features academic, yet accessible biographies of royal women—consorts, dowagers, royal mothers and female sovereigns—inclusive of all periods, cultures and geographic regions. These biographies include a deep engagement with the premise of queenship studies and the exercise of the queen's office (or equivalent), in addition to covering the lives of particular women. The series is divided into three sub-strands: Queens of England (blue), Queens and Empresses of Europe (purple), and Royal Women of the World (red).

Early English Queens, 850–1000
Potestas Reginae
Matthew Firth

Berengaria of Navarre
Queen of England, Lord of Le Mans
Gabrielle Storey

The Queens and Royal Women of Sweden, 970–1330
Their Lives, Power, and Legacy
Caroline Wilhelmsson

Envisioning the Empress
The Lives and Images of Japanese Imperial Women, 1868–1952
Alison J. Miller

ENVISIONING THE EMPRESS

The Lives and Images of Japanese Imperial Women, 1868–1952

Alison J. Miller

Routledge
Taylor & Francis Group
LONDON AND NEW YORK

Designed cover image: A Garden Refreshed by the Passing Rain (Ukasentei no zu), Toyohara (Yōshū) Chikanobu, 1888, multicolor woodblock print, Metropolitan Museum of Art.

First published 2025
by Routledge
4 Park Square, Milton Park, Abingdon, Oxon OX14 4RN

and by Routledge
605 Third Avenue, New York, NY 10158

Routledge is an imprint of the Taylor & Francis Group, an informa business

British Library Cataloguing-in-Publication Data
A catalogue record for this book is available from the British Library

ISBN: 978-1-032-45175-6 (hbk)
ISBN: 978-1-032-45237-1 (pbk)
ISBN: 978-1-003-37610-1 (ebk)

DOI: 10.4324/9781003376101

Typeset in Sabon
by Apex CoVantage, LLC

For my family

CONTENTS

ACKNOWLEDGMENTS

Writing a book is primarily a solitary project but one done in community, and I am grateful to have been surrounded by some exemplary people throughout this process. Before this was a book, it was a dissertation. My graduate school experience at the University of Kansas and the devoted members of my dissertation committee nurtured me in the early stages of research and writing and provided critical feedback and editing throughout. Maki Kaneko, Sherry Fowler, and David Cateforis gave countless hours of support in those early days. Michiko Ito, Kate Meyer, Halle O'Neal, Ashley Elston, Lara Kuykendall, and Emily Ryan were of a great help during my time in Lawrence, providing guidance and friendship through the process of research, grant writing, and general navigation of the university system.

Much of the core research of the dissertation was conducted while I was a Fulbright Graduate Fellow at the National Research Institute for Cultural Properties, Tokyo (Tobunken). Yamanashi Emiko assisted in providing introductions, showing me around the Tobunken library, and by asking critical questions that sharpened my thinking on empress images. Audiences at the Tobunken Research Forum and the Waseda Modern History Group provided helpful feedback. Professor Satō Doshin was kind enough to allow me to sit in on his courses at Tokyo Fine Arts University, where I learned a great deal about modern Japanese art, and librarians at Waseda University, the National Diet Library, the University of Tokyo Multi-media and Socio-information Studies

Archive, and the archives of the Imperial Household Agency provided essential support. Thanks as well to the Hall Center for the Humanities for summer funding that allowed me to finish the dissertation in a timely fashion.

After finishing my PhD, a year as an Andrew W. Mellon Postdoctoral Fellow at Bowdoin College allowed me the time and funding to start transitioning my dissertation into a book. Not only was Maine a beautiful place to live, but the supportive community I found in the Bowdoin art history department, Asian studies department, and among other post-docs was critical in launching my academic career. Thanks to Peggy Wang, Dana Byrd, Stephen Perkinson, Susan Wegner, Pamela Fletcher, Sakura Christmas, and Vyjayanthi Selinger for welcoming me into an extraordinary scholarly setting.

The majority of this book was completed at the University of the South, and a better academic home I could not wish to find. In the tiny mountain town of Sewanee, my art history and studio art colleagues have provided support and friendship, with Jeffrey Thompson and Pradip Malde providing additional assistance in getting this book to completion. Pollyanne Frantz, Scott Wilson, and Terry Papillon have given necessary support, as has funding from the Dean's Office, an IES Abroad Faculty Grant, Kennedy Faculty Fellowship, Barclay Ward Faculty Travel Fellowship, University Research Grant, and an Appalachian College Association Fellowship that funded a year of sabbatical. It was an unfortunate turn of fate that my sabbatical year coincided with the COVID-19 pandemic, but the librarians at Sewanee's DuPont Library went to extraordinary measures to keep the flow of books moving in the midst of impossible research circumstances. Prior to the pandemic, I conducted research for a blissful week at the Library of Congress thanks to a Florence Tan Moeson Fellowship, where I found fantastic resources and supportive librarians. The final stages of manuscript editing and preparation were undertaken while I was a Robert and Lisa Sainsbury Fellow at the Sainsbury Institute for the Study of Japanese Arts and Culture in Norwich, England. I am grateful for the incredibly warm scholarly community of 64 The Close and for the opportunity to be a part of such an esteemed institution.

Audiences at many conferences have provided helpful advice and asked informed questions that have pushed me to refine my arguments. Thanks to those who engaged with my work at the University of California, Berkeley Media and Transmission Conference, the Feminist Art History Conference, the Midwest Conference on Asian Affairs, the College Art Association Annual Conference, the Cambridge University Modern Monarchy Conference, the Asian Studies Conference Japan, the University of South Carolina, the SOAS Japan Research Centre, and the Yanai Initiative at UCLA.

Many scholars in the Japanese art history and Japanese studies community have provided intellectual support and concrete advice. Thanks to Alice Tseng, Mikiko Hirayama, Jan Bardsley, Kendall Brown, Namiko Kunimoto, Rhiannon Paget, Asato Ikeda, John Breen, Matt McMullen, Justin Stein, Ariel Acosta, Magdalena Kolodziej, Miriam Wattles, and Kit Brooks for your encouragement and for sustaining my curiosity at different points in the writing process. I am appreciative for the constructive and helpful comments provided by the anonymous reviewers of this book and for the supportive publication environment provided by series editors Louise Wilkinson and Elena Woodacre. Above all, I have to thank the group of strong women who read my words and provided feedback at a time when pandemic isolation was very real, including Ayelet Zohar, Hillary Pedersen, Sara Sumpter, Justine Wiesinger, Yang Wang, Sohl Lee, Doris Sung, and Amanda Wangwright. The members of the original penguin huddle, Kendra Strand, Eunyoung Park, and Paula Curtis, deserve extra credit for getting me through this book. Our meetings gave me energy and life in a time of darkness.

Finally, I have immense gratitude for my family and friends who were always there to provide distraction and remind me that there is more to life than writing a book. My parents Barb and Tom Miller have always been incredibly supportive and willing to help and gave me access to the world through a library card and countless museum visits. I credit my career in art history to all those free summer Tuesdays at the Art Institute of Chicago, where I first fell in love with Japanese prints and nineteenth-century art. Miles and Dylan, your questions about the world, willingness to try new things, and love of exploration keep me inspired. Above all, Joe Bruscato, who has been there since my undergraduate days, has patiently listened to me talk about empress images for over a decade and has been my companion in the outdoors, in travel, and in life. This book would not have happened without your limitless patience and support.

A NOTE ON NAMES AND ERAS

In Japan eras are marked by the *gengō* (元号) system. In the modern era this means the era name coincides with the period spanning the emperor's ascension to the throne and his death. The five modern periods—Meiji (1868–1912), Taishō (1912–1926), Shōwa (1926–1989), Heisei (1989–2019), and Reiwa (2019-present)—have each adhered to this system since the institution of the *issei ichigen* (one reign, one name, 一世一元) policy in the early Meiji period. In Japan dates are typically written in both the *gengō* system and the Gregorian calendar, with no year zero and an overlap for each era in the *gengō* system. For example, 1912 C.E. is also written as Meiji 45 or Taishō 1, as Emperor Meiji passed away on July 30. In the premodern era the *gengō* system (also termed *nengō,* 年号) was used but with many irregularities as eras changed according not only to reign but also cosmology and auspicious or inauspicious events.

Each emperor and empress can be referred to with multiple names. They received birth names and occasionally childhood names and were assigned imperial or posthumous names. During their reign, most were commonly referenced by title rather than name (皇后陛下・天皇陛下, *kōgō heika/tennō heika,* her majesty/his majesty). While Kōjun and Shōwa are often referred to as Nagako and Hirohito, Shōken, Meiji, Teimei, and Taishō are typically referenced with their posthumous names. Therefore, to maintain consistency, I will use the posthumous names of the emperors and empresses: Empress Shōken, Emperor Meiji, Empress Teimei, Emperor Taishō, Empress Kōjun, and Emperor Shōwa. A full chart of the names and dates of rule for central figures can be found in the Appendix.

INTRODUCTION

The Visual Monarchy

Monarchy is a visual phenomenon.

Portraits, be they painted, printed, or photographed, are the most common way of documenting, promoting, and interpreting the institution of monarchy over its long global history. Images, be they moving or still, previously hidden or always public, comprise our understanding of the individuals who constituted the ranks of royalty over time. Examples abound: today, Japan's Emperor Naruhito, Empress Masako, and Princess Aiko frequently appear in domestic and global news media; Queen Elizabeth II's visage as an icon of the British throne was one of the most recognizable on earth; King Maha Vajiralongkorn's image itself is protected by Thailand's infamously strict *lese majeste* laws. In Japan, the visual public monarchy is an entirely modern phenomenon, one which developed after the advent of photography, and in a time when royal portraits were being deployed as global propaganda. Previously hidden behind palace doors, the first modern Japanese royals, and those who managed their public image, had to invent every aspect of the visual monarchy in Meiji Japan, including what the new role of empress would be in both meaning and appearance. It was within this context that the public position of empress was fabricated in post-1868 Japan.

This book examines the political significance of the modern Japanese empresses in the context of visual monarchy, focusing on Empress Shōken (1849–1914, r. 1868–1912), consort of Emperor Meiji, and Empress Teimei (1884–1951, r. 1912–1926), consort of Emperor Taishō.[1] Visual monarchy is defined here as

DOI: 10.4324/9781003376101-1

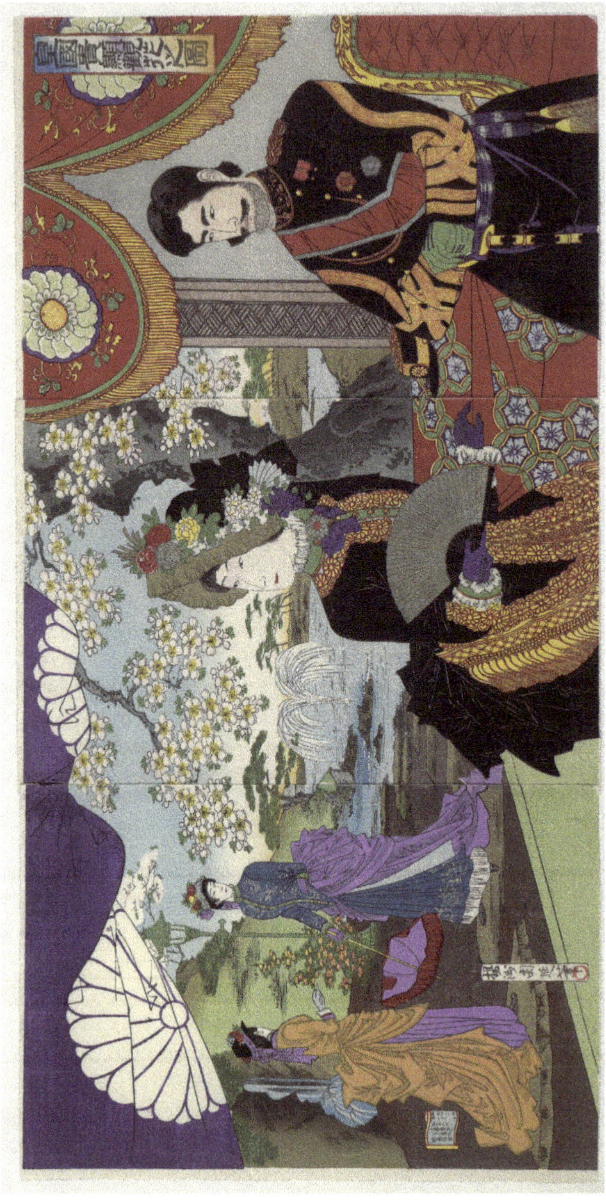

FIGURE 0.1 *Kōkoku kiken kanka no zu* (Dignitaries of the Empire Viewing Cherry Blossoms), 1887, Toyohara (Yōshū) Chikanobu, multicolor woodblock print, British Museum

the publicly relatable celebrity side of monarchy, established in two-dimensional vernacular media, with other means of accessibility limited. Amidst similar developments in global royal cultures of the nineteenth century, in the Japanese context it was Empress Shōken and Empress Teimei who were the personable face of the visual monarchy. The feminine tendencies of the visual monarchy in Japan were a result of the flexible role women sovereigns occupied: their positions did not hold the weighty religious and political connotations of the emperors, yet their close connections to the sacredness of their husbands and sons, combined with their glamorous fashions and aspirational lifestyles, made them popular figures in the cultural imagination. By tracing various discursive forms of visual materials featuring the empresses through time, and linking these images with biographical and historical details, this book shows how the modern empresses functioned as both royal celebrities and as role models of middle-class and aristocratic femininity and analyzes how they influenced women's gender roles in a broad social context. These images, and the empresses represented in them, had a strong impact on how common women understood acceptable feminine comportment over the modern period. As the chrysanthemum throne of the twenty-first century is thrust into public debates regarding female rulership, by establishing the visual monarchy, this book demonstrates that women have long been central to the Japanese monarchy and the public understanding of the institution.

Prior to the modern period there were many women of differing social status who served as the emperor's consorts—the *kōgō* (皇后, empress) was the highest ranking of these consorts. Before the Meiji period and the 1889 Constitution, women could serve as *tennō* (天皇, emperor) and did so on eight occasions between the seventh and eighteenth centuries.[2] Regardless of their rank or position, every woman of the pre-1868 imperial household was, like their male counterparts, invisible to the public. Thus, the formulation of the role of the empress as a public figure happened in tandem with the materialization of the Japanese imperial family as a visual monarchy, making it impossible to separate the empress' image from the modern empress role. Furthermore, all members of the Japanese imperial household as broadly understood in the public realm were performed roles; we do not know their true emotions, personalities, or beliefs, nor can we reconstruct their private views from the expurgated historical record. In the late nineteenth and early twentieth centuries, the imperial visage was censored and regulated, and even today the Japanese press regards the imperial family with a level of respect and distance not found in European nations. It was truly through these strictly controlled images that the public came to know their sovereigns: not as people but as personae. In short, the power of the image, or the visual monarchy, was the foundation of the modern institution of the Japanese imperial household.

In contrast to the abundance of images, the few historic occasions when the voice of the modern Japanese monarchy was audible were remarkable. For example, Emperor Hirohito's August 15, 1945 national radio address upon the Japanese surrender in World War II was notable to the Japanese public, as it was the first broadcast of the emperor's voice. Today, public addresses by the emperor remain rare and are always highly rehearsed, such as Emperor Akihito's 2016 televised speech, wherein he declared his desire to retire from his position. That monarchy is taciturn is particularly true for the Japanese empresses of the modern age.[3] On occasion empresses and princesses are forbidden from giving press interviews and have even suffered from periods of muteness, attributed to the stresses of their positions.[4] Despite recent forays into audio and film, monarchy is one of the oldest human institutions, with more than two millennia of history, most of which preceded recorded sound or video. Therefore, our received understanding of global monarchy is most often visual, whether oil portraiture, woodblock prints, or still photography, and with the two modern Japanese imperial couples, Meiji and Shōken, Taishō and Teimei, it was the primary medium of communication.

While officially playing a supporting role to their husbands, the empress' position should not be interpreted as purely secondary but rather as complementary. With the reorganization of the *kōkyū* (後宮, anterior court) in 1871, the empress gained a more central standing at court, and her position changed to be one half of the Japanese monarchy. In the years between 1868 and 1945, the Japanese emperors were viewed as a sacred presence, a long-established role that was brought into the public forum and as the head of the political and military structures, with these last two roles generally considered ceremonial in nature.[5] Although the empresses accompanied, mothered, and bore the males of the imperial household, they were not burdened with the same sacred, political, and social responsibilities as their male counterparts. However, they played a culturally central function through visual media, acting as celebrity role models and providing a conventional form of modern femininity that was acceptable to emulate, modeling being a common function of queenship the world over. These royal celebrity roles were articulated and performed in two-dimensional media during the Meiji and Taishō periods and later in moving images in the post-1920 decades. Through a close examination of these images in context, this book demonstrates that the empresses were, and are, lasting and constant cultural icons but are simultaneously a responsive symbol, adjusting to changing social norms and expectations through time.

As the biological or adoptive mother of the subsequent emperor, the modern and contemporary empresses play a critical role in the continuity of the imperial lineage. Consequently, they are celebrated for their maternity, often to a point of extreme personal stress. This is particularly of note for Empress Masako, who avoided the public eye in the early 2000s due to mental health issues resulting from her inability to produce a male heir. Over a century earlier, Empress Shōken also failed to produce a male heir and came close to divorce as a result.[6] In photographs of the 2019 Reiwa ascension ceremonies the gender imbalance between male and female members of the imperial household was remarkable. As Japan currently practices agnatic primogeniture, the visible gender disproportion points to a potential crisis in succession, an issue that first arose in 2005 when there was no clear male heir but which has since resolved with the birth of the emperor's nephew Prince Hisahito in 2006.[7] After 1947 the succession laws changed as part of the postwar constitution, leading to a renunciation of imperial status by the women of the imperial family upon marriage. Together with other policies and imperial laws that dramatically shrank the size of the Japanese nobility, the public expectations for, and perceptions of, the roles of princes and princesses have diverged with the dual status system. These roles were dynamic over the nineteenth and twentieth centuries, not only in response to changes in the political, legal, and social status of the imperial family but as expectations of motherhood, femininity, celebrity, and diplomacy were shaped by the women of the imperial household.

Today, it is widely understood that the women who accompany male leaders have a soft power influence in society, in both royal and political spheres. British royals Catherine, Princess of Wales, and Meghan, Dutchess of Sussex, hold celebrity status, lifting up both new and established designer labels with their sartorial selections and inspiring magazine articles, books, and social media accounts dedicated to following their activities. Japanese First Lady Akie Abe was outspoken on cultural issues that at times contradicted her husband's political positions, famously joining the Tokyo Pride parade in 2014 to promote equality and show her support for the LGBTQ+ community. While each of these twenty-first–century women have media handlers, provide television interviews, and are well versed in how to manipulate their social media image, the concept of how to use mechanical, mass-produced images to sculpt one's celebrity status was in its infancy when the modern Japanese imperial family first came into the public eye, and the careful use of fashion for monarchs and celebrities was an understood norm by the late nineteenth century. The Japanese empresses investigated in this book participated in the production of global modern royal celebrity culture as soft power as it was developing.

Although the visual culture of monarchy is a central source for understanding how royals were received by their subjects, the two-dimensional media that provided the stage for the creation of the imperial family was an unreliable source of truth. The woodblock and lithograph prints that constituted the early stages of imperial images were fabrications, and the photographs that made up their public image after the turn of the twentieth century were staged and limited. Photographs were republished for years after their creation, sometimes alongside images that were taken just days before, removing the immediacy and temporality of the genre.[8] All images were highly censored. Utilizing photography, as well as woodblock and lithograph prints, the Imperial Household Ministry (now Agency) invented an imperial persona with lasting power. While these images are manipulations that have varied through time, they are recognizable symbols that transcend and unify the modern period. Their public cultural meanings and interpretations adjusted in the differing social contexts of the modern era, just as the practices of court relationships, empress functions, and maternal roles changed, but the empresses maintained constant public visibility. The significance of the empress to her people shifted, but after being established in the 1870s, the optics remained relatively similar.

Chapter Outline

This book is composed of six chapters, covering the images of the modern empresses from the first stages of development in the 1870s to through the funeral of Empress Teimei in 1951, with a primary focus on the images of Empress Shōken and Empress Teimei between 1870 and 1930. Part One introduces the two empresses and their biographies and individual narratives, while Part Two looks at images of the women in comparison. Chapter 1 focuses on a history of the institution and image, while the remaining chapters focus on a specific medium or genre: woodblock prints, mass media photography, portraiture, fashion and global monarchy, and funerary images.

Chapter 1, "The Modern Imperial Family: Institutions and Images," outlines key facts from the history of the imperial system in the late nineteenth and early twentieth century. This chapter delineates how the institution of the Imperial Household Agency utilized images to mold the modern monarchy and highlights the importance of the newly redefined nobility that surrounded the emperor and empress. Chapter 1 provides fundamental theories for understanding the modern Japanese monarchy and reviews the origins of imperial imagery.

Chapter 2, "Mimesis and Multiples: Empress Shōken and the Power of Print in Establishing the Public Empress Persona," investigates representations of Empress Shōken in Meiji period woodblock prints. This era of the visual monarchy featured fantasy representations of the empress' domestic and court life, as well as her public appearances in new, modern locales such as government-sponsored events and ceremonies. Widely sold at accessible prices, these vernacular prints utilized a standard Japanese media in order to establish the new visibility and modern comportment of the empress in Meiji visual culture and validated her activities through the illusion of intimacy with her citizens. After introducing the biography of Empress Shōken and the theoretical frameworks of the chapter, prints are analyzed in categories of maternity, charity and work, and court and diplomatic events, globally common themes for royal women that were developed against domestic social values.

Chapter 3, "The Optics of Modernity: Empress Teimei, Photography, Mass Media, and Gender in the Imperial Likeness," provides biographies for Empress Teimei and Emperor Taishō and examines empress representations as published in the magazine *Fujin gahō* (Ladies Pictorial), a publication that was marketed to women of the upper and upper-middle classes. Chapter 3 establishes the ways which Teimei's image was strategically used as an imperial proxy at a time when the emperor fell ill and out of the public eye. I also demonstrate how she was presented as a military mother figure in the pages of the magazine in order to counter unpopular government policies.

Chapter 4, "Toward the Sacred and the Standard: Formality, Lineage, and Decorum in the Modern Japanese Imperial Portrait," discusses official studio portraiture of the modern Japanese empresses, explaining how imperial portraiture commenced and evolved between the Meiji Restoration (1868) and the end of the Taishō period (1926). Throughout the late nineteenth and early twentieth century, images of the emperors became increasingly standardized and sacred in nature, and the laws and norms which dictated the distribution and exhibition of imperial portraiture were codified. Simultaneously, images of the empresses became increasingly visible and took on an aura of "modernity." This chapter also looks at the *goshinei*, or sacred portrait, and its government distribution in small shrine structures built specifically for the portraits, the *hōanden* and *hōankura*. This chapter argues that the empress portraits played a significant role in establishing the visual culture of the modern monarchy and that the feminine presence in official lineage portraits and in the *hōanden* and *hōankura* points to the centrality of the empresses in the modern Japanese imperial family.

Chapter 5, "Fashion, National Identity, and the Community of Royals: Global Monarchical Visual Culture between the Meiji and Taishō Periods," begins by examining the empress' fashions in woodblock prints in the context of the newly globalized sphere of monarchy, considering clothing and national identity. It then contrasts this with images of global monarchy found in photography and amidst imperial expansion, positioning the empresses at a pivot point of Europe and East Asia. On the domestic front, in the early twentieth century in the context of the women's magazine *Fujin gahō*, images of the two modern empresses fit differing versions of the *ryōsai kenbo* (良妻賢母), or "good wife, wise mother," over three decades by taking a comparative and temporal approach to these images. The final section analyzes changes in the ideology and how these were modeled by the imperial women.

Chapter 6, "Mourning and Memory: The Visual Politics of Imperial Funerals and Memorial Sites," looks at imagery from the funerals of Empress Eishō, Emperor Meiji, and Empress Shōken, which innovated the modern form of the event. The chapter shows that visual culture of funerary events and memorial sites was critical to cementing the empress as a focal point in the modern imperial family and concludes with Teimei's funeral in 1951 as the first postwar imperial event, one which was covered in the domestic and international media, showing the transition to the era of the Japanese symbol monarchy.

Each of these chapters examines different media, audiences, and distribution channels for constructing the narrative of feminine imperial power in Japan while maintaining that the ultimate purpose of all of these images was to elevate the empress and to promote her image as a popular but conventional role model for the modern woman.

A Theoretical Framework of Monarchy, Celebrity, and Media

Empress images are not easily categorized. They exist betwixt and between academic boundaries: visually between art history, visual culture, and media studies and disciplinarily between history, women's and gender studies, religious studies, sociology, and the burgeoning fields of royal studies and queenship studies. In recent decades, the study of elites or royals was often perceived as perpetuating social inequality and hierarchy. Yet to ignore the story of the imperial family and their images is to allow the royal narrative to be written by those who extol their virtues or promote the imperial institution in an uncritical or nationalist fashion. This book focuses on the visual monarchy as the point of meeting between empresses and commoners, critiquing the façade of the royal image in Japan as that of a malleable, consumable celebrity and questioning the motivations for crafting the imperial persona in specific contexts at differing points in time. It also brings the visual analysis of women and their images to the fore: women remain understudied in the visual culture of the imperial family, and as the modern Japanese imperial family was a visual monarchy, it is of the utmost importance to view their images through the lens of art history.

The mediascape of the empresses covered by this book is enormous in scale. Ranging from woodblock and lithograph prints to photographs, paintings to film, it is an impossible task to analyze, or even list, every extant image of the modern empresses. Yet there are images that were repeated, themes that came to the fore, and photographs issued in widely distributed publications. The foundations of modern empress images can be found in woodblock and lithograph prints, but photography was also critical in the formative years of empress images and quickly became the central, constant source of visual information. Newsreels grew in popularity in the mid to late 1920s, ushering in the Shōwa era alongside a turn towards heightened militarism, expansion of the Japanese empire, and an increasingly conservative imperial family. As film brings in differing theoretical considerations, and because the reign of Shōwa and Kōjun lasted for over sixty years, witnessing the advent of television, this book looks exclusively at two-dimensional visual culture. As such, I focus on Shōken and Teimei, with brief forays into the Shōwa period to examine Teimei's funeral in 1951. This book uses two-dimensional media, visual analysis, and historical context to think through public reception, a notoriously difficult topic to ascertain.

As output from the Imperial Household Agency, empress images were political. Crafted with an eye towards the maintenance of the imperial institution, the images conveyed a specific message of how the Japanese royals were to be interpreted and understood by their subjects. As they were consumed by the public, empress images were culture. The true differential between the intended message and the received message is difficult to decipher; we do not have statistics on the public opinion of the late nineteenth and early twentieth century Japanese monarchy, and while there were instances of public critique of the imperial family, there was not a culture of criticism that surrounded them in the years prior to 1945.

The empress images were more than just pictures of monarchy; they were part of a nascent modern royal celebrity culture in Japan. Defined as having a commercial element and an aspect of fame, celebrity culture is often theorized as having a religious fervor. Celebrity and media are inseparable and mutually constitutive, "In 'housing' the values, beliefs, and norms of the day, celebrity coverage in the media—in newspapers, advertisements, films, television and so on—plays an essential role in organizing our perception of the world."[9] The literature on celebrity generally defines the years between 1890 and 1930 or 1940 as the period in which the celebrity as persona was systematized, with the origins of the concept in the eighteenth century.[10] For the imperial family, their royal celebrity status emerged between 1880 and 1910 in woodblock and lithograph prints, with photography dominating thereafter. Although projecting a drastically different value system, a thriving culture of celebrity and print media existed in Japan prior to the modern period, as evidenced in the thousands of woodblock prints featuring courtesans and kabuki actors that were widely sold during the Edo period (1600–1868). The celebrities featured in Edo prints, however, were of a low status and anonymous in physical appearance, while images of the Edo shoguns (military rulers) and emperors were explicitly banned. When the Meiji Restoration transformed Japanese political and social spheres, both the subjects and the optics of celebrity adoration shifted in tandem. The new media of newspapers and magazines that grew around the turn of the twentieth century no longer featured low-status performers but rather the nobility, the monarchy, military rulers, educators, and other high society role models who came to regulate the larger visual identity of Japaneseness in the modern period.

The visibility of celebrity is one of its central characteristics, as those who comprise the ranks of celebrities are not necessarily elevated for their accomplishments. Historically, fame was linked to the supernatural, or to an element of greatness, but celebrity marks the modernization of fame and a move toward media stars that were known in their lifetime.[11] The visibility that is critical to creating and maintaining celebrity as a phenomenon is dependent on repetition and the multiplication of images.[12] Because celebrity requires distance to maintain its allure and is only accessible through circulated texts, media as the agent of delivery is a necessary component.[13] Simultaneously, celebrities are intimately familiar, even if it is just the persona and not the person that we are acquainted with. As Sharon Marcus points out, twentieth-century German theorist Walter Benjamin famously critiqued replication in film as removing the aura, but he overlooked the allure of multiples, the positive factors found in the abundance and ease of transmission inherent in photography, and the singularity of celebrity that is intensified through copying.[14] In Japan, utilizing multiples and copies of images has historic roots in Buddhism, and the world of Edo celebrity expertly manipulated the multiplicity and reproducibility of woodblock prints, leaving Meiji Japan primed for a culture of highly visible, frequently reproduced, and intimately familiar aristocratic celebrities.

In the past, and today, the Japanese royals are covered in the press with a far greater reverence than their European counterparts; there are no gossip magazines or paparazzi devoted to cataloging their personal slip-ups. While rumors swirl around them from time to time, they are generally far less vitriolic than those that are attached to the British monarchs. As stated by one imperial correspondent, "If you want to argue that we protect the mystery (*shimpiteki na bubun*) of the imperial family, I think we do. But no matter what we do the family will have to reform. And the more they reform the more the mystery will decline. That's their dilemma."[15] Thus it can be said that the Japanese imperial family is treated with a level of public respect not found in many other nations.[16] The sense of mystery, the limited and censored visibility, and the often-repeated idea that the unbroken imperial lineage is part of Japan's "unique" culture validates monarchists and right-wing political groups. These same groups benefit by separating the imperial family from ideas of celebrity, as viewing the emperor and empress as distinct from regular people and above the fray of the gossip laden European monarchies affirms their ideas.

As the empresses were not bestowed with sacrality, and therefore had certain latitudes that the emperors did not, the women of the imperial household were central to the media presence of the modern royal family. The definition of mass media varies by geographic area and field of study but is generally viewed as a twentieth-century phenomenon. In the context of the images of the Japanese imperial family, the Meiji period marks the start of a mass culture: the woodblock prints, lithographs, and the *goshinei*, a sacred image, formed a nascent mass visual culture of royalty in Japan, which was relatively mature by the advent of magazines and newspapers in the early twentieth century. It was amidst the sheets of woodcuts and the pages of periodicals where private court rituals became "mediated celebrations of national identity which all citizens, wherever they may be, are able to witness and in which they are invited vicariously to take part."[17] The imperial family was conditioned by the very process of utilizing print to communicate their presence, for mass media does not simply represent cultural happenings, but it creates culture and becomes a cultural product in and of itself.[18]

Simultaneous with the rise of celebrity and the ubiquity of the imperial visage in the mass media, the *goshinei* was presented and utilized in a similar fashion to a religious icon. Paradoxically, the *goshinei,* discussed in Chapter 4, was often utilized in non-official contexts. Therefore, it is impossible to clearly separate the sacred and secular images of the imperial family. Instead, we should recognize the continuum of royal prints, photographs, and paintings as a spectrum of communications and visual access. This stream of disparate representations signals that the seemingly singular nature of the emperor and empress in the modern era was dependent on widespread mechanical reproduction. In the context of the *goshinei*, the meaning of the image was dependent on its indexical quality. Despite Emperor Meiji's *goshinei* being a reproduced Conté crayon drawing, and notwithstanding the widespread unsanctioned usage of the *goshinei* in later years, the intention of these official portraits was to activate the link between the reproduced image and the actual presence of the person in the portrait, or that which is indexed by the image. In East Asia, the idea that the image holds a trace of the person has historic precedent in Buddhist theories on the power of icons, and while the larger theoretical history of nineteenth-century Japanese photography is beyond the scope of this book, suffice it to say that the *goshinei* was, in theory, less about verisimilitude and more about the vestige of the physical presence.[19] Yet the presence and popularity of the mass media photographs tells us that there was more than one way to view images of the imperial family. Differences in the representations, reproductions, and display of the emperors, empresses, princes, princesses, and larger nobility will be elaborated upon over the course of this book, but for as many means of image distribution that existed, we can further intuit that there were many ways of interpreting these divergent images of the Japanese royal house.

The links between modern monarchy, gender roles, and portrait photography are inseparable. In 1842, Prince Albert sat in a studio in Brighton, England, for the first royal portrait photograph, only three years after photography was invented.[20] When Queen Victoria sat for her first photograph a few years later, an image which is no longer extant, she positioned herself as a mother, not as the sovereign of a global empire. Yet these earliest royal portrait photographs were not intended for public consumption. It was not until 1857 that Prince Albert's photograph was displayed at the Art Treasures exhibition in Manchester and 1860 that Queen Victoria allowed her photograph to be sold.[21] Photography came to Japan in 1848, and by the time imperial images grew to national levels of distribution and consumption in the 1870s, the use of public images of royalty to justify and promote their rule was widely, globally understood by those disseminating them. Just as Prince Albert preceded Queen Victoria in the public eye, so did Emperor Meiji enter the public forum of photography before Empress Shōken, and just as Victoria first held a conventionally feminine role in photography, so did Shōken. The order and content of these images was not coincidental and demonstrates the intentions of the Imperial Household Agency: to maintain women's roles within the monarchy as separate and complementary.

Monarchy is often derided as outdated and prized as timeless, yet the survival of this system shows that it is neither. Throughout this book, the images of the modern empresses strike a balance between propaganda and popular media, noble philanthropy and upper-middle class role model, royal celebrity and mother of the nation. By examining how the empress image was exalted and approachable, and how it shifted in meaning over time, this book illuminates dynamic and powerful female figures who impacted not only women in their own time but whose influence extended to later generations of the imperial household, creating a greater role for imperial women and elevating the status of women's roles at a crucial juncture in Japanese history.

Notes

1 See front matter on naming conventions.
2 Paula R. Curtis, "Japan's Once and Future Female Emperors," *Nursing Clio*, April 30, 2019, https://nursingclio.org/2019/04/30/japans-once-and-future-female-emperors/.
3 Masako Kamiya, "Is the Japanese Monarchy in Crisis Due to Its Gender Bias?" *Royal Studies Journal* 7, no. 2 (2020).
4 Empress Michiko was mute for two months at the end of 1993 and for a period in 1963. The first bout was attributed to pressures from her mother-in-law, the second from stresses related to unfavorable press coverage. T.R. Reid, "The Empress Speaks," *The Washington Post*, December 13, 1993.
5 1868 marks the start of the restoration of imperial rule in Japan and the opening of the nation to international trade. This is widely considered the start of the modern era in the field of Japanese studies. I am using the end of the Pacific War, 1945, to mark the transition from the modern era into the postwar. The postwar period in Japan is defined by the US occupation (1945–1952) and the US occupation of Okinawa

(1945–1972) and was a vastly different political landscape than that under consideration here. For the full lineage of emperors, see: Kunaichō, "Genealogy of the Emperors of Japan," www.kunaicho.go.jp/e-about/genealogy/koseizu.html.

6 Mamiko C. Suzuki, *Gendered Power: Educated Women of the Meiji Empress' Court* (Ann Arbor: University of Michigan Press, 2019), 4.

7 It is still widely recognized that the line of succession is not sustainable, and government panels have been convened on occasion over the past few decades with the goal of altering the system. For a historian's take that includes proposals for a female palace, revival of adoption, and changes to official duties, see: Toroko Isao, *Kōi keishō no arikata: "josei, boeki tennō" wa kanō ka* (Tokyo: PHP, 2006).

8 Alice Y. Tseng, "Imperial Portraiture and Popular Print Media in Early Twentieth Century Japan," *Journal of Japanese Studies* 46, no. 2 (2020).

9 Jessica Evans and David Hesmondhalgh, eds., *Understanding Media: Inside Celebrity* (Berkshire: Open University Press, 2005), 2.

10 In Edo Japan woodblock prints were utilized for the promotion of specific beauties and actors. For a study of celebrity and kabuki, see: Christine Guth, "Memorial Portraits of Kabuki Actors: Fanfare in the Floating World," *Impressions*, no. 27 (2005): 22–41. In England, the connection between early celebrity performers and portraiture is explored in: Heather McPherson, *Art and Celebrity in the Age of Reynolds and Siddons* (University Park, PA: Penn State University Press, 2017).

11 Charles L. Ponce de Leon, *Self-Exposure: Human-Interest Journalism and the Emergence of Celebrity in America, 1890–1940* (Chapel Hill: University of North Carolina Press, 2002), 14. In the Euro-American context, modern celebrity often meant a move away from the aristocracy, yet in Japan, the nobility was expanded and the Meiji period, and a central part of late nineteenth and early twentieth century celebrity visual culture.

12 Sharon Marcus, *The Drama of Celebrity* (Princeton: Princeton University Press, 2019), 19–26.

13 Evans and Hesmondhalgh, *Understanding Media*, 19.

14 Marcus, *The Drama of Celebrity*, 126.

15 Media coverage of the imperial family is still not completely open. David McNeill and Herbert P. Bix, "Trouble at the Top:

Japan's Imperial Family in Crisis," *Asia-Pacific Journal: Japan Focus* 2 (2004). Ken Ruoff, *The People's Emperor: Democracy and the Japanese Monarchy, 1945–1995* (Cambridge, MA: Harvard East Asia Monographs, 2001).

16 The monarchs of Thailand or the Middle East are treated with a similar level of respect; however, they are still part of their respective national power structures, whereas the Japanese imperial family is a constitutional monarchy and is forbidden from influencing politics or expressing political opinions.

17 John B. Thompson, *The Media and Modernity: A Social Theory of the Media* (Stanford: Stanford University Press, 1995), 201.

18 Amy Bliss Marshall, *Magazines and the Making of Mass Culture in Japan* (Toronto: University of Toronto Press, 2019), 5–7.

19 Maki Fukuoka, *The Premise of Fidelity: Science, Visuality, and Representing the Real in Nineteenth-Century Japan* (Stanford: Stanford University Press, 2012).

20 Anne M. Lyden, *A Royal Passion: Queen Victoria and Photography* (Los Angeles: The J. Paul Getty Museum, 2014), vii.

21 Lyden, *A Royal Passion*, 107.

PART I

1

THE MODERN IMPERIAL FAMILY

Institutions and Images

Against a bright vermillion background and surrounded by yellow and gold paulownia and chrysanthemums, seven imperial portrait rounds make up the design of a small postcard, produced after 1907 (Figure 1.1). The striking color is reminiscent of a *torii*, the gate of a Shinto shrine, the flowers symbolic of the imperial family, with buds showing flourishing growth. Connected by the foliage, the visual metaphor of lineage is made clear—from Meiji, through Taishō, the future of the imperial family lay at the bottom center of the card with the imminent young Shōwa emperor. Addressed to "my dear Mason" from N. Sugie, the message states in English, "I am sending to you a book of photographs of our dearest H.M. the emperor," along with well wishes for the receiver and a hope that the photographs arrive in good condition. Yet despite the sender's message, this is not a purely masculine image: the empresses are present, the visual equals of their husbands, and just as important for the stability of the family tree. A postcard with imperial portrait photographs of the emperor and empress, crown prince and princess, and their three young sons was not an extraordinary object but a standard part of early twentieth-century Japanese visual culture. It was through these common objects that the Japanese citizenry knew their sovereigns and through repeated visual encounters that the biographies of the imperial family were written in the public forum. These stories were calculated in nature and always in service of the mission of the Imperial Household Agency (formerly Ministry) and their goals of maintaining respect for the emperor, empress, and larger imperial family. Subtle differences in

DOI: 10.4324/9781003376101-3

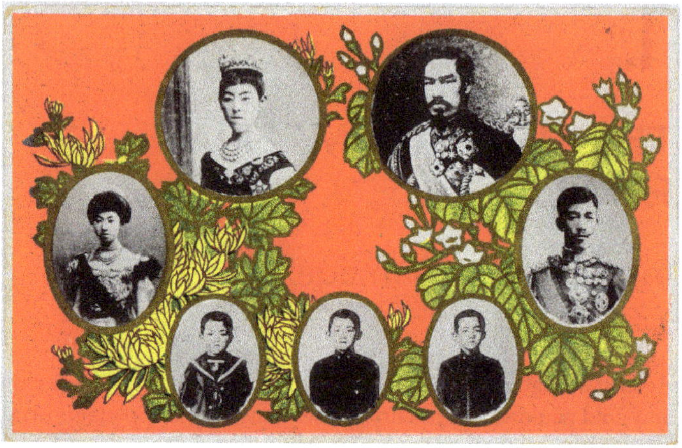

FIGURE 1.1 Meiji tennō, kōgō, tennōkei (Meiji emperor, empress, imperial family), after 1907, postcard, Art Research Center Collection, Ritsumeikan University, akkPC0001–001

representation and reception, owing to both the varied interests and backgrounds of the family members themselves as well as the changing societal expectations about women's roles, led to divergences in how the stories of the individual family members were communicated in the public realm.

The three modern empresses, Shōken, Teimei, and Kōjun, like the other members of the modern Japanese imperial household, are constructed figures. Throughout the course of written history, the imperial lineage of Japan experienced no interregnum. Although at times there were creative means by which the line of descent was sustained, the mythical roots of the imperial family extend over 2,500 years into the past. During this lengthy history the treatment and understanding of the imperial family by the ruling classes and the public widely varied. In the modern era it was their representation in the public forum—as the visual monarchy—that fabricated what was known about them. Although there was, and still is, some element of gossip and rumor that surrounds the media presence of the royals and their retinue, negative comments were strictly suppressed by the state censorship machine. In the late nineteenth and early twentieth centuries, the imperial family typically did not make statements during their public appearances, and their personal thoughts were not, and are not, available to the public.[1] As the imperial family was thought to exist "above the clouds," interrogating their media representations to find their true personalities was likely not something that the general public craved or desired: the visible institution was what was known and what mattered. Therefore, the empresses as examined in this book are the imagined empress personae who were consumed by the public through images such as prints and photography. Here, the lives and roles of Shōken and Teimei as seen in the forums of newspapers, print culture, and magazines will be put under the lens in order to demonstrate how the visual monarchy was presented to the public, as it was through these images that the empresses' biographies were communicated to their subjects.

This chapter begins with background information on the Japanese imperial system, including the modern conceptions of the imperial family, the role of the Imperial Household Agency, and touching upon imperial intersections with Shinto. The subsequent sections explore key theories of monarchy as an institution and examine imperial gender roles, providing critical background for the remainder of the book, with the final section providing a review of the pre-history of modern imperial portraiture.

The Japanese Imperial System

Since the Meiji Restoration in 1868, the Japanese imperial family has been a central institution in Japanese culture with a significant impact on Japanese society, but it is also an organization in constant flux. Today, all members of the family are active in philanthropic, scholarly, and cultural pursuits, and prior to 1945 the men of the house were active in Shinto, the military, and politics. However, this social and political influence and presence was a post–nineteenth-century phenomenon.

During the Meiji, Taishō, and early Shōwa periods, the imperial family—in their institutional roles—was one component in the larger project of constructing nation and nationalism among the Japanese citizenry. Throughout this time the emperors were characterized as descendants from the sun goddess Amaterasu and framed by a belief system premised on their divine origins.[2] The modern era was a distinctive time for the imperial family; in the premodern and early modern eras, they were largely invisible to the public eye, and in the years post-1945, the emperors rescinded their political status, acting as figureheads and cultural icons rather than in positions of power. Furthermore, many of the performed rituals of the imperial family, activities which are now incorporated into a basic understanding of their role in society, were constructed during the modern era.[3]

The modern Japanese imperial system had its start in the years after the Meiji Restoration of 1868. After the overthrow of the Tokugawa shogunate, which ruled for over 250 years, Japan's new leadership restored the imperial institution to a central role in the Japanese society and state. Prior to 1868, the emperor and his court lived in seclusion in the old capital of Kyoto. During the period of military rule, which began with the transition to the shoguns in 1185, the emperor and the court were at times half of a diarchy and at times held at the will of the ruling powers. The Japanese imperial family traces its roots back to the legendary first emperor, Emperor Jinmu (c. 660–585 B.C.E), and from there to the sun goddess Amaterasu.[4] Historians and archaeologists debate the origins of the Japanese emperors; extant records point to the female ruler Himiko ruling the land of Wa around the third century, but it was not until the eighth century that kingship arose under Shōmu (r. 724–756) as the first *tennō*.[5] Imperial history was not widely known by the Japanese populace until the modern era, when it was incorporated into educational materials and visual culture as a means of justifying and validating the position of the modern imperial family.

In Japanese history the concepts of legitimacy and lineage were understood in a different fashion than they are today; only half of the historic emperors were sons succeeding their fathers, and with concepts of monogamy, marriage sacrament, and inheritance being more flexible than in contemporary understandings, the premodern imperial lineage was more enigmatic than it is today.[6] During the course of over 1,500 years of imperial history, the emperor of Japan was primarily a ceremonial position, with brief exceptions for direct rule in the seventh and fourteenth centuries.[7] A full narrative of the lineage is too complex to detail here, but it is crucial to note that for the entirety of premodern imperial history, the emperor was never a public figure. He did not embark on tours of the nation and did not appear before the masses. It is questionable how much the general populace was even aware of the imperial presence, as he was not seen in distributed visual culture until the modern period.[8] Yet the accumulated and often imagined narrative of premodern imperial history was collected in the modern imperial institution, and the legitimacy of the modern emperors and empresses is built on a cultural understanding of this premodern foundation.

The idea of a single empress who acted as part of a couple with the emperor was not part of the structure of the imperial household prior to 1868; rather emperors had many concubines to serve them at the Imperial Palace. Women could take the throne prior to the modern period and did so on eight occasions. Of these eight, six female *tennō* (天皇, emperor) acted in the Nara period (710–794) or earlier.[9] Timon Screech argues that the omission of two women emperors from the official dynastic portraits of the Edo period indicates that the women who served as emperor during the early modern Edo period (1600–1868) were not perceived as strong leaders.[10] Other scholars such as Hitomi Tonomura disagree. Tonomura observes that "Women's involvement in political affairs is not as alien to Japanese history as is frequently supposed, and the Meiji government 'domesticated' women (including royal women) to a degree that obscures an earlier, wider scope of female activity."[11] Tonomura further argues that the patrilineal system of royal inheritance did not exist prior to the eighth century, and in these early years of imperial history, royal status was derived from both the maternal and paternal sides.[12] The omission of women from the historical and art historical record and the reinterpretation or revision of their historic roles to dim their importance is a common practice across cultures and should not be read at face value. Empresses, queens, and women generally were often written out of history the world over. Later chapters will show how images of Empress Shōken and Empress Teimei reveal their popularity and cultural power, yet often today their names and faces are forgotten in a history that has prioritized ever more conventional binary gender roles for the imperial family.

The present-day laws that regulate the imperial family were only enacted starting in the late nineteenth century, with the term imperial family (天皇家 *tennōke*) not widely used until the Shōwa period, as the emperor was not affiliated with a family in the premodern era.[13] Within the system of modern imperial law, the first draft as written in 1882 allowed for women to take the throne; however, as women did not have suffrage, the concept of a female leader was viewed as contradictory, and thus the law was changed in subsequent drafts. By 1889 when imperial law was made official, women were excluded from taking the throne, a provision that continues to this day.[14]

The creation of the majority of the modern imperial system was undertaken over the course of more than two decades in the mid-nineteenth century, with some structures not being codified into law until almost forty years after Emperor Meiji came to the throne. However, it was in the first decade of the Meiji period that the emperor and the imperial family became a central, visible part of Japanese society. Emperor Meiji became a paramount military, religious, and political figure in the late nineteenth century, taking on the public role of the model nuclear family together with his primary wife Empress Shōken and his son Crown Prince Haru. The construction of the imperial family as undertaken in the Meiji period was intertwined with the lives of Shōken and Meiji as the founding family of Japan's modern imperial lineage. The roles and responsibilities that both Meiji and Shōken adopted were completely new in the course of Japanese history; with the institution of the emperor at the head of society, entirely new rituals, ceremonies, institutions, and societal norms had to be created in order to cement the emperor's position as the head of the modern Japanese nation. Every aspect of imperial life needed to be documented and put into the legal code, including the way imperial events such as weddings, enthronements, and funerals were commemorated; the messages depicted in imperial portraiture; national holidays in honor of the emperor; and private religious rites, all of which had to be defined and presented to the public in an authoritative fashion. Most of these imperial activities were portrayed and promoted to the public with an air of historicity yet were only loosely based on ancient precedent: the rites, rituals, and public performances of the emperor and the imperial family were primarily creations of the modern age.

Among hundreds of similar images, the 1887 woodblock print triptych *Kōkoku kōki kagami* (Mirror of Imperial Nobility) (Figure 1.2) by Toyohara (Yōshū) Chikanobu (楊洲周延 1838–1912) worked to make the imperial family familiar to their public and to solidify their authority.[15] Featuring Empress Shōken, Crown Prince Haru, and Emperor Meiji, the print presents the illusion of a nuclear family, surrounded by symbols of the throne such as the chrysanthemum seal on the purple drapery and the phoenix on the patterned tablecloth, as well as signs of the family's cosmopolitanism such as the European-style books on the table and their elaborate red and gold chairs. This print, like so many others, presents the imperial personae as an institution, with women playing a central role.

After the initial dramatic changes that took place in the 1870s, the position of the imperial family in public life transformed three additional times between 1889 and the postwar period. Emperor Taishō and Empress Teimei cemented the imperial roles which were invented in the Meiji period, but these roles would change with the regency period (1921–1926) when the emperor fell ill and out of the public eye. Chapter 3 details the strategic presence of Teimei's image amidst Taishō's concealment and prior to Hirohito's marriage in 1924, making the regency a time when the empress was the dominant public representative of the monarchy. The public personae of the imperial family changed once again with their successors, Emperor Shōwa and Empress Kōjun, as the nation marched towards imperialism and greater nationalism in the late 1920s and into the 1930s. Emperor Shōwa's image was marked in the age of empire by his role as the head of the military in the pre-war years and transformed yet again in the postwar era, when his societal status adjusted to fit the needs of the postwar political state.

The flexibility of the Japanese monarchy while maintaining the appearance of timeless tradition is critical to their survival

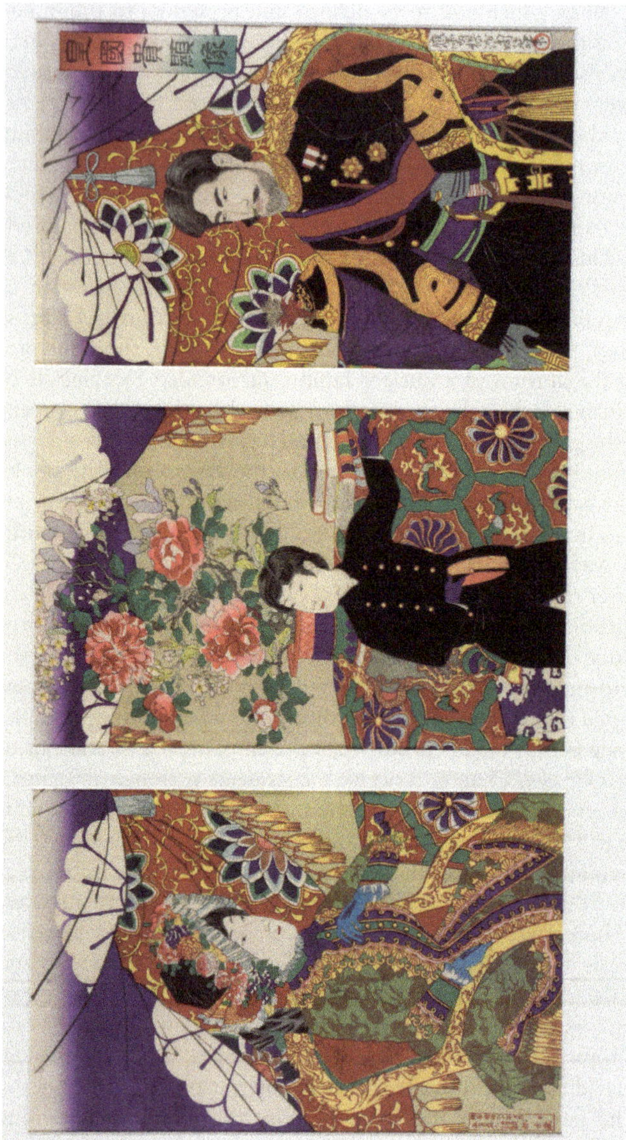

FIGURE 1.2 *Kōkoku kōki kagami* (Mirror of Imperial Nobility/Illustrious Nobility of the Empire) 1887, Toyohara (Yōshū) Chikanobu, multicolor woodblock print, Spencer Museum of Art, University of Kansas, Museum purchase: Lucy Shaw Schultz Fund, 2006.0034.a,b,c

as an institution. As Hikari Hori points out, in the pre-war era, "The emperor system relied on and at the same time continually constructed the notion of the sacred imperial lineage, ideals of gendered imperial subjecthood (women as mothers and men as soldiers), and social stratification of class and ethnicity."[16] An image such as *Mirror of Imperial Nobility* does just this—it envisions Shōken as demure, her tiny gloved hands and delicate facial features contrasting with the far more substantial bodily presence of Meiji. The emperor and his heir are linked visually by their black military-style clothing, with Meiji displaying his status and masculinity through conspicuous medals, sashes, and the sword he grips in his left hand. The constricting form of the empress' attire and the busy floral patterns of her costume blend in with the chair and the background, reinforcing her femininity through her reserved appearance, and thus her differential status. Represented here as a nuclear family, it was a widely known fact that the crown prince's biological mother was a palace concubine and one who also held a public position. At the time this triptych was printed in 1887 the imperial family had been visible to their people for less than twenty years, yet in the print, despite the newness of their familial structure and the novelty of their dress, they appear stable and timeless, an illusion that their successors would maintain with each change of the modern monarchy.

Throughout the modern era, the system and organizational structure which surrounded, and surrounds, the imperial family was controlled by the government agency charged with state matters related to them, the Imperial Household Agency (宮内庁 *kunaichō*).[17] The Agency, which still acts as an Independent Administrative Institution, is not regulated by legislation, as is standard for other institutions of the same governmental position. In addition to maintaining the customs of the imperial family and managing their affairs, the Agency is charged with the care of the Privy Seal, the official seal of the emperor, and the State Seal of Japan. The Agency was established between the seventh and eighth centuries, growing to a massive bureaucracy through the years. Throughout the Meiji period, from the establishment of the modern Ministry of the Imperial Household in 1869 to the reorganization in 1908, the departments, functions, and power structures of the Ministry changed frequently. As part of the State Shinto system, Shinto affairs fell under the structure of the Ministry during the Meiji, Taishō, and early Shōwa periods, but upon the imperial proclamation in 1945 renouncing the emperor's sacred status, Shinto was separated from the Ministry and from state governance. Between 1947 and 1949, the Agency was reformed, and the staff was cut by over eighty percent, down to 1,000 workers and officers. The Imperial Household Agency still exists today. The Agency website states:

> The Imperial Household Agency, as a government organization placed under the Prime Minister, takes charge of the state matters concerning the Imperial House. In addition, among the Emperor's acts in matters of state stipulated in Article 7 of the Constitution of Japan, the Agency assists His Majesty in receiving foreign ambassadors and ministers and performing ceremonial functions. It also keeps the Privy Seal and State Seal.[18]

Aside from overseeing the activities and affairs of the emperor, empress, and their extended family, the Agency also oversees the Archives and Mausolea of the Imperial Family, the properties and gardens of the family, and two museums: the Sannomaru Shōzōkan (三の丸尚蔵館, Museum of the Imperial Collections) in Tokyo and the Shōsōin Treasure House (正倉院) in Nara.

It is critical at this point to recognize the system and social network which surrounded the imperial family in the modern era, that of the peerage, or nobility. The nobility (華族, *kōzoku*) which formed the social group that surrounded the imperial family included between 400 and 1,000 families and reached its height in the years of the Pacific War. A smaller peerage system existed pre-Meiji, but the modern *kōzoku* was created by law in 1884. The members of the nobility were well known as public figures and celebrities in the late nineteenth and early twentieth centuries and functioned as a group to protect the interests of the imperial household and serve in the upper house of the government.[19] They frequently surrounded the imperial family in photographs, at public appearances, in their education, and at social events. This group was disbanded in 1947, at the end of the Pacific War.

Today, the continued usage of “emperor” and “empress” in English to refer to the contemporary Japanese sovereigns is problematic, as Japan does not have an empire. Historically, however, and within the era covered in this book, the terms are appropriate, as Japan did possess imperial territories in the Meiji, Taishō, and Shōwa periods.[20] It was during this period that the transliterated term *mikado* (帝, emperor), used in English in the nineteenth century to refer to the Japanese monarchs, fell out of favor in the Anglophone world and was replaced with the term emperor.[21] Developed to contrast the Japanese emperor with that of other nations (specifically China), the Japanese word *tennō* refers only to the Japanese emperor rather than the term *kōtei* (皇帝, emperor), which refers to any emperor. The Japanese imperial system was initially developed between the mid-sixth and early eighth centuries during a period when the influence of Chinese culture, and specifically Confucianism, was particularly strong.[22] Under Confucian philosophy, merit is a core value, and the overthrow of unjust rulers who lack merit is warranted. Because the Japanese monarchy draws their legitimacy and power from their deified lineage, not from worldly merit, it was necessary to create a distinction between the Japanese system and those of other nations.

Additionally, the imperial household, as it was conceptualized between 1868 and 1945, was tightly interwoven with the ideology of Shinto. During this time, the emperor was promoted as a sacred presence, or a *kami* in human form (*aramikami*, *akitsumikami*, 現御神), a descendant of the sun goddess Amaterasu, and was envisioned as a political, sacred, and national leader: a father figure of the Japanese state. The emperor’s importance to rituals provided them with a crucial and unique role, one which could not be usurped by political leaders; the emperors of the Meiji, Taishō, and early Shōwa periods were reliant upon their advisers, ministers, and the *genrō* (元老, an extraconstitutional palace oligarchy), as true political power and authority in these periods rested with the bureaucracy; the military; and the heads of the House of Peers, the Privy Council, and the House of Representatives.[23] While the emperors of the modern era were presented with the aura of political and military authority, their primary importance remained in their roles as figureheads and ritual leaders.

Similarly, the modern empresses were primarily symbolic in nature, but their absence in sacred and ritual realms meant that their personae functioned predominantly as that of a royal celebrity. The term *kōgō* has historic roots in the Japanese language but came to be used for the empress consort in the Meiji period as this new role developed. Unlike *tennō*, *kōgō* can be used for the empresses of other nations but is generally reserved for empress consorts of East Asia, with *jotei* (女帝) used for empress regnant of other regions, such as Catherine the Great, empress of eighteenth-century Russia. In English, use of the term empress for the Japanese women royals mirrored the use of *kōgō* in Japanese, as there was not widespread English publication on the women of the Japanese imperial household prior to the nineteenth century. For both *tennō* and *kōgō*, *heika* (陛下, majesty) is the honorific suffix utilized to refer to the living sovereign and designated by Imperial Household Law.

Outside of a few examples of 1880s woodblock prints of Emperor Meiji visiting the Yasukuni Jinja, where Japan's military dead are enshrined, it was not until the Taishō and early Shōwa periods that the imperial family was widely visually linked with Shinto in visual culture; during the Meiji period the connections were primarily made through slogans and state-promoted concepts such as *saisei itchi* (祭政一致, shrine rites and imperial rule are one), by distributing amulets, and by promoting the Ise Grand Shrine (伊勢神宮) as an imperial mausoleum for Amaterasu, among other activities.[24] That the modern imperial family utilized Amaterasu, a female *kami*, as one source of their legitimacy while simultaneously denying women female emperorship cannot be ignored. This gendered duality: that the sacred power of the imperial family was derived from Amaterasu, yet women were, and are, excluded from official Shinto ceremonies and structures at the imperial level, arose from Meiji period gender ideology.

As Meiji state structures were formed in the 1870s and 1880s, gender discrimination on all levels was justified through a process of mutual reinforcement of Shinto, state, and emperor. Imperial law was constructed to allow only for male emperors, looking to a variety of historic texts and select global royal precedents, as well as broad patriarchal structures within Meiji society at large.

At the same time, household law used the male imperial lineage to rationalize unequal laws for average citizens.[25] While changes in Japanese laws have led to greater gender equality in the postwar period, the Shinto foundations of the imperial family remain an obstacle to women emperors, meaning that religious rites will need to transform to allow for female rule.[26]

The various nineteenth century attempts to define and codify Shinto resulted in three major variations of the practice—state/emperor, local/ritual, religious/sectarian—all of which shared nationalist conceptions of Shinto as Japan's pure indigenous belief system.[27] The Japanese term for religion, *shūkyō* (宗教), was coined during the Meiji period, and as the word developed in relation to Euro-American concepts, *shūkyō* connoted a belief system that included doctrine and personal piety, concepts that were not considered applicable to Shinto.[28] In the same era, state-supported shrine Shinto involving emperor worship was officially deemed non-religious in character after 1882.[29] The idea of Shinto as non-religious remains contentious: in 2018 lawsuits were filed against the Japanese government claiming that spending public money on the imperial enthronement ceremonies was a violation of the separation of religion and politics.[30]

In the modern era, bureaucrats combined the power of the Shinto system with that of the patriarchal state to create an infallible and highly powerful government.[31] This was based on the principle of *saisei itchi*, reflected in the initial Imperial Rescript from 1867, which abolished the shogunate and called for imperial rule in the style of the mythological first emperor, Jinmu. The Rescript associated Buddhism with the failed Tokugawa shogunate and acted as a hedge against the spread of Christianity in Japan.[32] Furthermore, it cemented the centrality of the emperor and worked to create additional national unity.[33] It also furthered the conventional male–female gender binary that was promoted through government family policies.

Parallel to Shinto thought, Neo-Confucianism was the preferred intellectual paradigm in eighteenth and nineteenth century Japan, but with a layer of Japanese symbolism. Within Confucian philosophy, leadership is selected through merit and revolution, yet the selection of rulers in Japan was superseded by the importance of the imperial bloodline and the connection of the emperor to the sun goddess Amaterasu.[34] The system that emerged in the late nineteenth century resulted from these hybrid religious and philosophical beliefs and was, in essence, Confucian ancestor worship with the imperial family at the national center, per Shinto mythology.[35]

As the Meiji period went on, Shinto developed as an ideology and strengthened ties to the symbol of the emperor. The second phase of state-managed Shinto, which Shimazono Susumu defines as the "period of completion of the doctrine," lasted from the Promulgation of the Imperial Constitution in 1889 through the end of the Russo-Japanese War in 1905.[36] It was during this period that Shinto "became a supra-religious national ritual system under the Imperial Constitution."[37] It was also during this second phase that the *goshinei* (御真影, imperial portrait), a sacred image which will be discussed in Chapter 4, was distributed and enshrined within schools and government offices. Just after the Promulgation of the Constitution, the *Kyōiku ni kansuru chokugo* (Imperial Rescript on Education) was released and sent to schools to be stored together with the *goshinei* in small structures that often resembled Shinto architecture, thus further promoting the emperor and Shinto in official contexts. The empress was also part of the official *goshinei* visual program.

Building upon the nascent visual ties of emperor, empress, and Shinto in the Meiji period, in the Taishō and early Shōwa periods, the graphic connections of Shinto and the imperial family grew increasingly explicit. A number of lithograph scrolls showing aerial views of Meiji Jingū, where Meiji and Shōken are enshrined, together with portraits of the emperor and empress and scenes from palace and government functions, were produced in the early Taishō period.[38] Widely accessible materials such as postcards also unified Shinto and the imperial family; in an example from 1920 (Figure 1.3), Shōken is represented with the gate of Meiji Jingū and a graphically vague scene of a railing, lantern, clouds, and pines, referencing the bridge into the shrine and the expansive forested grounds. Created six years after her death and at a time when Emperor Taishō was out of the public eye, this postcard juxtaposes what was then a thirty-year-old photograph

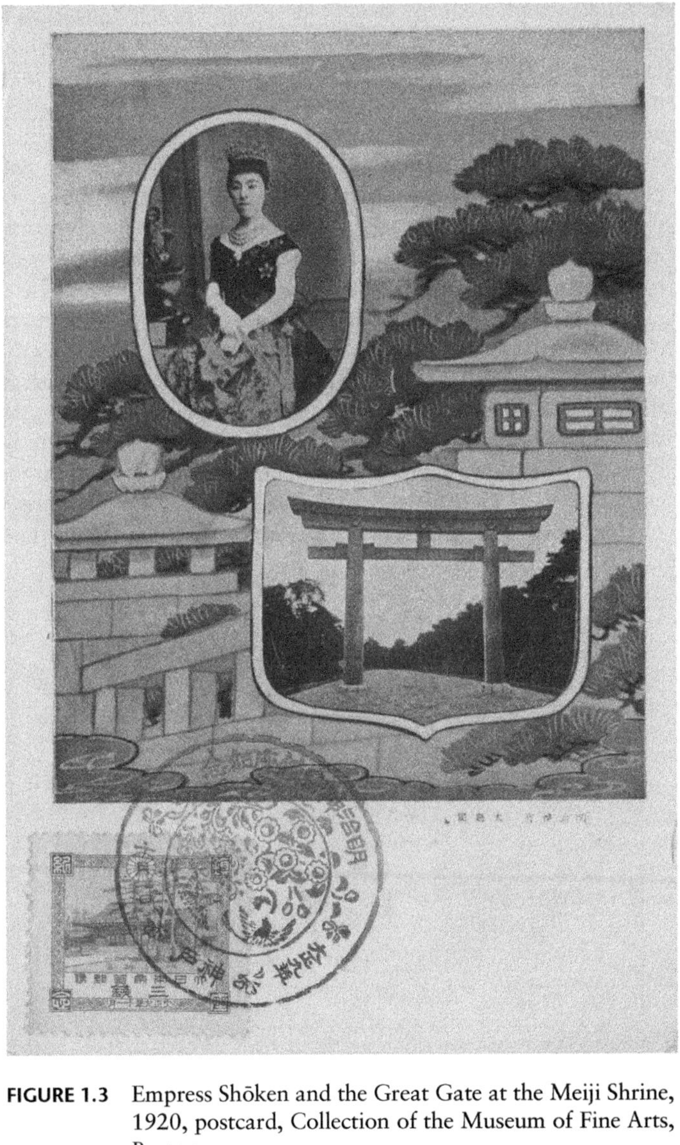

FIGURE 1.3 Empress Shōken and the Great Gate at the Meiji Shrine, 1920, postcard, Collection of the Museum of Fine Arts, Boston

of Shōken with a shrine that holds a significant physical position in the capital. The image shows both her connections to Shinto vis-à-vis the space where she is enshrined, as well as how ingrained the Meiji imperial family, and specifically the empress, was in the broader field of Japanese visual culture.

Seven years later, at the time of his enthronement, Kōjun and Hirohito's portraits were placed on a postcard with an image of the Daijōkyū, the temporary shrine complex used in the enthronement ceremonies, and a phoenix design in the background tying together the varied parts of the composition (Figure 1.4). The elegant gold and silver coloring harmoniously blends with the monochrome portraits and landscape and presents the couple as the inheritors of the imperial lineage, connected to Amaterasu through the Daijōsai, or Great Thanksgiving rite, that took place in the shrine. The use of Amaterasu in imperial lineage portraits will be further addressed in Chapter 4, but here it suffices to say that the empresses were increasingly represented in Shinto-oriented imperial images over the course of the modern period. The connections

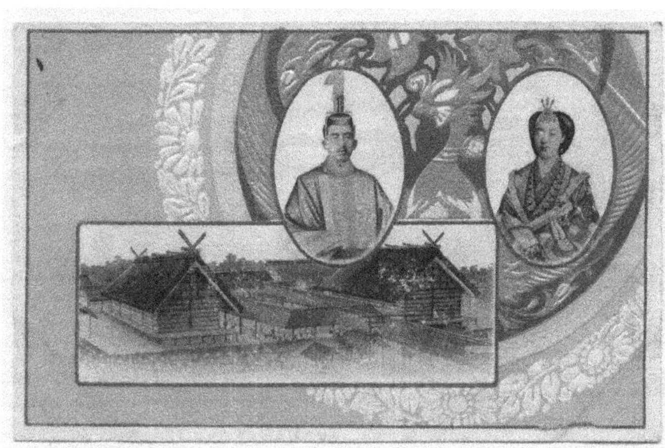

FIGURE 1.4 Daijōkyū, Shōwa Emperor and Empress, c. 1928, postcard, Special Collections & College Archives, Skillman Library, Lafayette College

of the imperial family, Shinto, and the state combined to show that women had an important role to play in both imperial and Shinto structures. While both institutions were, and are, highly patriarchal, the duality of gender implied and visualized in Shinto and the imperial household should not be ignored, as the presence of women contributed to ideas of corporate monarchy and to the active involvement of women in modern Japanese society.

Key Theories for Constructing the Modern Imperial Family

The imperial family has long held somewhat contradictory positions in society, positions which in the modern era are inherent in their public visual representations. Erwin von Bälz, the German physician who cared for the imperial family's medical needs in the early twentieth century, famously stated, to the Japanese people the emperor is, "not so much an individual as the incarnation of an idea."[39] In the realm of images, this conceptualization supports the conventional promotion of the *goshinei,* or the unchanging sacred presence, a realistic image distributed to schools and government buildings. Yet, from an examination of print and photographic imagery in the late nineteenth and early twentieth centuries, and even through to the present day, it is apparent that the modern emperors of Japan were very much represented as individuals—from Emperor Meiji through to Emperor Naruhito, the distinctive interests and activities, as well as divergent dispositions, of the five modern emperors were, and are, an important component of their public personae. When Baelz was working for the imperial family, Emperor Meiji's strong, stoic personality was central to his reputation as a leader and to the justification of him as the leader of the nation.

This contradictory notion—of the emperor as an individual and as a representative of a timeless ideal—has long been of interest to scholars of the imperial household. Historically, a number of specialists across disciplines investigated how the emperor and the imperial institution acted as a timeless symbolic representation of the nation-state of Japan rather than as an individual in the narrative of nation or history.[40] More contemporary scholars have detailed the individual characteristics and biographical and personal elements of the modern emperors, marking them as matchless personages, shaped by their historical moment and unique place in Japanese society.[41] In considering the position and role of the empress, particularly in the context of the imperial family, it is crucial to understand these seemingly inconsistent capacities of the emperors who were constrained by their role as sacred authorities in the imperial lineage, yet in the era after 1868, the imperial family was also promoted as a role model of modernity and the nuclear family, particularly in images.[42] Alice Tseng examines this contradiction and how official images "commanded unconditional reverence on the one hand and conjured casual curiosity on the other."[43] This book argues that the sacred/secular paradox of imperial representation was resolved through the use of empress images; by presenting complimentary gendered royals, the citizenry had multiple means to approach their sovereigns.

A variety of theories surrounded the establishment of the modern imperial family, provided constraints on and expectations of their behavior, and were referenced in the writing of Imperial Household Law including theories on the king's two bodies and those of *kokutai*. These theories are vital for understanding images of the empress.

In the realm of Japanese language scholarship, the imperial family is often studied through the lens of sociology. Yoshimi Shunya has theorized that, at its core, the emperor system is about the reception and consumption of a mass media institution. He states, "the modern emperor system is the media organization itself, which records the effects of interpretations of the emperor's body, regardless of its presence, at the national level. There is no 'essence' of the emperor outside of nation-wide media acceptance."[44] Migita Hiroki also argues for the centrality of the media in creating a secular role for the imperial family, one that was in opposition to the religious fervor of government-sponsored *kokutai*, or national polity ideology, and led to a popular perception of the emperor's persona as dualistic in nature.[45] These scholarly evaluations of the media as critical to the existence of the modern imperial family support the concept of the visual monarchy, but they neglect the role of the empress and her position as a royal celebrity and do not address how the women of the imperial household, part of, yet simultaneously outside of, the emperor system, promoted and sustained the monarchy as an institution.

Subsequently, it is critical to theorize the imperial family not just as a media product created for consumption but as an entity with multiple parts that responds to public demands, one which has agency in how it is represented and is inseparable from media representations. Within the emerging interdisciplinary field of royal studies, as stated by Elena Woodacre,

> the idea of "corporate monarchy," that the exercise of royal power is a collaborative process which incorporates not only the sovereign but their consort, core members of the dynasty and even favorites and mistresses has become increasingly influential in recent years.[46]

The Japanese imperial family has the added influence of the Imperial Household Agency as a mediating force and as an intermediary between the royals themselves and the mass media that distributes images and ideas.

In regard to understanding images, art historical studies on the Japanese imperial family are extant, but they are relatively few in number compared with visual studies of European monarchies and tend to focus on the male members of the family.[47] Probable reasons for this gap are the intermedial nature of the images, primarily available in photography and print, as paintings and sculptures of the imperial family are rare and often inaccessible to the public or to scholars. An exception is art historian Wakakuwa Midori, who argued that the icon of Empress Shōken was as critical as that of Emperor Meiji in establishing the modern Japanese state and that Shōken's image was central in creating ideals of womanhood and maternity.[48]

As new concepts of gender were instituted in the Meiji period, notions of the timelessness of the male imperial lineage and the distinct roles of emperor and empress, in line with a conventional male/female gender binary, were also established. While these roles were somewhat flexible over time, intellectuals in the Meiji and Taishō periods established the perception of the emperor and empress as strict father and lenient mother, two royals as one complementary unit, thus providing a role for the empresses within the imperial structure.[49] Scholar, journalist, and politician Suematsu Kenchō (末松 謙澄,1855–1920) and ethnologist and literary theorist Origuchi Shinobu (折口 信夫,1872–1953) provided two important voices among many whose writings on Japanese society and culture included notions of duality in imperial rule.[50] Suematsu, who spent three years studying law at Cambridge University, wrote about the English theory of the king's two bodies as a means to conceptualize the Japanese monarchy in the late nineteenth century.[51] He states:

> The king is said to be one who never dies. . . . This does not mean that the life of the king is in reality undying but that when the sovereign dies his power and majesty as king are immediately conveyed to the royal heir. Because it is deemed that not a moment intervenes, it is said that while there is a replacement of the old king's physical body (*shintai*) by the new, it is as if there has never been a change in the king's spirit (*seishin*).[52]

As this was part of a report to the Imperial Household Ministry which Suematsu completed while posted in London as part of the official Japanese diplomatic mission, it is clear that those who were formulating and constructing the concepts of the modern imperial structure were aware of the theory of the king's two bodies as interpreted by Suematsu.[53] Undoubtedly, significant differences existed between systems of European and Japanese kingship, but Meiji intellectuals ignored these differences in their writing and thus actively constructed the dualism of the modern emperor.[54] A delicate balance was required: the emperor had to maintain an element of being "above the clouds," mysterious and mystical, yet he could not be so far removed from the people so as to lose relevance.[55]

Although the emperor's duality may be a tidy way of fashioning the theories of imperial power, it is an overly simplistic one and does not tell the full story. It was the role of the empresses that complicated this narrative—as seen in visual culture—and that provides a third, complexifying presence. Theresa Earenfight argues for monarchy as a partnership between king and queen, stating, "The densely interconnected personal, cultural, social, economic, and political milieu of queenship is part of a gender system of political action that is not culturally static, but rather has a political dimension that varied geographically and temporally."[56] The empresses had a public role, but it was not always as a soft, domestic counterpart to the emperors. This is true for Empress Shōken, who was the central subject of hundreds of woodblock prints, and for Empress Teimei, who maintained imperial power and legitimacy through her role as an imperial proxy. Furthermore, the empresses and the other members of the imperial household provided an important human element to the emperor. The empress and the children of the emperor were a sign of the conjugal relations of the emperor and thus a reminder of his humanity. The empress and imperial children therefore assisted in connecting the emperor to his people; the emperors acted as the timeless imperial ideal inside the palace walls and governmental structures, while the empresses provided the citizenry with a human connection to the monarchy.[57]

The bureaucratic objective of establishing the monarch as a social ideal and not an individual became a serious quandary at points in the modern era, with the presence of the empresses acting as a solution. For example, during the regency years of the early 1920s and in the midst of public updates on Emperor Taishō's health status, the emperor could not be invisible to the populace as a personage; on the contrary, his reticence due to illness highlighted the frail nature of his humanity. Thus, Taishō's malady and the subsequent flow of information to the people regarding the details of his health meant that the citizenry could not ignore that there was a human being at the apex of the imperial household, one who was ailing in the same mundane and mortal fashion as his subjects. It was in the midst of this predicament that Empress Teimei came to the fore as a stand-in for the emperor during public appearances.

In the context of the regency, this would allow for the *seishin* (精神), or the king's spirit, to continue on, unbroken in lineage and unaffected by the illness that Emperor Taishō was experiencing in his physical body, or *shintai* (身体). In practical terms, the concept of the king's two bodies allowed for the invisibility of Emperor Taishō—his power lay in the unseen *seishin*, or spirit, rather than in the mortal *shintai* form—and thus Empress Teimei could act as the visible face of the monarchy. Decades later, a similar argument was put forth by Origuchi Shinobu, who postulated that the imperial body was merely a receptacle, or *iremono* (入れ物), which housed the *tennōrei* (天皇霊), or imperial spirit.[58] Within this theoretical context, because the corporeal body was merely a physical placeholder, or signifier of the more vital, timeless spirit, the visibility of the emperor's body in front of the citizenry was not necessary for maintaining the imperial narrative. As such, these theories of the dual imperial body were crucial for positioning the empresses and allowed for imperial continuity in a variety of situations.

Kokutai (国体), or national polity, is yet another key concept that was distinct in meaning during Japan's modern era. Generally translated as national polity or national essence, the term literally means national body. Defining *kokutai* is notoriously difficult; the term has its roots in the premodern period, and the nuance in the meaning of the term quickly evolved in the modern era. In essence, *kokutai* refers to the "unique" Japanese system of governance, social structure, and rule. Closely linked with the emperor, who was envisioned as the father figure of the nation, *kokutai* was, in the nineteenth century, a means for justifying the continuation of the monarchy, the expansion of state-managed Shinto, and the promotion of the legendary origins of Japan and the imperial family while simultaneously maintaining a constitutional democracy in the style of the European powers.[59] As time progressed, the use of *kokutai* to keep these two systems blended into an overarching philosophy of single governance, with the emperor at the head of state.

In 1925, at the end of the Taishō era, the Peace Preservation Law was passed, criminalizing the critique of the *kokutai* and the property system and making criticism of the emperor a capital offense.[60] By 1937, with the publication of *Kokutai no hongi* (国体の本義, Cardinal Principles of the National Polity), the system reached its zenith; the manifesto promoted the emperor as central to Japanese life, stating:

> Our country is established with the emperor, who is a descendant of Amaterasu Ōmikami, as its center, as our ancestors as well as we ourselves constantly have beheld in the emperor the fountainhead of her life and activities. For this reason, to serve the emperor and to receive the emperor's great august will as our own is the rationale of making our historical "life" live in the present; and on this is based the morality of the people.[61]

Communal interest, military values, and serving the nation above all else were promoted as part of the text, which was distributed to school children throughout the nation. Over the period covered in this book, the concept of *kokutai* was steadily developing, its influence growing greater with time. Regarding the study of empress images, the promotion of *kokutai* in the modern period means that it is exceedingly difficult to find critiques of the imperial family in the historical record. The images under examination in this book were created and disseminated under state control, and any questioning of the imperial family or the system that surrounded them was swiftly suppressed. Likewise, the majority of the written record invokes praise when mentioning the imperial family.

Gender and the Throne in Meiji and Taishō Japan

A common observation on the Japanese imperial family is the highly conservative, Confucian, and patriarchal nature of the institution. Undoubtedly, the monarchy's penchant for tradition is true; the women of the imperial household are officially held in an inferior position through the system of primogeniture, and certainly the draconian politics and policies of the Imperial Household Agency worked to assert a level of control over the individual members of the family. Yet, while the imperial institution is extremely conventional, examining the images and public personae of the imperial family shows that women have played a central role through time. For example, between 1965 and 2006, the imperial family did not produce a single male heir. In the late 1990s and early 2000s, prior to the birth of Prince Hisahito, a great deal of concern was expressed by the general public, in political circles, and indirectly by the Imperial Household Agency about the lack of a male heir and the potential need to change the law of agnatic primogeniture to one of male preference or absolute primogeniture.[62]

Pivotal to this discussion was Empress Masako, who was forbidden to give press interviews in the months leading up to her 1993 wedding and was made over with an entirely new, yet highly conventional, princess-worthy wardrobe.[63] While Masako's public persona and image were decided for her, she herself was still essential to the narrative of the imperial family during the early years of her marriage. As a Harvard-educated career diplomat, Masako left her career upon marriage and faced immense public criticism when she gave birth to a single daughter. That there are parallels between average women and the imperial women related to the decrease in fertility and pressure to sacrifice their own interests and careers for the sake of continuing a patriarchal lineage is not lost on the Japanese public. As will be further revealed throughout this book, these parallels in women's issues rang true throughout the modern period, with the empress image consistently used to promote and model state gender ideology but simultaneously elevating the women as popular celebrity figures.[64] The station of Japan's imperial women is decidedly orthodox and often lies outside of their control, but it is a position which the women have used, in their own ways, to create differing meanings.

The parallels between the plight and issues of average women and imperial women and the alternating feminist critiques contrasting with the co-opting of the imperial institution as a symbol of women's issues in Japan are not unique to Masako. A 2005 publication on the succession predicament surrounding Masako and Naruhito's offspring stated,

> This crisis has sparked a lively discussion in Japan among the general public, media, and pundits over how it should be resolved. Even feminists, who have remained aloof from discussion of imperial matters (seeing the throne as a remnant of Japan's militaristic past), have entered the debate.[65]

While this quotation references feminists of the early 2000s, at points in the past feminists such as Hiratsuka Raichō (平塚らいちょう, 1886–1971) were in full support of the Japanese imperial institution.[66] Women's relationships with and views of the imperial institution were, and are, complex. Empresses were often involved in issues and affairs that were relevant to their female subjects; the imagined role of the empress, dynamic through time, has constantly reinforced official ideals of what women's roles should be while simultaneously being critiqued and co-opted by common women.

While it is widely understood that familial gender roles and broad social conceptions of gender underwent dramatic changes in the Meiji period, what is less studied is how these conceptualizations were applied to the empresses.[67] Scholars have debated both the feminization of the emperor and the motherly nature of Empress Kōjun, but Shōken and Teimei and the subtleties of how their femininity, maternity, and imperial power were expressed in the visual realm have received little attention.[68] The visual monarchy as constructed between 1870 and 1930 at times defied feminine and maternal gender constructions; the imaging of Shōken and Teimei was complex and changing, establishing what feminine and maternal meant in the context of modern Japan and against the global visual standard of European monarchy. This conceptualization negotiated concepts of biological, adopted, and national motherhood for the empresses, allowing Meiji imperial concubines to be public figures. By means of visual culture the empress image was utilized to establish palace customs in the nineteenth century, tie tradition to femininity, and invent a national maternal role. It adeptly validated the emperors by linking them to a sacred female ancestor, while policy simultaneously denied women the right to become *tennō* or, in the realm of the citizenry, to hold basic privileges such as voting.

During the 2019 Reiwa enthronement ceremonies, the media brought attention to the lack of women's participation in the rites and rituals that ushered the monarchy to the throne, while surveys indicated that over 80% of the Japanese public supported female emperors and a similar number felt a personal affection for the emperor.[69] The laws and standards that brought the imperial family to the place where they are today changed on multiple occasions throughout the past 150 years and will change again in the future. The flexibility of the monarchy, with its rites and rituals that appear ageless and eternal, is what has allowed it to endure through eras of divergent cultural and political norms.

The Foundations and Development of Imperial Portraiture

In addition to these key theories, it is crucial to review a brief history of the human likeness in Japanese visual culture to further appreciate the ground-breaking nature of the material covered in this book. Portraiture, defined here as a visual representation of the human likeness, has a long and rich history in Japan, but for most of this time the predominant portrait subjects were men. By establishing the masculine precedents for imperial portraiture, we can understand how revolutionary it was to witness the advent of portraits and images of imperial women in the Meiji period.

The earliest Japanese portraits, dating from the eighth century, presented the likenesses of Buddhist monks.[70] After contact with Song dynasty China in the twelfth and thirteenth centuries, representations of monks began to appear with greater frequency in painting and sculpture.[71] Although these images were principally of spiritual men, they establish a historical precedent of naturalistic portrait imagery, one which had an impact on and legacy in imperial portraiture.[72] These idealized portraits were not, however, comparable to modern secular portraits in their use or patronage. They were not intended for everyday viewing and were not displayed for personal use in the home or for public consumption. Rather, they were usually created by devout followers upon the death of the monk and were displayed during memorial ceremonies and later upon the anniversary of the death of the sitter. These norms of usage, too, would have an impact on the way imperial portraits functioned in the modern era.

As the women of the imperial household were hidden from public view prior to the Meiji period, their likenesses were not recorded in portraits that are known to us today. Empress consorts and courtesans were absent from portraits partially due to their low social status among a patriarchal court culture but also owing to cultural ideas and norms that precluded most living people from being represented in a realistic fashion. Even after these standards changed, women's ancillary positions at court meant that their countenances remained private until the early Meiji period.

The development of the *nise-e* (似絵, copy picture) in the mid-twelfth century and the portrait of the retired Emperor Toba (鳥羽天皇, 1103–1156) at the same historical moment mark the innovation of imperial Japanese portraiture.[73] The *nise-e* generally depicted secular figures with individualized faces but similar bodies.[74] It is accepted among scholars that prior to the twelfth century, there was a belief that realistic or naturalistic imagery could result in a supernatural curse.[75] The potential for the growth of portraiture was unleashed once these beliefs changed. *Nise-e* of the emperors were extant but rare. The earliest was created in 1338, of Emperor Hanazono (花園天皇, 1297–1348), yet these were not publicly displayed until well into the nineteenth century.[76] As six of the eight premodern female *tennō* ruled before the eighth century, their likenesses were not recorded in *nise-e*, and extant portraits of the remaining two female *tennō* from their lifetime are either unknown or do not exist. Throughout the same time, the shoguns, male military leaders who ruled from 1185–1868, were represented in portraiture with similar conventions to Buddhist monks, as were men of the warrior class and occasionally female poets and nuns.[77]

In a dramatic turn of representation, the first Japanese ruler to be photographed was Tokugawa Yoshinobu (徳川慶喜, 1837–1913), the last leader of the shogunal government. The earliest photographs of him dated to the mid-1860s, with a reproduction of one of the images published in the *Illustrated London News* on August 10, 1867.[78] Although photographs of the shogun from the year prior are extant, the 1867 image was the first to be widely viewed by the public, but notably this public was outside of Japan; the image received virtually no domestic distribution.[79] The *Illustrated London News* portrait was taken by amateur British photographer Frederick William Sutton, in Japan with the Royal Navy to document the meeting of the Shogun and the visiting British Minister Extraordinary and captains of the

Royal Navy vessels docked in Osaka in April of 1867.[80] An additional image of Yoshinobu from the 1860s depicts him in a military uniform that was a gift from Napoleon III. Although these images were not widespread in their reproduction or distribution, as Mikiko Hirayama states, they "clearly indicate a conscious attempt to present a positive image of the then-shaky shogunal authority overseas."[81] It is also important to note that the single published image was taken by a foreign photographer. Although in these early days of public portraiture of Japanese rulers the concept of authority was decidedly important, Japanese government officials had yet to codify and standardize a visual strategy for representing leadership. The international character of the clothing choices, distribution channels, production, and reproduction of these initial images foreshadows the global nature of modern imperial portraiture in Japan, which would always have close connections with foreign, and specifically British, monarchies.[82]

The lack of a unified imperial visual strategy and relative absence of women's portraits continued into the early Meiji years. With the Meiji Restoration in 1868, it was deemed critical to the national project to situate Emperor Meiji as the unquestioned leader of the nation and for him to hold an aura of authority. Coinciding with the ascent of Emperor Meiji to the throne the distribution of news was in the midst of major adjustments due to technological advancements in communications, printing, and transportation that led to the development of mass media. Simultaneously, the developing field of photography was impacting the way portraits were conceived and created.[83] Combined with social changes in how gender was conceived, these fluctuations would have a great impact on the development of imperial portraits as a genre.

The first Japanese royal photograph was of Emperor Meiji, captured by the Czech photographer Baron Raimund von Stillfried-Ratenicz in January of 1872. Upon the occasion of Emperor Meiji visiting the city of Yokosuka to tour industrial facilities, Stillfried surreptitiously placed his camera behind a canvas sail with a small hole in it, so as to capture the emperor and his entourage while they took a break from their tour.[84] In the image Emperor Meiji wears formal Japanese-style robes, as do only three of the twenty men who accompany him. Immediately, the illicit photograph caused a stir. The *Japan Weekly Mail* reported the incident,

> On the occasion of the recent visit of the Mikado to Yokoska, an enterprising photographer managed to secure a view of the scene, including a portrait of His Majesty. The Japanese, fearful of the universal diffusion of the portrait, sent down to Yokohama to buy up the copies which had been struck off and the negative itself. This they have done at a large price, the photographer clinging, not unnaturally, to his rights.[85]

Stillfried attempted to market the image but was quickly embroiled in an international controversy, complete with the involvement of Japanese diplomats, the British Consul, and the Austrian Minister Resident, the result of which was the confiscation of the negatives and the censorship of the photograph.[86] The commotion surrounding the photograph was widely reported in the press and promptly led to discussions on the need for a visible, visual monarchy in Japan, something which was not a priority throughout the previous millennia of imperial history.

Among government bureaucrats, there were many concerns about the weak appearance of Emperor Meiji in the early days of the Restoration. As Meiji's youth was spent in isolation, he had little experience or training in how to act as a public figure; in early visits with European dignitaries many commented on his odd way of walking, his hushed voice, his highly made-up face, and his sartorial antiquity.[87] At the encouragement of his advisers and diplomats and with the support of his handlers, Emperor Meiji quickly transformed his public persona. In fact, less than six months after Stillfried's image was created, the Japanese government responded with an image of their own. With interest in the emperor—and critically the empress—gaining traction with commoners and making appearances in popular *nishiki-e* multi-color woodblock prints that will be covered in Chapter 2, the government sensed the need to distribute an official image, thus providing a modicum of control over the likenesses in circulation and planting the seeds for the development of the visual monarchy. It is this first official photograph, and the other official studio portraits of Emperor Meiji and Empress Shōken, that will be covered in Chapter 4.

This chapter has provided vital context for the remainder of the book on the development of the modern imperial system, theories of Japanese monarchy, and gendered rule, particularly as related to Shinto and the position of the emperor and empress in the years between 1868 and 1930. Due to the many restrictions on information surrounding the Japanese imperial family, the modern empresses are not figures who we can truly know; however, their public personalities and constructed personae were central to ideas of femininity and women's comportment between the Meiji and early Shōwa periods. The following chapters will examine empress images in prints, photography, mass media, and portrait representations, all of which were part of constructing their biographies in the larger public forum.

Notes

1 There are a variety of biographical books written on each of the empresses, which tend to be deferential and sympathetic in style and offer an uncritical narrative of the lives of the women. Examples include: Shufu no tomo, *Teimei kōgō* (Tokyo: Shufu no tomo, 1971), or Itoko Koyama, *Nagako: Empress of Japan* (New York: John Day Company, 1958). Also, the poetry of the imperial family was frequently published in newspapers, magazines, and special publications, but this was part of their intentionally crafted public personae. Gossip-style books and magazines do exist, but nothing on the scale of the paparazzi-driven media surrounding the British monarchy.

2 In English, the modern emperors are often referred to as deities; however, there is some cultural translation which requires clarification in this regard. The divinity of the emperors was promoted in the modern period, building throughout the Meiji, Taishō, and Shōwa periods, and eventually included in morality texts in the 1930s and 1940s. This divinity arose from the ancestry of the emperors and from their connections to the sun goddess Amaterasu. The emperors were not regarded in the Euro-American sense of a god, but they were

viewed as mediums, and their ritual actions could impact the world around them. When Emperor Shōwa announced the end of the war with his August 15 radio broadcast, the *Gyokuon-hōsō* (玉音放送, Jewel-voice broadcast), he said nothing of his personal divinity. With his January 1, 1946, broadcast, he touched upon the subject but did not specifically renounce his divinity. Ben Ami Shillony recounts that he stated, "The ties between him and the people did not 'depend upon mere legends and myths' and were not 'predicated on the false conception that the emperor is divine.' He confirmed the fact that his sacred position did not derive from the belief that he was god, but from the belief that he was a descendant of Amaterasu Ōmikami." In short, Hirohito did not renounce his divine descent, as it provided the legitimacy for the imperial family, but did step back from the wartime escalation of his status. See: Ben-Ami Shillony, "'Restoration,' 'Emperor,' 'Diet,' 'Prefecture,' or: How Japanese Concepts were Mistranslated into Western Languages," in *Ben-Ami Shillony-Collected Writings* (Abingdon: Routledge, 2004), n.p.

3 Throughout this book I utilize Takashi Fujitani's concept of the "construction of tradition," which states that during the late nineteenth century the Imperial Household Ministry created public rituals, processions, and rites which were loosely based on tradition and which worked to legitimize and validate the position of the emperor at the head of society. Takashi Fujitani, *Splendid Monarchy: Power and Pageantry in Modern Japan* (Berkeley: University of California Press, 1996).

4 The lineage from Jinmu to Amaterasu can be found in the *Kōjiki*. As the *Kōjiki* was a pseudo-historical narrative, written in the eighth century at the request of an empress, it is not considered an accurate historical source. *Kōjiki*, trans. Donald L. Phillipi (Princeton: Princeton University Press, 1969). For the full lineage, see "Genealogy of the Emperors of Japan," *Imperial Household Agency*. The 2,600-year history is widely disputed but still permeates official imperial household functions, Kenneth J. Ruoff, *Imperial Japan at its Zenith: The Wartime Celebration of the Empire's 2,600th Anniversary* (Ithaca: Cornell University Press, 2010), 185–187.

5 Joan Piggott argues for the development of early kingship culminating in the rulership of Emperor Shōmu as the first true *tennō*, Joan R. Piggott, *The Emergence of Japanese Kingship* (Stanford: Stanford University Press, 1997), 236–279.

6 In the record of 120 emperors, only 60 were a son succeeding his father, and many of those were not the eldest or legitimate sons. It should be remembered, however, that in the Japanese tradition, monogamy and a sacrament of marriage did not exist, thus leaving the legitimate/illegitimate line quite unclear. In short, the story of Japanese succession was not as tidy as the modern narrative might lead one to think. Ernst Lokowandt, "The Imperial House Law and Its Meaning for the Position of the Tennō in the Meiji State," in *Leaders and Leadership in Japan*, ed. Ian Nery (Surrey: Japan Library, 1996), 132–133.

7 Kenneth J. Ruoff, *The People's Emperor: Democracy and the Japanese Monarchy, 1945–1995* (Cambridge, MA: Harvard University Asia Center, 2001), 17–19.

8 Bob Tadashi Wakabayashi, "In Name Only: Imperial Sovereignty in Early Modern Japan," *Journal of Japanese Studies* 17, no. 1 (Winter 1991): 25–57.

9 Lokowandt, "The Imperial House Law and Its Meaning for the Position of the Tennō in the Meiji State," 128–146, 132. Another example is the female Emperor Kōken, a powerful figure often misrepresented in the historical record, Paula R. Curtis, "Japan's Once and Future Female Emperors," *Nursing Clio*, April 30, 2019, https://nursingclio.org/2019/04/30/japans-once-and-future-female-emperors/.

10 One instance of a woman ruler during the Edo period was Okiko (posthumously Meishō), who began rule in 1629. She was the daughter of Kotohito (posthumously Go-Mizunoo), who tried to seize power from the new shogun, failed, and then resigned, allowing his last-but-one daughter Okiko to become emperor. Another instance was Toshiko (posthumously Go-Sakuramachi), emperor from 1762–1771, during the first half of Ieharu's reign. Timon Screech states of these women, "Something of the depleted sense of a woman shujō can be surmised from the fact that she [Toshiko] and Okiko were omitted from the official dynastic portraits." *Shujō* (主上) is the honorific (keigo) term for emperor. Timon Screech, *The Shogun's Painted Culture: Fear and Creativity in the Japanese States, 1760–1829* (London: Reaktion, 2000), 149. See also Kuroda Hideo, "Kinsei no tennō to shōgun no shozōga," in *Ō no shintai ō no shōzō* (Tokyo: Heibonsha, 1993), 286–287.

11 Hitomi Tonomura, "Royal Roles, Wider Changes: Understanding Japan's Gender Relations from a Historical Perspective," in *Japanese Women: Lineage and Legacies*, ed. Amy McCreedy Thernstrom (Washington, DC: Woodrow Wilson International Center for Scholars, 2005), 13.

12 Tonomura, "Royal Roles, Wider Changes," 19.
13 The concepts surrounding the imperial family as a unit were, however, initiated in the late nineteenth century. As such, I will use the term *tennōke* throughout this book. See: Yokoo Yutaka, *Rekidai Tennō to Kōgōtachi* (Tokyo: Kashiwa Shobō, 1987), 53.
14 Toyama Shigeki, *Tennō to kazoku, nihon kindai-shisō taikei*, vol. 2 (Tokyo: Iwanami, 1989), 132, *Kōshitsu tenpan*, https://elaws.e-gov.go.jp/document?law_unique_id=322AC0000000003.
15 This print can be found under the alternate title Illustrious Nobility of the Empire or in a slightly different version as *Fūsō kōki kagami* (A Mirror of Japan's Nobility) at the Metropolitan Museum of Art.
16 Hikari Hori, *Promiscuous Media: Film and Visual Culture in Imperial Japan, 1926–1945* (Cornell: Cornell University Press, 2017), 28.
17 Prior to the late 1940s, the agency was termed the Ministry of the Imperial Household (宮内省 *kunaishō*).
18 Kunaicho, "Organizations and Functions of the Imperial Household Agency," www.kunaicho.go.jp/e-kunaicho/soshiki.html.
19 The nobility was a hereditary peerage and was a merging of the *kuge*, the court nobility, and the *daimyo*, or feudal lords. Takie Sugiyama Lebra, *Above the Clouds: Status Culture of the Modern Japanese Nobility* (Berkeley: University of California Press, 1993), 28–61.
20 When Korea became a part of the Japanese empire in 1911, the Korean nobility was brought into the larger community of the Japanese nobility. The same was true for Okinawan royals in the 1870s. Bruce Batten also argues that ancient Japan was an empire. Bruce Batten, *To the Ends of Japan: Premodern Frontiers, Boundaries, and Interactions* (Honolulu: University of Hawai'i Press, 2003).
21 Ben-Ami Shillony calls for the transliterated use of *tennō*, as *mikado* was not commonly used by the Japanese themselves, and emperor is not an accurate translation. Ben-Ami Shillony, " 'Restoration,' 'Emperor,' 'Diet,' 'Prefecture'," *Ben-Ami Shillony-Collected Writings*, n.p.
22 Imatani Akira, "The Strange Survival and Its Modern Significance," n.p, in *The Emperors of Modern Japan*, ed. Ben-Ami Shillony (Leiden: Brill, 2007). Joan R. Piggott, *The Emergence of Japanese Kingship* (Stanford: Stanford University Press, 1997).
23 Bernard S. Silberman, "Conclusion: Taishō Japan and the Crisis of Secularism," in *Japan in Crisis: Essays on Taishō Democracy*, ed. Bernard S. Silberman and H. D. Harootunian (Princeton: Princeton University Press, 1970), 244.

24 Mark Teeuwen and John Breen, *A Social History of the Ise Shrines: Divine Capital* (London: Bloomsbury Shinto Studies, 2017), 172–173.
25 Hiromi Sasamoto-Collins, "The Emperor's Sovereign Status and the Legal Construction of Gender in Early Meiji Japan," *The Journal of Japanese Studies* 43, no. 2 (Summer 2017); Susan L. Burns and Barbara J. Brooks, eds., *Gender and Law in the Japanese Imperium* (Honolulu: University of Hawai'i Press, 2014); Marnie Anderson, *A Place in Public: Women's Rights in Meiji Japan* (Cambridge, MA: Harvard University Asia Center, 2010); Hayakawa Noriyo, *Kindai tennōsei to kokumin kokka* (Tokyo: Aoki Shoten, 2005).
26 Masako Kamiya, "Is the Japanese Monarchy in Crisis Due to Its Gender Bias?" *Royal Studies Journal (RSJ)* 7, no. 2 (2020): 127.
27 John Breen and Mark Teeuwen, *A New History of Shinto* (West Sussex, England: Wiley-Blackwell, 2010), 18–19.
28 Jason Ānanda Josephson, *The Invention of Religion in Japan* (Chicago: University of Chicago Press, 2012), 1–8. Trent E. Maxey, *The 'Greatest Problem': Religion and State Formation in Meiji Japan* (Cambridge, MA: Harvard University Asia Center, 2014).
29 Mark W. MacWilliams and Okuyama Michiaki, *Defining Shinto: A Reader* (New York: Routledge, 2020), 14.
30 *Japan Times*, "Lawsuit Filed against Japan's State-Funded Ceremonies to Mark Imperial Enthronement," www.japantimes.co.jp/news/2018/12/11/national/crime-legal/lawsuit-filed-japans-state-funded-ceremonies-marking-imperial-enthronement/.
31 Shimazono Susumu, "State Shinto in the Lives of the People: The Establishment of Emperor Worship, Modern Nationalism, and Shrine Shinto in Late Meiji," *Japanese Journal of Religious Studies* 36, no. 1 (2009): 95. Sheldon Garon, *Molding Japanese Minds: The State in Everyday Life* (Princeton: Princeton University Press, 1997), 5–6.
32 Breen and Teeuwen, *A New History of Shinto*, 7–9.
33 As Breen and Teeuwen state, the radical reforms, "drew on a wave of nostalgic nativism that idealized Japan's age of antiquity as a divine era of natural harmony and innocence." Breen and Teeuwen, *A New History of Shinto*, 8.
34 Hara Takeshi, *Kōgōkō* (Tokyo: Kodansha, 2015), 363. Svend M. Hvass, *Ise: Japan's Ise Shrines, Ancient Yet New* (Holte, Denmark: Aristo, 1999), 142.
35 Breen and Teeuwen, *A New History of Shinto*, 8–9. In recent years there has been a scholarly debate over the term State Shinto as a way to define this system. The term

is now mostly disregarded, and "state managed" is used to refer to the late nineteenth-century relationship between government and shrines. See: Murakami Shigeyoshi, *Kokka Shintō* (Tokyo: Iwanami shinsho, 1970); Helen Hardacre, *Shinto and the State, 1868–1988* (Princeton: Princeton University Press, 1989); Shimazono Susumu, *Kokka Shintō to Nihonjin* (Tokyo: Iwanami shoten, 2010); Helen Hardacre, *Shinto: A History* (Oxford: Oxford University Press, 2017), 355–359.

36 Shimazono, "State Shinto in the Lives of the People," 95.

37 Shimazono, "State Shinto in the Lives of the People," 95.

38 Kanagawa kenritsu hakubutsukan, *Oke no shōzō: Meiji kōshitsu arubamu no hajimari* (Yokohama: Kanagawa kenritsu rekishi hakubutsukan, 2001), 74–75.

39 Toku Baelz, ed., *Awakening Japan: The Diary of a German Doctor, Erwin Baelz* (Bloomington and London: Indiana University Press, 1974), 395.

40 William Elliot Griffis, *The Mikado: Institution and Person* (Princeton: Princeton University Press, 1915).

41 Stephen S. Large, *Emperors of the Rising Sun: Three Biographies* (Tokyo: Kodansha International, 1997), Donald Keene, *Emperor of Japan: Meiji and His World, 1852–1912* (New York: Columbia University Press, 2002), Hara Takeshi, *Taishō Tennō* (Tokyo: Asahi shinbunsha, 2000), and Herbert P. Bix, *Hirohito and the Making of Modern Japan* (New York: Harper Collins, 2000).

42 For an analysis of the emperors as "manifest destinies," see Large, *Emperors of the Rising Sun*, 10. For additional information on pictorial magazines such as *Kōzoku gahō* (*Royal Pictorial*), see Aoki Junko, "Zasshi "Kōzoku gahō" ni miru kindai kōzoku fuasshon no imeji," *Contentsu Bunkashi Kenkyū* 8 (2013).

43 Alice Y. Tseng, "Imperial Portraiture and Popular Print Media in Early Twentieth Century Japan," *Journal of Japanese Studies* 46, no. 2 (2020).

44 Yoshimi Shunya, *Karuchuaru tān bunka no seijigaku e* (Kyoto: Jinbun shoin, 2003), 239.

45 Migita Hiroki, "'Kōshitsu gurabia' to 'goshinei': Senzenki shinbun zasshi ni okeru kōshitsu shashin no tsūjiteki bunseki," *Kyoto shakai gakunenhō* 9 (2001).

46 Elena Woodacre and Cathleen Sarti, "What Is Royal Studies?" *Royal Studies Journal* 2 (2015): 16. Woodacre and Sarti also cite: Theresa Earenfight, "Without the Persona of the Prince: Kings, Queens and the Idea of Monarchy in Late Medieval Europe," *Gender and History* 19, no. 1 (2007).

47 Hara Takeshi, *Kōgōkō* (Tokyo: Kodansha, 2015). Jordan Sand, *House and Home in Modern Japan* (Cambridge, MA: Harvard University Press, 2004). For examples of English language studies on the image of Emperor Meiji, see: Mikiko Hirayama, "The Emperor's New Clothes: Japanese Visuality and Imperial Portrait Photography," *History of Photography* 33, no. 2 (2009), and Yuki Morishima, "Political and Ritual Usages of Portraits of Japanese Emperors in Eighteenth and Nineteenth Centuries" (PhD diss., University of Pittsburgh, 2014). In an additional example of previous scholarship, Morris Low writes on the Shōwa Emperor, with reference to the Meiji Emperor, yet only mentions Taishō a few times. Morris Low, *Japan on Display: Photography and the Emperor* (New York: Routledge, 2006).

48 Wakakuwa Midori, *Kōgō no shōzō: Shōken Kotaigō o hyōshō to josei no kokuminka* (Tokyo: Chikuma Shobo, 2001). Shōken did not have biological children.

49 Mikiyo Kanō, *Tennōsei to gendā* (Tokyo: Inpakuto, 2002), 190–200.

50 For additional biographical information on Suematsu Kenchō, see: Ian Ruckston, "Suematsu Kenchō, 1855–1920: Statesman, Bureaucrat, Diplomat, Journalist, Poet and Scholar," in *Britain and Japan: Biographical Portraits*, vol. 5, ed. Hugh Cortazzi (Folkestone: Global Oriental, 2005). For a biography of Origuchi Shinobu, see: Nakazawa Shin'ichi, *Kodai kara kuta miraijin: Origuchi Shinobu* (Tokyo: Chikuma Primer Shinsho, 2008). Although no biography of Origuchi Shinobu exists in English, the following article introduces his philosophies and background: Alfonso Falero, "Origuchi Shinobu's *Marebitoron* in Global Perspective: A Preliminary Study," in *Classical Japanese Philosophy*, ed. J.W. Heisig and R. Raud, Frontiers of Japanese Philosophy 7 (Nagoya: Nanzan Institute for Religion and Culture, 2010), 274–304.

51 For further information on Suematsu's formative years studying in Britain, see: Noboru Koyama, *Japanese Students at Cambridge University in the Meiji Era, 1868–1912: Pioneers for the Modernization of Japan*, trans. Ian Ruxton (Raleigh, NC: Lulu, 2004). Suematsu's writings while he was studying at Cambridge were created as reports to the Imperial Household Minister. Suematsu Kenchō, "Eikoku teishitsu shorei kansatsu hōkoku," no. 1, 1881, Shoryōbu, Imperial Household Agency, Tokyo.

52 Suematsu, "Eikoku teishitsu shorei kansatsu hōkoku" as translated and published in Fujitani, *Splendid Monarchy*, 155–156.

53 For more on the European conceptualization of the duality of the monarchs, see: Ernst H. Kantorowicz, *The King's Two Bodies: A Study in Medieval Political Theology* (Princeton: Princeton University Press, 1998).
54 Fujitani, *Splendid Monarchy*, 158.
55 Fujitani, *Splendid Monarchy*, 160–161. Marius Jansen, "Monarchy and Modernization in Japan," *Journal of Asian Studies* 36 (August 1977).
56 Theresa Earenfight, *The King's Other Body: Maria of Castile and the Crown of Aragon* (Philadelphia: University of Pennsylvania Press, 2009), 4. See also: Theresa Earenfight, "Without the Persona of the Prince: Kings, Queens and the Idea of Monarchy in Late Medieval Europe," *Gender & History* 19, no. 1 (April 2007): 1–21.
57 Mikiyo Kanō discusses the empress as the better half of the royal unit that had a public appeal, *Tennōsei to gendā*, 197.
58 Origuchi Shinobu, "Daijōsai no hongi" (1928), collected in *Origuchi Shinobu zenshū* (Tokyo: Chūō Kōronsha, 1966), 3:174–240.
59 Carol Gluck, *Japan's Modern Myths: Ideology in the Late Meiji Period* (Princeton: Princeton University Press, 1985), 138–146.
60 Gregory J. Kasza, *The State and Mass Media in Japan, 1918–1945* (Berkeley: University of California Press, 1988), 41; Richard H. Mitchell, *Thought Control in Prewar Japan* (Ithaca: Cornell University Press, 1976), 56–68; Andrew Gordon, *A Modern History of Japan* (New York: Oxford University Press, 2009), 170.
61 Selections from *Kokutai no hongi*, 1937, from *Sources of Japanese Tradition*, ed. Wm. Theodore de Bary, Carol Gluck and Arthur L. Tiedemann, 2nd ed., vol. 2 (New York: Columbia University Press, 2005), 968–969, 975.
62 Nakano Masashi, *Josei tennōron: shōchō tennōron to Nippon no mirai* (Tokyo: Asahi Shinbunsha, 2004).
63 Jan Bardsley, "Japanese Feminism, Nationalism and the Royal Wedding of Summer '93," *The Journal of Popular Culture* 31, no. 2 (Fall 1997).
64 Of note here is the system of *tennōsei* (天皇制), or the ideology of the emperor (in the context of the modern Japanese state), which was a product of the years between 1890 and 1945. This system of thought used nationalist rhetoric to conceptualize the Japanese state as a large family under the emperor and positioned Japan as uniquely superior, justifying their colonial control over neighboring states. While often excluded from discussions of *tennōsei*, the empresses played an important part in

instituting and promoting this system; images of the imperial family worked to promote conventional gender roles along a male–female binary, while the empresses supported the masculine *tennōsei* ideology from their complimentary position. Carol Gluck, *Japan's Modern Myths: Ideology in the Late Meiji Period* (Princeton: Princeton University Press, 1985), 5.

65 Amy McCreedy Thernstrom, ed., *Japanese Women: Lineage and Legacies* (Washington, DC: Woodrow Wilson International Center for Scholars, 2005), 1.

66 On Hiratsuka Raichō and her support of the imperial project and emperor system: Yoneda Sayoko (trans. Hiroko Tomida), "Hiratsuka Raichō's Idea of Society: Nature, Cooperation and Self-Government," in *Japanese Women: Emerging from Subservience, 1868–1945*, ed. Hiroko Tomida and Gordon Daniels (Kent: Global Oriental, 2005), 34–35. For a compilation of scholarship on gender and views of the imperial institution: Kanō Mikiyo, ed., *Josei to tennōsei* (Tokyo: Shisō no kagakusha, 1979).

67 Jason G. Karlin, *Gender and Nation in Meiji Japan: Modernity, Loss, and the Doing of History* (Honolulu: University of Hawai'i Press, 2014).

68 Takashi Fujitani argues for a gendered duality of emperor and empress, Takashi Fujitani, *Splendid Monarchy: Power and Pageantry in Modern Japan* (Berkeley: University of California Press, 1996), 171–192. Kanō Mikiyo discussed separating gender from the sexed bodies of the emperor, Kanō Mikiyo, " 'Omigokoro' to 'hahagokoro': 'Yasukuni no haha' o umidasu mono," in *Josei to tennōsei*, ed. Kanō Mikiyo (Tokyo: Shisō no kagakusha, 1979). Kanō later argued for the imperial family modeling 'strict father/nurturing mother' roles, Kanō Mikiyo, *Tennōsei to gendā* (Tokyo: Inpakuto shupansha, 2002), 190–200. Others have argued for the emperor and empress in the 1930s to have complimentary roles, with the empress as maternal, Sally A. Hastings, "Empress Nagako and the Family State," in *The Emperors of Modern Japan*, ed. Ben-Ami Shillony (Leiden: Brill, 2008), 242, and Ueno Chizuko, "In the Feminine Guise: A Trap of Reverse Orientalism," in *Contemporary Japanese Thought*, ed. Richard F. Calichman (New York: Columbia University Press, 2005), 239. And in the postwar context arguing for the feminized emperor, Yoshikuni Igarashi, *Bodies of Memory: Narratives of War in Postwar Japanese Culture, 1945–1970* (Princeton: Princeton University Press, 2000), 27–35.

69 Motoko Rich, "As a New Emperor Is Enthroned in Japan, His Wife Won't Be Allowed to Watch," *New York Times*, April 29, 2019. *Japan Times*, "Nearly 80% in Japan Support Having Women on the Throne and 82% Feel Affection for New Emperor," May 2, 2019.

70 Yukiya Kawaguchi traces early Japanese portraiture to the eighth century realistic wood sculpture of Ganjin. Yukiya Kawaguchi, "Portraits of the Self: Characteristics and Development of Asian Portraits," in *Self and Other: Portraits from Asia and Europe*, ed. Kenji Yoshida and Brian Durrans (Tokyo: Asahi Shinbun, 2008), 264–266.

71 Tokyo Kokuritsu Hakubutsukan, *Nihon no shōzōga* (Tokyo: Asahi Shinbun, 1991); Yamato Bunkakan, *Nihon no shōzōga* (Nara: Yamato Bunkakan, 1991).

72 Portraits of women did exist but were less common than those of men. For more information on premodern portraiture of nuns and nobility: Miyajima Shinichi, *Shōzōga no shisen* (Tokyo: Yoshikawa kōbunkan, 1996), 170–183, and Naruse Fujio, *Nihon shōzōgashi* (Tokyo: Chūōkōron bijutsu shuppan, 2005), 132–136.

73 Miyajima, *Shōzōga no shisen*, 37.

74 Japanese Architecture and Art Net Users System, "nise-e," www.aisf.or.jp/~jaanus/deta/n/nisee.htm. Accessed June 15, 2019.

75 Yamamoto Yōko, "Tennō o egaku koto o habakaru hyōgen no shūen," *Myōjyō daigaku kenkyū kiyō* 9 (2001): 21.

76 Mikiko Hirayama, The Emperor's New Clothes: Japanese Visuality and Imperial Portrait Photography," *History of Photography* 33, no. 2 (2009): 168. Timon Screech, *The Shogun's Painted Culture: Fear and Creativity in the Japanese States, 1760–1829* (London: Reaktion Books, 2000), 111–166.

77 Miyajima Shinichi, *Shōzōga* (Tokyo: Yoshikawa kōbunkan, 1994), 232–248.

78 Masato Miyachi, *Tokugawa Yoshinobu, Akitake, Yoshikatsu shashinshū: Shogun tonosama ga totta Bakumatsu Meiji* (Tokyo: Shin Jinbustu Ōraisha, 1996), 98.

79 The earlier images, including those of Tokugawa Yoshinobu in Napoleonic-style military dress, Japanese dress of two differing styles, and a European-style suit, as well as later images of the shogun, can be found in: Masato Miyachi, *Tokugawa Yoshinobu*, 96–106. This publication also includes photographs of Tokugawa Akitake, the younger half-brother of Yoshinobu, whose image was recorded around the same time, 1867, which coincided with Akitake's visit to France.

A woodcut copy of Akitake's portrait was also published in the *Illustrated London News*, in December of 1867.

80 Sebastian Dobson, "Frederick William Sutton, 1832–1883: Photographer of the Last Shogun," in *Britain and Japan: Biographical Portraits*, ed. Hugh Cortazzi, vol. 4 (London: Japan Society, 1994), 289–302.

81 Hirayama, "The Emperor's New Clothes," 166.

82 Rachel Peat, ed., *Japan Courts and Culture* (London: Royal Collection Trust, 2020).

83 One early Meiji example of the changing presentation of news was the *nishiki-e shinbun*, or brocade print newspaper. These single-sheet multi-color woodblock prints, which began publication in the mid-1870s, featured a graphic illustration of a news story, often violent in nature. Chiba-shi Bijutsukan, *Bunmei kaika no nishikie shinbun: Tōkyō nichinichi shinbun, yūbin hōchi shinbun zen sakuhin* (Tokyo: Kokusho kankōkai, 2008). Japanese newspapers had their roots in single-sheet woodblock prints of the seventeenth century, with modern newspapers developing in the 1860s and early 1870s.

84 Luke Gartlan, *A Career of Japan: Baron Raimund von Stillfried and Early Yokohama Photography* (Leiden: Brill, 2016), 73–104.

85 *Japan Weekly Mail*, January 13, 1872, published in Gartlan, "A Chronology of Baron Raimund von Stillfried-Ratenicz," 131.

86 Gartlan, "A Chronology of Baron Raimund von Stillfried-Ratenicz," 132.

87 Donald Keene, *Emperor of Japan: Meiji and His World, 1852–1912* (New York: Columbia University Press, 2002), 211.

2

MIMESIS AND MULTIPLES

Empress Shōken and the Power of Print in Establishing the Public Empress Persona

Awash with vibrant aniline reds and rich purples, *Wakin haru no kotobuki* (Spring Felicitations in Japanese Brocade) (Figure 2.1), 1885, by Toyohara (Yōshū) Chikanobu (楊洲周延, 1838–1912), is a typical triptych woodblock print representing Meiji court ritual. Like many similar scenes, the print represents the interior of the imperial palace and is filled with familiar symbolism: the plum blossoms on the hulking, craggy tree just outside, a sign of hope as the first flowers to bloom at the end of winter, the pine bow on the ceremonial tray, showing resilience through winter and representing the new year, the paulownia flowers on the textiles that drape from the ceiling, an emblem of the imperial family. Emperor Meiji sits in his military uniform at the far right, the lone male figure in the scene. Empress Shōken stands near him, the motif of her robes reflecting her phoenix crown. Less than twenty years after the start of the Meiji period and the advent of the modern visual monarchy, multi-color woodblock triptych prints such as this one were widespread, commonplace media. The masculine gaze and presence of Emperor Meiji across visual culture of the late nineteenth century has been extensively studied, but what the collected print culture of the era shows, and what has been largely ignored in the scholarship, is the high visibility of Empress Shōken and the largely feminine palace environment of the visual monarchy. In numerous examples from the decades of the late nineteenth century, the power of print was utilized to create a sense of familiarity with the intimate world of the inner

DOI: 10.4324/9781003376101-4

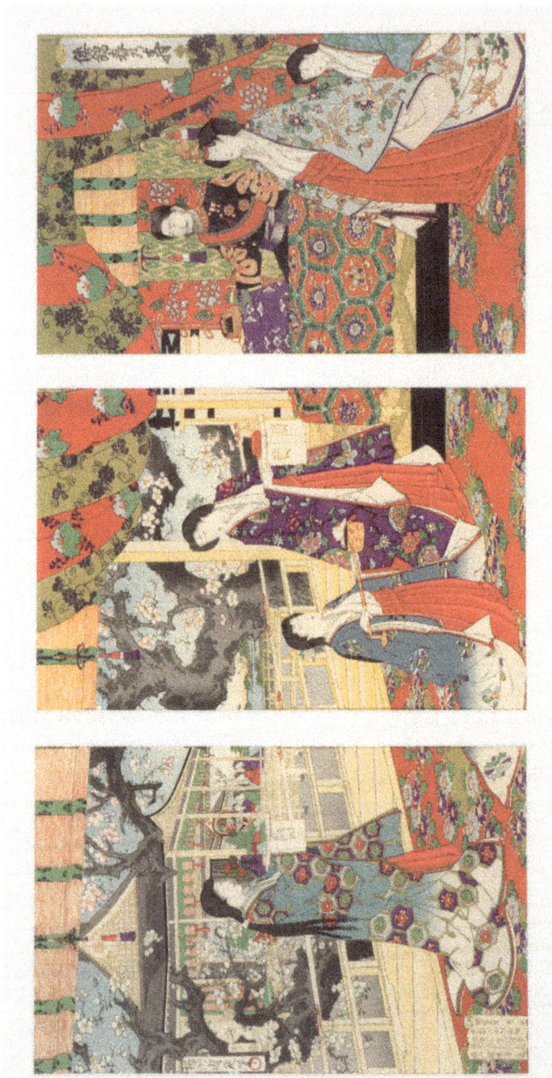

FIGURE 2.1 *Wakin haru no kotobuki* (Spring Felicitations in Japanese Brocade), 1885, Toyohara (Yōshū) Chikanobu, multicolor woodblock print, Spencer Museum of Art, University of Kansas, Museum Purchase: Lucy Shaw Schultz Fund, 2007.0066.a,b,c

palace, the multiplicity and ease of print reproduction allowing for the Japanese citizenry to form parasocial relationships with their sovereigns through repeated mediated visual encounters, as the very construction of the public understanding of the office of the empress was shaped in visual culture.[1]

This chapter investigates representations of Empress Shōken in Meiji period woodblock prints. This era of the visual monarchy featured fantasy representations of the empress' domestic and court life, as well as her public appearances in new, modern locales such as government-sponsored events and ceremonies. Widely sold at accessible prices, these vernacular prints utilized a standard Japanese media in order to establish the new visibility and modern comportment of the empress in Meiji visual culture and validated her activities through the illusion of intimacy with her citizens. After introducing the biography of Empress Shōken and the theoretical frameworks of the chapter, prints will be analyzed in categories of maternity, charity and work, and court and diplomatic events, globally common themes for royal women that were developed against domestic social values. There are hundreds of examples of the imperial family in Meiji prints, meaning a comprehensive study is beyond the scope of this chapter, but like other aspects of the visual monarchy, the images are relatively formulaic and predictable, therefore allowing meaningful conclusions to be drawn from a representative sample.

Institution as Biography/Biography as Institution: Shōken and Meiji

Every activity of Empress Shōken and Emperor Meiji is detailed in the two lengthy, multi volume official chronicles, *Shōken kōtaigō jitsuroku* (昭憲皇太后実録, Annals of Empress Shōken) and *Meiji tennō ki* (明治天皇記, Record of the Emperor Meiji).[2] Emperor Shōwa's account, *Shōwa tennō jitsuroku* (昭和天皇実録, Annals of Emperor Shōwa), was released in recent years, but those of Empress Teimei or Empress Kōjun have yet to be published.[3] Emperor Taishō's record is contested and only available at the Imperial Household Agency Archives.[4] While the full details of the empress and emperor's public lives were documented with extreme attention to minute detail, the stories of their inner personal lives and personal thoughts are relatively unknown. As Theresa Earenfight stated in 2008, "elite women's public visibility can mask them;" uncovering their stories can be surprisingly tricky.[5] As such, the combination of detailed daily imperial records with the constructed and imagined prints, paintings, and photographs investigated in the subsequent chapters of this book builds a biographical account of the monarchs as representatives of the imperial institution, not as individuals. With special attention to standard ceremonial events such as coronations and weddings—major moments which were uniform but also gave the citizenry an opportunity to connect with their sovereigns in a public forum—this section argues for the unity of image and biography in forming the public understanding of the Japanese monarchy in the modern era.

The posthumously named Empress Shōken, who took the name Haruko (春子) upon her 1867 engagement to Emperor Meiji, was born to the Fujiwara clan on April 17, 1849, as Ichijō Masako (一条勝子, 昭憲皇后).[6] The Fujiwara maintained a powerful role throughout much of Japanese history, as the women of the imperial household came from the lineage for over 1,000 years. As she was three years older than her husband, an inauspicious difference in age, her official birth year was changed to 1850 upon her marriage into the imperial household in 1869.[7] She was the first to take the title *kōgō* (皇后) in the modern era. The term *kōgō*, translated as empress consort, or empress, was given to non-ruling women who acted as the primary wife of the emperor. While employed with frequency in the tenth through fourteenth centuries, the title had decreased significantly in use, with only a few women holding the position in the centuries prior to the Meiji period.[8] With Shōken began the contemporary use of the term *kōgō* to refer to the wife of the emperor, as conceived in the model of the Euro-American nuclear family. Although Emperor Meiji had access to concubines or other women of his choice in the privacy of the palace, he appeared in public with Empress Shōken, and it was she who acted as the representative female face of the monarchy.

As part of the new public, modern model of proper feminine comportment, Empress Shōken took on a variety of charity and philanthropic activities. Although charity, virtue, and piety are common queenly values the world over, in the case of Japan the visible expression of these principles for the recently redefined role of empress was something new. She was frequently at her husband's side during state functions and hosted official diplomatic visits of women dignitaries throughout her reign. Among her primary philanthropic interests were hospitals for the poor and for the military, women's education, and the Red Cross. Shōken was instrumental in supporting the Red Cross Organization in Japan. The charity continues to receive the support of the Japanese empress today, and empresses act as the symbolic leaders of the organization.[9] As part of her work she established the Empress Shōken Fund in 1912, the first fund of its kind to be dedicated to the peacetime activities of the Red Cross.[10] The fund is still active in the twenty-first century, supporting a diverse array of global humanitarian aid projects.

Empress Shōken was also a well-respected writer of *waka* poetry, composing over 30,000 *waka* poems in her lifetime. *Waka* are composed in five lines, with syllables of 5/7/5/7/7, and written to express one's emotions. It is through these poems that we can gain some understanding of the daily life and concerns of Empress Shōken.[11] Topics covered in this work range from observations of nature on her official travels to concern over her husband's alcohol consumption.[12] Although the vague nature of the poetry does not provide as much detail as an autobiography or detailed diary account, the expanse of available poetry does offer a glimpse into her personality, expressed as elegant, compassionate, and refined through her poetry, which was of course part of her imperial façade.[13] Furthermore, her involvement and interest in poetry was represented in visual art, with paintings of poetry gatherings at the Meiji Memorial Picture Gallery, a propagandistic museum dating from the Taishō and early Shōwa periods that documents the lives of Meiji and Shōken in eighty permanently displayed paintings. This artistic pursuit of *waka* was the start of creative and intellectual activity as a core endeavor of the empresses.

Together and as individuals, Shōken and Meiji undertook a variety of actions which were new to the imperial household: they were the first imperial couple to meet with European people, live in the new capital of Tokyo, and have their images widely displayed in public. Each of these activities and the numerous other firsts that they participated in led to a standardization and ritualization of the imperial behaviors as performed for the public, foreign, and domestic dignitaries, and palace visitors.

Meiji was born as Sachinomiya (祐宮) son of Emperor Kōmei (孝明天皇, 1831–1867) and Nakayama Yoshiko (中山慶子, 1836–1907), a *gon no tenji* (典侍), or imperial concubine.[14] His birth came at a time of harrowing political change for the Japanese rulers, as within a year Commodore Matthew Perry would enter the harbor at Uraga (1853), near present-day Tokyo, bringing a forceful request for a trade treaty from the president of the United States.

Emperor Meiji spent his childhood cloistered in the Imperial Palace in Kyoto, surrounded by the traditional world of palace and court life. In 1860, at age eight, he was given the name Mutsuhito (睦仁) when titled Crown Prince. Throughout his youth, he continued his education in the classical tradition at the palace, learning poetry and Confucian classics, among other topics, but without exposure to contemporary politics or statesmanship. He was the last emperor educated in this manner. Accounts of his childhood are rife with contradictions about his health and temperament, and most were written at a later date, leaving many questions unanswered or unanswerable.

Emperor Kōmei suddenly passed away in his mid-thirties in 1867, leaving the teenaged Mutsuhito to take the throne as the 122nd emperor of Japan under the rule of the last shogun, Tokugawa Yoshinobu (徳川慶喜, 1837–1913). Meiji's youth was spent in Kyoto against the backdrop of intense political drama; the reign of the shoguns, which lasted for 200 years prior, was coming to a close. In the midst of the signing of new international treaties and extraordinary economic hardship upon entering the global economy, the shogunate was in a weakened position and faced challenges to their rule from young samurai, particularly those of the Satsuma and Chōshū regions. These samurai led a revolt in 1867, allied with the imperial court. In 1868 the young Emperor Meiji, who took the throne only one year earlier, declared an Imperial Restoration, abolishing the shogunal system together with a coalition of Japanese leaders who desired political revolution. The regime change that resulted from this coup came with domestic battles and much political maneuvering and marked the start of the modern imperial system.[15]

Marking this change, on September 12, 1868, Emperor Meiji was crowned in an elaborate ceremony based on Shinto rites. Previous coronations were believed to be modeled on Chinese ceremonials, and the bureaucrats at the Ministry of Shinto worked to revise the ceremonies in what they felt was an authentically Japanese fashion, which served as the model for future coronation ceremonies.[16] The ascension ceremonies were not public and were not observed outside of the palace confines, although officials and laborers were given a holiday to mark the occasion. This was the last time that a coronation happened in such a secluded fashion; beginning with Emperor Taishō, the ascension ceremonies were large publicized events on a national scale, with an extensive visual record. Just a few months later Meiji was married to Shōken on January 11, 1869. This was also the last time that an imperial wedding occurred in isolation.

With the new regime came a change in the geographic center of power. On November 26, 1868, Emperor Meiji arrived in Tokyo on his first trip to the city, becoming the first emperor to travel this distance and to see the sights along the way, including the Pacific Ocean and Mount Fuji.[17] Shōken and the entirety of the imperial household made the move to Tokyo just one year later. The city, established as Edo for more than 250 years as the center of power for the shoguns, would be renamed and remade as a modern imperial capital. The former Edo Castle, the central symbol of military rule, sustained great damage in the previous century. Over the course of the first decades of the Meiji period, the site became the grounds of the Imperial Palace and remains as such to this day. This process was not completed quickly, however. The transfer of power from Kyoto to Tokyo took over eight months, stretching from the September 3, 1868, edict proclaiming Edo henceforth be called Tokyo (東京, Eastern Capital) to Meiji's residence in Edo Castle, then renamed *kōkyo* (皇居, Imperial Palace) on May 9, 1869. Many in the elite classes viewed the new capital as a temporary site for up to twenty years after the Emperor's arrival in Tokyo.[18] Although the physical transformation from the low, wooden city of Edo to the modern brick metropolis of Tokyo, crisscrossed by trains and dotted with imperial monuments, took decades, by the time of the Taishō ascendancy to the throne, the restyling of urban life would be remarkable and the city unrecognizable from its form when Meiji and Shōken arrived just forty years prior.

Early in his reign, Meiji conducted imperial tours throughout the nation and together with Shōken made frequent appearances on the streets of Tokyo in the imperial carriage, a vehicle which became a symbol of the modern monarchy. For those not fortunate to catch a glimpse of the carriage, woodblock prints provided a glance at the pomp of the imperial procession in images such as Utagawa Kunitoshi's (歌川国利, active 1847–1899) 1889 *Gohōren no zu* (Illustration of the Imperial Carriage) (Figure 2.2). The print places Shōken and Meiji in the carriage in front of their home, the Imperial Palace, with the famed Nijūbashi bridge in the middle ground and Mount Fuji in the distance, cementing their institutionality, biography, and iconography in one image. Kunitoshi presents an invented perspective in the print, giving the viewer multiple angles that allow more to be seen in the print than in reality.

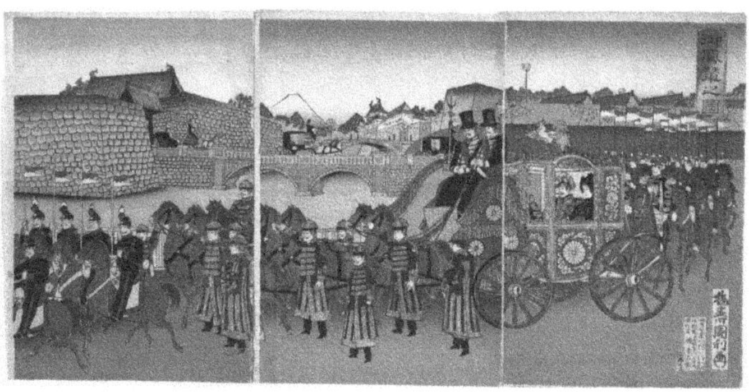

FIGURE 2.2 *Gohōren no zu* (Illustration of the Imperial Carriage), 1889, multicolor woodblock print, Utagawa Kunitoshi, Metropolitan Museum of Art

The trope of Mount Fuji in the distance is common for images set in Edo, later Tokyo, and the single arched bridge behind the double arched bridge is too distant to be seen from a single vantage point. The fisheye view expands the scene, giving the viewer further depth into the palace than is possible when standing in front of Nijubashi. All of this combines to give the illusion of truth, with just enough accurate detail to convince the viewer that the scene is based in reality. It is noteworthy that Shōken is the only woman visible in the print.

Emperor Meiji fathered fifteen children during the course of his reign, but only five of them lived to adulthood, and the only male child to survive was the future Emperor Taishō. Meiji sired children with five different concubines of the imperial house but never produced an heir with Empress Shōken, who was biologically childless. This would also be a historic last, for beginning with Emperor Taishō and Empress Teimei, monogamy was the preferred family structure for the Imperial Household, and maintaining concubines ceased to be an imperial practice.

Late in the evening on July 30, 1912, Emperor Meiji died of heart failure. Immediately, the sacred objects—mirror, sword, and jewel—were passed to his son, Emperor Taishō, in the confines of the Imperial Palace in Tokyo. There was no gap in leadership and no interregnum, and the large-scale public funeral of Emperor Meiji was already in the planning stages, as his health had been waning for many months. His was the first public ceremonial event commemorating the death of the monarch in the modern period, and many of the details of the rites were written into the law only a few years earlier, with the Edict on Imperial Household Mourning (皇室服喪令, *Kōshitsu fukumo no rei*) in 1909. The funeral of Meiji's father, Emperor Kōmei, was held in 1867 and was a Buddhist affair, the last of its kind for an emperor. Empress Dowager Eishō's funeral in 1897 gave precedent for Meiji's memorial, but it was a much more private, small-scale affair than the funeral of the first modern Japanese emperor.[19] Empress Shōken's funeral would follow only a few short years later, with her playing a visible role in transitioning between the two eras in the two-year period between Meiji's passing in 1912 and her own death. She passed away on April 9, 1914, and the preparations for her funeral delayed the Taishō enthronement ceremonies, as the state bureaucracies put off the coronation in order to allow for a period of mourning and for a proper state funeral. Both Meiji and Shōken were buried at the Fushimi Momoyama Imperial Mausoleum (伏見桃山陵, *Fushimi no momoyama no misasagi*) near Kyoto.[20] Their graves are based upon the simple Buddhist designs which were standard for the emperors of Japan since the twelfth century: a small square base structure beneath a low, round mound. The burial sites are encircled by a low fence with a Shinto *torii* (gate) at the front and surrounded by forest. Meiji and Shōken were the last emperor and empress to be buried near Kyoto. The visual culture of modern funerals will be further covered in Chapter 6.

As Emperor Meiji reigned over Japan during a long period of intense changes, and as he was promoted as a father figure, political leader, and head of the Shinto system, many citizens developed a personal connection with him and felt an emotional bond to him as the leader of their nation. Although most writings address his death as an era change, we can imagine that many citizens felt similarly connected to Shōken. Meiji was intrinsically linked with modernity itself, and with his death, there were concerns about the future direction of the Japanese state. The Promulgation of the Constitution, a turning point in national image, was only twenty-three years past, and the military victories of the Sino-Japanese War (1894–5) and Russo-Japanese War (1904–5), which truly catapulted Japan to its status as a global power, were seventeen and seven years past, respectively. The global political situation in the early 1910s was growing increasingly unstable, and the change in the monarchy represented a potential moment of weakness for the state. The Taishō emperor was unproven as a leader, and the state-constructed narrative of national modernity which revolved around Emperor Meiji as a cult of personality had to be repositioned to center around Emperor Taishō. Yet what is frequently overlooked is that the empresses remained a stable visual component of the imperial family. During Meiji's funeral, Shōken persisted as a continuing presence into the early Taishō years, just as Teimei would ease the transition to the Shōwa monarchy.

The Gaze, the Multiplicity of Print, and Parasocial Relationships

Two seemingly dialectical concepts frame the discussion of late nineteenth-century empress prints: the panopticon and the gaze and mimesis and reproduction. Yet these concepts operated not in opposition but in tandem; as stated in the introduction, the allure of multiples gave the Japanese citizenry a feeling of closeness to their sovereigns, one which was cultivated vis-à-vis reproduced images. The plethora of widely available vernacular prints gave imperial subjects the opportunity to look upon the empress and emperor at their leisure. This act of looking was replicated within the images themselves, as the pictured members of the court regarded each other, but also set up a multi-directional observation between the emperor, empress, and citizenry that was mediated by the two-dimensional surface of the print.

In an image such as *Spring Felicitations in Japanese Brocade* (Figure 2.1), the viewer, or the owner of the print, has visual access to the private confines of the imperial palace and can examine the details of the figures and spaces at their leisure, in the private environment of their home. How should we interpret the power held by the citizenry as they "owned" a woodblock print—an image—of the imperial family in their most intimate inner palace rooms? In this print the gaze of Shōken and Meiji direct us towards the central ritual and the plum blossoms, but in many images the empress is the object of the gaze, her visual emphasis making her a vital symbol within the images. Here the viewer is given the option of relating to multiple figures within the composition, either the luxuriously clad celebrity empress; the powerful, masculine emperor who surveys the scene; or the attendants, but Shōken remains central to each position, a grounding presence at the right of the scene who directs our attention to the action at the center and left.

In his examination of Emperor Meiji's masculine imperial gaze, Takashi Fujitani argues for a nuanced understanding of the work of philosophers such as Michel Foucault and Pierre Bourdieu in the context of the late nineteenth century Japanese monarchy.[21] Fujitani's application of Foucault's theories of the panopticon, the disciplinary regime of power, and the culture of surveillance are applicable in the context of the gaze of the Meiji Emperor, who was cultivated in the media as a strong, military-oriented, charismatic, and highly masculine figure. Emperor Meiji's public image was one of staunch discipline met with a piercing gaze. He almost always appeared in public in military costume, and his paternalistic stare was represented in prints as one of strength and authority.[22] Ozawa Asae further argues that Emperor Meiji's gaze was not only seen in portraiture, as he looked upon his citizens, but also in landscape photographs taken from his viewpoint, literally recreating the scene before his eyes.[23] Both of these interpretations assist in dissecting Emperor Meiji in *Spring Felicitations in Japanese Brocade*, but how can we understand the role of the recipients of his observations within the print, the women of the imperial household that surrounded Emperor Meiji in the palace interior, and how can we incorporate Empress Shōken into the optical paradigm?

All of the images examined in this chapter were created as mass-produced multiples, part of a cultural milieu of mimesis and reproduction. The imperial family is often thought of in a singular fashion, but it was the power of multiplicity, the ability to have an abundance of images, and a repetitive public exposure that made the visual monarchy recognizable and powerful. The woodblock prints examined here show an imagined and fabricated reality which attempted to project an aura of truth. Yet in the spirit of celebrity, the imperial family maintained a layer of separation by means of the medium of print. Over the course of the decades that Meiji woodblocks were produced, photography was widespread but not yet viable for mass reproduction and distribution. Figural mimesis in woodblock prints meant an idealized interpretation of reality: the empress' visage is recognizably consistent in these images, but the images do not provide significant detail; the scenes are based upon biographical events, but as they were produced in advance of any given occasion, they are not an accurate historical record. There is also a substantial emphasis on the elaborate colors and patterns that make up Shōken's clothing and millinery, which provides an additional layer of distance. Chapter 3 will address how photography introduced different issues in reproduction, but in the Meiji period as covered in this chapter, woodblock prints provided the illusion of intimacy and familiarity for the citizens who both viewed and purchased these commercial objects.

The soft power aspect of these multiples and the ability of vernacular images to nudge culture was well understood by the imperial bureaucracy. Alongside woodblock prints for primarily domestic distribution, photographs of royals from Europe, Asia, the Pacific, and the Middle East were globally distributed as calling cards, and internationally, the concept of royal-as-celebrity was fairly well developed in the late nineteenth century. The Imperial Household Ministry observed how other crowned heads manipulated their public personae and reputations, absorbed these lessons, and acted upon them in their crafting of imperial images. Both the public and private activities that Shōken participated and was imaged in, such as sericulture, charity, childrearing, and official government activities, impacted the social understanding of what acceptable women's comportment was. For example, *Ueno daisankai naikoku kangyō hakurankai gyokō no zu* (Visit of the Empress to the Third Industrial Promotional Exhibition at Ueno Park), by Chikanobu, 1889, shows Shōken as she sets a standard for attendance at public events, modeling proper, modern conduct for her citizenry.[24] The exhibition was held between April 1 and July 21, 1890, but this print was released in December of the previous year in order to generate interest in the upcoming event. As Shōken exits the imperial carriage, adorned with the chrysanthemum seal, her ladies-in-waiting assist. Emperor Meiji stands at the center, with a crowd of onlookers in the distance, the architecture of the exhibition building framed by festive lanterns, cherry blossoms, and international flags. The clothing of the imperial women is the highlight of the print, showing a variety of patterns and designs, but, while Shōken's fashions may have been aspirational, her activities were attainable. Images of the celebrity-as-role-model empress were intended to motivate the actions of everyday citizens; in this example, attending an exhibition was an activity that upper middle-class people could participate in. Parasocial relationships, defined here as one-sided relationships with celebrities wherein viewers come to feel that they personally know the famous, were created through the medium of print leading the empress image to inspire work habits, leisure activities, and patriotism among the women and men of Meiji Japan.

Art and visual culture played a significant part in communicating the messages of the new, modern systems; woodblock prints in particular promoted the various slogans of the Meiji government such as *fukoku kyōhei* (富国強兵), rich country, strong military; *shokusan kōgyō* (殖産興業), encourage new industry; or *bunmei kaika* (文明開化), civilization and enlightenment. Women had limited realms where they could exercise their power, but in the areas of the court, silk production, education, and hospitals, women had significant roles to play. Each of these areas of influence is represented in woodblock prints, specifically with representations of Empress Shōken as a role model of modern femininity. The outliers here are images of government and official events: average women were not afforded a role in these functions, but Shōken was frequently envisioned as attending such affairs. Arguably, like the fantasy glimpses of life at court, placing Shōken within images of government and official events allowed average women to gain a glimpse of the political side of Meiji life and allowed them to feel as if they had a place at the proverbial table.

Starting in 1875 censorship laws governed imperial images, meaning most of the Meiji woodblock prints of the imperial family were flattering in form. But exceptions to this complimentary standard existed.[25] For example, Chikanobu's 1877 *Mitate shō chikubai no uchi: Matsutake gari* (Inside a Pine-Bamboo-Plum Parody: Pine Mushrooms) shows the women of the imperial household on an outing to gather mushrooms. The fungi are sexually explicit in their forms and appear to be caressed by the some of the women. While the empress herself sits in the background, removed from the action, this erotic humor was offensive to standards of imperial propriety. Chikanobu avoided the authorities, but his contemporary Tsukioka Yoshitoshi (月岡芳年, 1839–1892) was arrested for his 1878 print series *Mitate shichi yōsei* (Parody on Beauties of the Seven Nights), examined later in this chapter.[26] Critique of the monarchy was a very real, yet seriously constrained, part of Meiji life and culture.[27]

A final note: due to space restrictions, this chapter will not be addressing the lives and oeuvres of the artists who created these prints. While the artists certainly had agency over their work and made creative decisions that led to the distinct characteristics and styles of these images, they also operated within a market and censorship system that narrowed their choices and expression when creating imperial representations. The artists acted together with publishers to determine what subject matter would be saleable but still meet legal restrictions.

Empress and *Gon no tenji*: Images of Maternity and Issues of Lineage

While the visibility of the empress was a dramatic change, much of the power of Meiji imperial women resulted from their maternity, a historic and universal role for queens and empresses. Within Japan, the female progenitors of the lineage were historically drawn from the Fujiwara clan, giving immense power to the family. Empress Shōken was from the Fujiwara nobility, yet she was biologically childless, and the agnatic primogeniture of Japan's modern era could be interpreted as leaving palace women, particularly those without biological heirs, in an inferior position.[28] Yet despite her fertility issues, Shōken's adoption of and apparent devotion to Meiji's heir, the future Emperor Taishō, was what kept her in a central court position. Likewise, Empress Teimei's role as a mother to four boys similarly worked in her favor. In short—maternity, biological or adopted, brought power to the women of the imperial household.[29]

It was widely known that palace women gave birth to Emperor Meiji's fifteen children, women who made appearances in visual culture. In *Yorozu toshi sakae no kotobuki* (Long, Long Life of Glory), a colorful triptych woodblock print by Utagawa Kunitoshi, 1877, the palace concubine Yanagihara Naruko, biological mother to Emperor Taishō, is shown in a small inset square.[30] Her face is revealed, while her body remains behind a curtain, with the baby Prince Takenomiya Yukihito held by an attendant. Eight attendants flank Yanagihara, with common symbols represented throughout, including Mount Fuji outside the terrace in the distance, stylized chrysanthemums on a water pot, and phoenixes on the draperies, with a globe and clock showing the international character of the imperial family. The young prince did not live to see childhood, but this celebratory print tells us that there was a market for both images of concubines and those commemorating an imperial birth. An image such as this shows that multiple and varied types of maternity were simultaneously accepted and celebrated: that of concubines and empresses, biological and national in their positions, and replete with symbolism and façade that was readily accepted and understood by the citizenry.

Palace concubines were represented as single figures as well. In 1878, Yoshitoshi published the series *Mitate shichi yōsei* (Parody on Beauties of the Seven Nights), which led to the artist's arrest.[31] In the title of the series, *shichi yōsei* (七曜星) refers to the seven luminaries: sun, moon, Mercury, Venus, Mars, Jupiter, and Saturn, and each of the seven prints includes a kanji reference to one of the seven astronomical features.[32] Six of the prints include *gon no tenji*, or imperial concubines, labeled with their names, and each with a visual play on the character represented, such as *Hachiue no do* (鉢植えの土, Potting Soil) representing Takakura Toshiko (高倉寿子, 1840–1930), a concubine, and utilizing the character for the planet Saturn (土星, *dosei*) but in the context of a different term—here *hachiue no do*, which means potting soil.[33] Half of the composition shows Takakura and the other half a large potted peony, a symbol of nobility and wealth. While the concubines were accepted as a necessary part of the imperial household structure, there was a certain furtive manner required of their position. Donald Keene states of the Yoshitoshi series featuring the women,

> Although it was not a disgrace to be a *gon no tenji,* these women were shadowy presences, and there was something clandestine about them. They so seldom left the palace or were exposed to sunlight that their faces were said to have a ghastly pallor.[34]

Here, this secretive nature of the women, combined with the wordplay of potting soil, can be interpreted as a metaphor for

Takakura's supporting role for the emperor and the palace, allowing them to flourish while she remains out of sight, an allusion to sexuality and the fertility of imperial concubines.

The mother of Emperor Taishō, Yanagihara Naruko, was another of the concubines represented in the series. In *Mitate shichi yōsei: Tōdai no hi* (灯台の火, Flame of the Lighthouse), Yanagihara is labeled with her rank, name provided in a light yellow cartouche (権の典侍正五柳原愛子, Yanagihara Naruko, Gon no Tenji of the Fifth Rank).[35] She is envisioned in a suggestive position, preparing to extinguish a large candle-lit lantern and holding a packet of tissues in her mouth in what was a sexually evocative gesture. The image was so controversial that it was banned by the authorities but nevertheless shows the importance of imperial women for their roles in both imperial succession and widespread popular appeal.

In addition to the sexual allusions of imperial concubines, the series also included an image of Empress Shōken. *Mitate shichi yōsei: Asahi* (朝日, Morning Sun, Figure 2.3) does not explicitly label the represented figure as the empress, but her crown, hair, clothing, and fan are reminiscent of Uchida Kuichi's 1872 photograph of Shōken (see Figure 4.4). The exceedingly large red sun at the left of the print, complete with radiant crimson rays, is suggestive of both the Japanese Army's Rising Sun Flag and also representations of the sun that refer to Amaterasu, as seen in images of the Ise Grand Shrine. With her attendant kneeling at her side, the symbolism of the print is powerful: Shōken is linked to the female *kami* at the root of both the imperial lineage and Shinto belief. The abstracted sun and rays can also be read as a stand-in for the emperor, as Shōken gazes in the direction of the rising orb. Viewed in the context of the *Mitate shichi yōsei* series, it was the connection of the empress print to that of the sexually available concubines that made the subject controversial and worthy of attention from the authorities, but the reproductive and pleasurable functions that caused these concerns also show the centrality of women to the continuation of the imperial lineage and the public curiosity surrounding inner palace life.

The print series, and the broader acceptance and awareness of the sexual relationships of the emperor and his concubines, gives

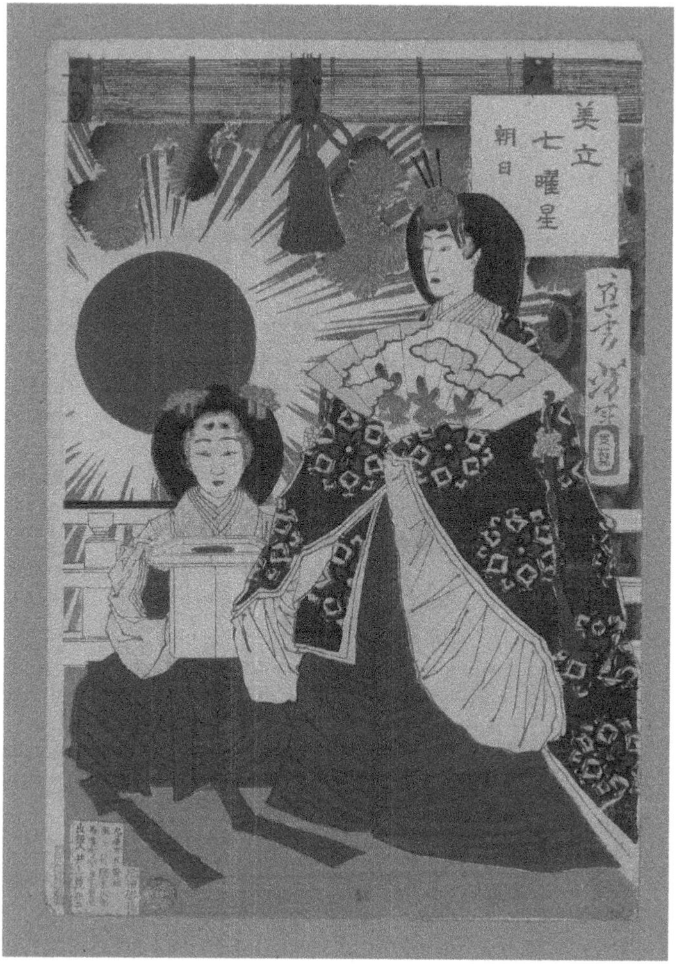

FIGURE 2.3 *Mitate shichi yōsei: Asahi* (Parody on Beauties of the Seven Nights: Morning Sun), 1878, Tsukioka Yoshitoshi, multicolor woodblock print, Tokyo Metropolitan Library, C198C11

us insights into the social understandings of succession and feminine imperial relationships. Aside from the *Mitate shichi yōsei* series, the empress was frequently represented in prints alongside the imperial concubines. In one specific recorded instance of the relationships between the empress and imperial concubines, Shōken's annals state that she sent a box of Nara dolls to the concubine Yanagihara on Boys Day in 1878 to celebrate Prince Hana no Azuma, a child born to Yanagihara in 1877.[36] In 1878 the prince was the sole surviving heir of Emperor Meiji, preceded in death by one male and two female children. The gift was commemorated in the woodblock print *Hana no Azuma oji Onagusame no zu* (Emperor Meiji with Family and Court Ladies: Prince in a Baby Carriage), but sadly the prince passed away just two months later.[37]

While instances were rare, Shōken did occasionally transgress into political activity, something which may have constituted a small act of rebellion against the empress' constrained sexuality, contrasted with the emperor's sexual liberation as seen in Meiji's relationships with concubines.[38] Scholar Hayakawa Noriyo explores these palace relationships stating that concubines were accepted because under *kokutai* the "males of the male line" were critical to the imperial lineage.[39] Historically across the region, concubines that served the male ruler both sexually and as progenitors of the male line were the standard court structure, with examples to be found both in the shogun's Ōoku (women's quarters) and in Korean and Chinese court examples.[40] It is impossible to know if Shōken was distressed by her husband's open relationships with palace concubines or if she did indeed rebel against this standard palace procedure, but we do know that Shōken spent time with Meiji's courtesans, traveled with them, and sent them gifts, all as a part of normal palace life and much of which is reproduced in woodblock prints.

While Shōken is represented together with either Meiji's courtesans or the Crown Prince, and often both, a final example illuminates her importance to the lineage: Chikanobu's *Honchō haiji kiō kagami* (Mirror of Our Country's Revered Deities and Esteemed Emperors) (Figure 2.4) from 1878. In the print, Shōken and Meiji are identifiable through their clothing

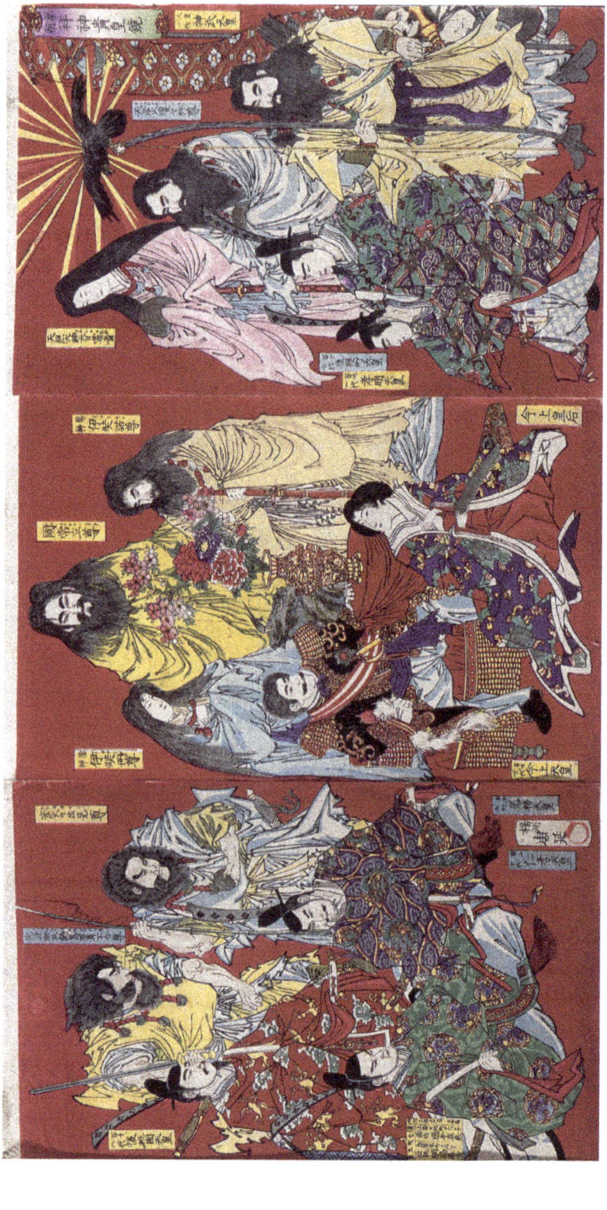

FIGURE 2.4 *Honchō haiji kiō kagami* (Mirror of Our Country's Revered Deities and Esteemed Emperors), December 1878, Toyohara (Yōshū) Chikanobu, multicolor woodblock print, Scripps College Collection

and the cartouches that label them as the current empress and emperor but not their physiognomy. They are surrounded by imagined portraits of historic *tennō* and *kami*, including Amaterasu holding a mirror and wearing pink at the upper right and the primordial *kami* Kunitokotachi and their children Izanami and Izanagi just above the modern imperial couple.[41] At the far right the legendary first emperor Jinmu stands with his Yata crow, which helped guide him as he conquered Japan, comma-shaped jewels adorning his torso. The early modern emperors in the foreground are distinguished by their patterned robes, including Meiji's father Kōmei, while Chikanobu's dynamic line quality provides a sense of energy to the image. In this image, the imagined group portrait genre lends lineage and legitimacy to the contemporary monarchs, and it is notable that women have a significant presence among the imperial figures and *kami* that are deemed central to the Japanese national story. Each of the three panels forms a discrete composition, but when viewed together, the focus of the image is on Meiji and Shōken, the gaze of their predecessors leading the eye to the imperial couple. Once again, maternity as a source of women's royal power is the focus of the print, be it biological or adoptive in nature.

Encouraging Women in Charity and Work: Schools, Factories, and Hospitals

Like the cross-cultural associations of queenship and maternity, charity and work are also common virtues for empresses to encourage, practice, and model. Examples abound across time and space, but in the late nineteenth century Queen Victoria stood as the preeminent "Mother of the Empire," projecting a model of middle-class wife and mother, despite her heavy involvement in political affairs, an aspect of her rule that her subjects did not see.[42] The public images of both Queen Victoria and Empress Shōken functioned to encourage middle-class women in the domestic sphere; in Japan this meant the promotion of education, sericulture, and wartime nursing in successive decades of the Meiji period.[43]

The growth of women's education and status was a central project of the Meiji state. In an 1871 speech, Emperor Meiji stated:

> We lack superior institutions for high female culture. Our women should not be ignorant of those great principles on which the happiness of daily life frequently depends. How important the education of mothers, on whom future generations almost wholly rely for the early cultivation of those intellectual tastes which an enlightened system of training is designed to develop!
>
> Liberty is therefore granted wives and sisters to accompany their relatives on foreign tours, that they may acquaint themselves with better forms of female education, and, on their return, introduce beneficial improvements in the training of our children.[44]

As shown in Chapters 3 and 5, this social-educational responsibility for mothers continued into the twentieth century and was modeled by the empress in her public image as a military mother and in the context of *ryōsai kenbo*.

In Toyohara Kunichika's (豊原国周, 1835–1900) 1887 *Kōgōgū gosei shōka* (Song Composed by the Empress, Figure 2.5), Shōken teaches a group of young girls to sing as they sit around a table. The girls are aristocratic children, and the song was based on a poem that the empress presented to the Peeresses' School (Kazoku joshi gakkō) in March of the same year.[45] The poem, printed at the upper left, was based on Benjamin Franklin's virtue of industry, part of his twelve virtues, which Shōken had learned of from the Confucian palace tutor Motoda Eifu (1818–1891), and the imaging of music reinforced other prints visualizing singing and playing instruments.[46] That education was the realm of women's responsibilities was not intrinsic to Japanese culture, as it was in other parts of the world.[47] In the Edo period men were tasked with ensuring the education of their offspring, and there was social concern that educated women would enter the political realm.[48] In the decades following the publication of this print, the *jogakusei* (school girl) would become a major figure in Japanese culture, and around the turn of the century, school girls would

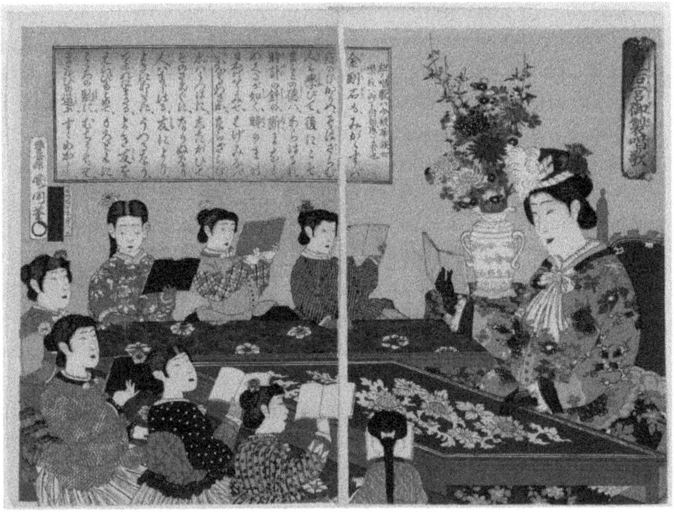

FIGURE 2.5 *Kōgōgū gosei shōka* (Song Composed by the Empress), September 8, 1887, Toyohara Kunichika, multicolor woodblock print, Collection of the Museum of Fine Arts, Boston

be envisioned with a subversive tone.[49] In this diptych, though, we see the use of the empress image as a flex of cultural power; despite these girls being of the nobility, the mimicry of the act of a woman teacher with a group of girls would be played out across the archipelago in the mid-Meiji years. Shōken's role in elevating girls' education was so central to her position and had a lasting national impact, to the degree that her role as an educational leader is represented in two of the eighty paintings in the Meiji Memorial Picture Gallery.

On May 24, 1881, Empress Shōken attended a concert at the Women's Normal School conducted by Luther Whiting Mason, an American who taught at four Tokyo schools and worked with the Music Study Committee (Ongaku Torishirabe Gakari).[50] This committee was headed by Izawa Shūji, principal of the Tokyo Normal School, and produced textbooks for schools, including

Shōkashū, the first elementary music textbooks in Japan, while court musicians attached to the Tokyo Women's Normal School wrote *hoiku shōka* (songs for education) that were part of official school curriculum.[51] Shōken's patronage of women's education, specifically at the Peeresses' School, allowed for women to be educated in Euro-American music and for women to eventually become music teachers. It also made it acceptable for women to perform not just in school settings but at the Rokumeikan, a site of diplomatic state events.

Whereas the empress' association with and promotion of education and music provided new opportunities for women, her link to sericulture positioned Shōken between a historic domestic practice and modern global manufacturing. Silk production was a critical Meiji industry, and one which brought in significant amounts of foreign currency. The government operated a number of silk filatures, which were predominantly staffed by young women. The difficult labor conditions of the silk mills, and the need for girls to travel and live away from their families, made recruiting and retaining workers a difficult task, and woodblock prints frequently featured not just silk production at court but also showcased the mill structures, the factory girls, and the silk machinery which was demonstrated at domestic industrial exhibitions.[52] The use of Shōken's image in Meiji sericulture prints shows that the visibility and activities of the imperial family were used to manipulate social norms for the greater project of national economic development.

Throughout the Meiji images of silk production, the imperial family was an important and constant presence. Empress Shōken began ritual silk production in 1871, at the same time that government silk filatures were promoted in woodblock prints. The imperial ties to sericulture have very early precedents, including a mention in the *Nihon Shoki*, a mythological history written in the eighth century, and are part of a distinctively East Asian queenship practice. In China the invention of sericulture is credited to the legendary ancient empress Leizu, and Chinese empresses practiced state sacrifices of silk from the second century BCE through the Ming dynasty, while the Joseon queens ritually cultivated silk to encourage silk farming.[53] Yet silk production as part of the imperial public image was a Meiji innovation, and one that was distinctly feminine.[54]

Utagawa Kunitoshi's 1877 *Dai Nihon kokusan no uchi yōsan tenran no zu* (Picture of the Imperial Viewing of Sericulture Production) is a busy scene filled with women wearing floral textiles representing different seasons, including a particularly fantastic iris pattern at the far left, morning glories at the bottom center, and maple leaves on black at the center left.[55] As was standard in earlier prints, the fabrics include lines and blocks of pattern representing folds to show how the textiles would drape on the human form, but the patterns do not necessarily follow the folds or the contours of the body, thus allowing the viewer to fully read the flattened patterns. In the Edo period this was done because kimono makers had close relationships with printmakers and desired to show off their wares through woodblock prints; here it works to promote the Meiji textile industry as a whole, in both a mercantile and patriotic way.[56] Empress Shōken, wearing her crown, enters from the right side to oversee the production of silk, explicitly showing both her position by means of the crown and her supervisory role by means of her position in the composition. The triptych is a hectic, busy scene filled with women working, the overlapping patterns and abundance of bright colors making it challenging for the viewer to read the activity. The stages of silk production are visible: from collecting the eggs at the bottom left to reeling at the upper right, with some outdoor activity in the shadows of Mount Fuji in the far distance. Yet, due to the chaotic composition, it takes both a previous understanding of sericulture and some effort from the viewer to interpret the specific steps of preparation.

In sericulture prints of the 1880s, the links to the imperial family would increase, and the Meiji Emperor would also be included in the images. The 1883 Chikanobu triptych *Fūki no shunsan no hanei* (The Riches of Spring Silkworm's Prosperity) (Figure 2.6) (alternately translated as *Emperor Observing Sericulture*) includes Emperor Meiji in full European-style military costume and Empress Shōken in historically inspired court dress but also two cartouches, the one at the left with Kinugasa daimyōjin (絹笠大明神), a silk *kami*, the one at the right with Wakumusubi no kami (和久産巣日神),

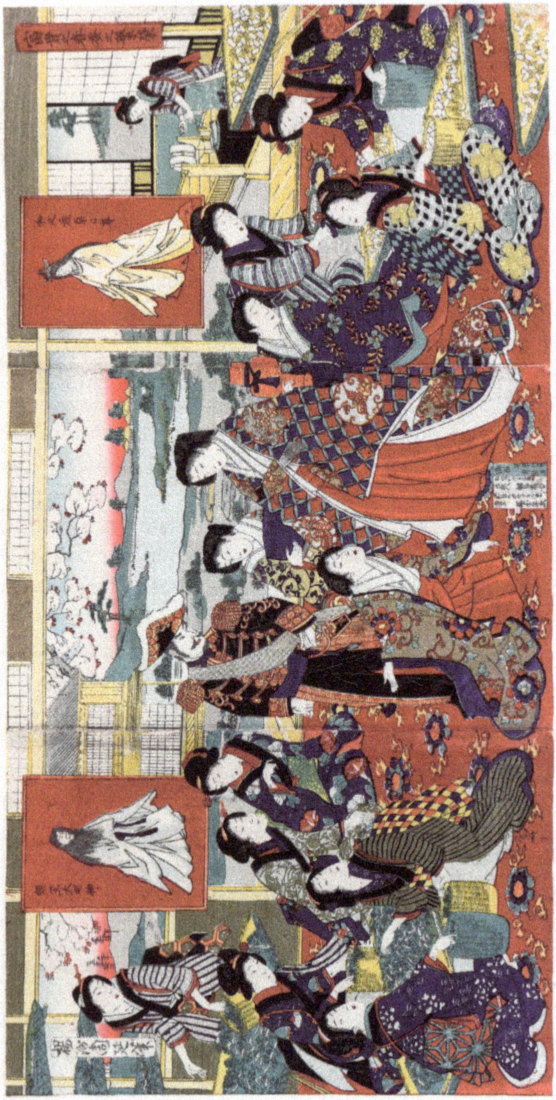

FIGURE 2.6 *Fūki no shunsan no hanei* (Emperor Observing Sericulture), 1883, Toyohara (Yōshū) Chikanobu, multicolor woodblock print, Nature and Science Museum, Tokyo University of Agriculture and Technology

an agriculture *kami* with connections to silk worms. The sericulture production is pushed to the sides of the image to place the imperial couple at the center, linking the two institutions and tying history to the present day. Like most Meiji prints, the colors and patterns are fantastic, and here the process of sericulture is discernable from the triptych. What is important to note in the Chikanobu print is the way the imperial couple is highlighted, their forms and Shōken's clothing reflected in the *kami* that float in the cartouches at each side, and the feminine environment of silk. Building on the anachronistic feel of earlier sericulture prints, Chikanobu's includes Shinto connections to the imperial family in the image, making for a powerful mix of the sacred, the historical, the political, and the economic.[57] It also reinforces the patriarchal structure of both Meiji Japan and the silk industry: Emperor Meiji's masculinity is reinforced by his military costume, complete with a sword, and his height above the women workers and Empress Shōken. He supervises the activity as they work and is not directly addressed by the woman, who seemingly speaks to the empress. Yet, as in many imperial images, Shōken has a larger physical presence in the print, likely to highlight both her beautiful textiles and her connections to the industry, and the emperor stands amidst an all-female environment, evidence of the critical roles women played in Meiji society and court.

A final later example is Hasegawa Chikuyō's (長谷川竹葉, active 1876–1889) 1888 *Kyūchū yōsan no zu* (Illustration of Sericulture at the Imperial Court), which represents Emperor Meiji and Empress Shōken in the right panel, both dressed in European-style clothing, as they observe five upper-class women in full corset and bustle, dressed in the latest Parisian styles of the day, while they take the production of silk from raising the eggs to reeling the thread from cocoons against a plain background.[58] As the busy palace setting is now removed, it is easier to clearly see the silk production process, including the worms on the leaves and the gentle feather used to brush down the eggs. This print also takes the process to the final stage of weaving. Similar to other contemporary prints of sewing from the 1880s, we see women of the upper classes undertaking work that was, by this time, low-paid work reserved for women of limited means and status. This genre of print, with separated female figures set against a plain background, was similar to earlier fashion plates and illustrations from neo-Confucian manuals of feminine deportment.[59] Into the 1880s, as the silk filatures changed from places where the noble daughters would go to learn the craft of modern machine-reeled silk production to undesirable occupations for the lower classes that were fueling the Japanese economic rise, the visual link to the imperial family became an important means to legitimate the work of the factory girls and to encourage their work by means of a celebrity monarch.

Today, ritual silk production continues at the imperial palace, but as in the Meiji period, it is a fantasy of labor. Just as the work being done in these images would not have been possible while wearing the elaborate fashions shown, the empresses of the twenty-first century do not have the time and knowledge to cultivate and reel silk without the assistance of highly skilled labor. By incorporating the empress into these prints, the nineteenth century silk industry received both promotion and acceptability. Domestically, silk was revered in Meiji Japan for its role in economic development, linking these prints to the *shokusan kōgyō* (encourage new industry) slogan. Empress Shōken visited the Tomioka Silk Mill in the 1870s, encouraging the girls for their hard work and writing them a celebratory poem. Today a stone monument stands outside the factory building as a marker of her visit, gracing the factory with the imperial aura. Just as Empress Shōken helped to legitimize Meiji sericulture for domestic audiences, Empress Michiko played a significant part in bringing back historic varieties of silk in the twentieth century and revitalized sericulture as an elevated craft industry. The sericulture images featuring Shōken are in many ways the closest to propaganda, but in promoting factory work—a new manner of modern female activity and comportment—they utilized the soft power of the empress to nudge Japanese culture in the midst of changing roles for women.

Likewise, as industrial work was a new role for women that benefitted from imperial validation, public-facing charity work in service of the modern military was also new. As the Japanese empire grew, women were needed to work as nurses, serving nationalist agendas that were expanded upon in the Meiji period and which supported the *fukoku kyōhei* (rich country, strong military) slogan. Women of the working classes were needed in labor positions, and women of the nobility and upper classes were needed to raise funds and provide social support for military causes. Shōken buoyed these roles through her charity work, as she frequently visited hospitals and prints of her performing acts of goodwill increased in the 1890s as the politics of expansion changed in the years surrounding the Sino-Japanese War. The idea of caretaking as a primary role of the empress was, and is, a common characteristic of global queenship, and while official visits to wounded soldiers and their caretakers are a constant visual theme of modern monarchy, the Japanese imperial women's relationship to the military would grow significantly in the twentieth century, and will be covered further in Chapter 3.

The idea of women as nurses in Euro-American-style hospitals was slow to gain acceptance in the early decades of the Meiji period. Like with the woman factory workers, early Meiji nurses came from the wealthy classes, as training required the means to pay for an education.[60] With the increase in international travel, and subsequent reports of woman nurses working in European and American hospitals, the idea of female nurses caring for people outside of their immediate family combined with the growth of new possibilities for public work for women and led to nursing as an accepted female profession. Empress Shōken contributed to this through her monetary contributions to the Hakuaisha association starting in 1883 and their hospital in 1886. When the association became the Japanese Red Cross in 1887, Shōken's contributions increased more than tenfold: this explicit imperial approval lent credibility to both the organization itself and to the relatively new occupation of nursing.[61]

As Japanese imperialism grew, the state's interest in the body and also the care of the men fighting on the frontlines also expanded. In Kobayashi Kiyochika's (小林清親, 1847–1915) 1895 *Sanbō honbu gyōkei no zu* (Illustration of the Empress Visiting the General Staff Headquarters), Shōken presents a gift of bandages while seated above the other people in the room.[62] The print is highly feminine, showing the nursing side of war but without any direct references to injury or sacrifice. The white bandages are reminiscent of mochi donations for New Year's, and the sterile environment has no references to hospital or battlefield conditions. The print can be understood alongside the popular Sino-Japanese War triptychs that represented land and naval battles in a more masculine setting. Shōken was involved in founding the Japanese Red Cross in 1877 and would later, in 1912, establish a fund in her name to underwrite international aid projects, a fund that still exists today. What was critical about the increased imaging of charity visits in the 1890s was the onset of the Sino-Japanese War and Japanese imperial expansion efforts. Just as the sericulture prints functioned to encourage women to work in service of a national industry, images of empress visits to hospitals urged women to send their sons and husbands to war, as they envisioned the respect that the imperial family had for military service and also inspired women to service in nursing professions. Furthermore, with the march of time, the style of these prints changed as well. The busy patterns and elaborate, crowded scenes of the 1870s and 1880s gave way to a more streamlined style of print, including the use of shadow and light on the carpet, showing the visual impact of photography as it became more widespread.

In the example *Yasen byōin gyōkō no zu* (Illustration of the Empress Visiting a Field Hospital [in Hiroshima]) by Kobayashi Kiyochika) (Figure 2.7), injured male soldiers and their attending female nurses fill the left half of the scene, outfitted primarily in crisp white clothing, the instantly recognizable symbol of the Red Cross attached to the women's uniforms. In the foreground are two military officers and four women of high class, evidenced by their clothing. Empress Shōken stands at the center, dressed in light purple with gold trim on her fashionable dress, fitted with corset and bustle. Her three attendants, also dressed in resplendent, colorful outfits, surround her as she walks into the hospital environment, where she is greeted by one of the military officers and two nurses. The nurses assist a soldier who sits in bed, wrapped in bandages, attempting to respectfully bow to the empress with the nurse's help. In the background, which is framed by a bright red curtain, we see additional nurses and another soldier seated in bed. Though it may seem like a straightforward image of charity, the expansion of Japanese imperial ambitions

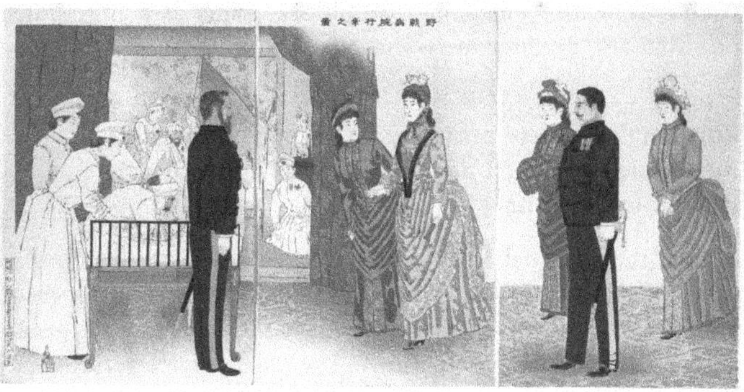

FIGURE 2.7 *Yasen byōin gyōkō no zu* (Illustration of the Empress Visiting a Field Hospital [in Hiroshima]), 1895, Kobayashi Kiyochika, multicolor woodblock print, Metropolitan Museum of Art

was implicit in the subject of this print. While Empress Shōken did visit wounded soldiers, this print allows this scene to be experienced by a far wider swath of the Japanese citizenry than would otherwise be possible.[63] Kobayashi Kiyochika was known for his polished style, use of light and shadow, and incorporation of subtle details. In addition to cityscapes, he created many *senso-ga*, (戦争画) or war prints, during the First Sino-Japanese War of 1894–95. While most of these prints are battle scenes, Illustration of the Empress Visiting a Field Hospital shows the many, gendered sides of war and, by extension, empire. In this print we see women as caretakers in a variety of roles: as a national symbol, as attendants to the empress, as physical support for the bodies of the wounded soldiers, and as emotional buoys for male fighters and the empress as a female cultural leader. Queens were frequently viewed as a counterbalance to conflict, conventionally understood to be natural diplomats and peacemakers, able to heal divisions of many varieties. Prints of medicinal charity are more limited than the other categories addressed in this chapter, as they were late to develop and as lithography grew in popularity and photography became easier to reproduce around the turn of the twentieth century, meaning woodblock prints as a mass media phenomenon declined in production.

Public Diplomacy and Private Palaces: Invented Intimacies of Court and Government in Woodblock Prints

Beyond the maternal and charity functions of the empress images, many of the woodblock prints of the Meiji royal couple were set in the interior rooms of the imperial palace, spaces that the general public could not access, and showing intimate, private family scenes. Yet these cloistered settings are always formal in nature, with prim comportment and decorous clothing selections. It was not until 1890 that the emperor and empress made their first public appearance together, but in the imagined world of woodblock prints, they were envisioned together frequently, as early as the 1870s.[64]

In most print depictions Shōken appears demure, often with a dainty upturned and bent wrist or an angled turn of the head, averting her eyes downward, and clothed in the latest elaborate Parisian fashions, as in the 1888 *nishiki-e* woodblock print *Baien shōkazu* (Chorus in the Plum Garden) (Figure 2.8) by Chikanobu. Shōken appears at the center of the triptych print, leaning on a bright red chair with Crown Prince Yoshihito to her side. Her tight corset and large bustle force her figure into a posture which compromises any assertiveness and which emphasizes the female anatomy while obscuring any individual physical bodily features. The print does not explicitly label Shōken, but her central position, elaborate clothing, and the elite setting, together with the Crown Prince, indicate her identity. Her face is reminiscent of Edo-period *bijin* from woodblock prints—unindividuated, idealized, sparse on details, and completely lacking the contours and shading of three-dimensional visual representation. Empress Shōken is surrounded by palace ladies, the Crown Prince, a luxurious imperial interior in European style, and an expansive garden in the background. Two of the four palace ladies play an instrument—violin and pump organ–while the other two sing as they hold sheet music.[65] In the Meiji period, musical imagery included both Japanese and European instruments and

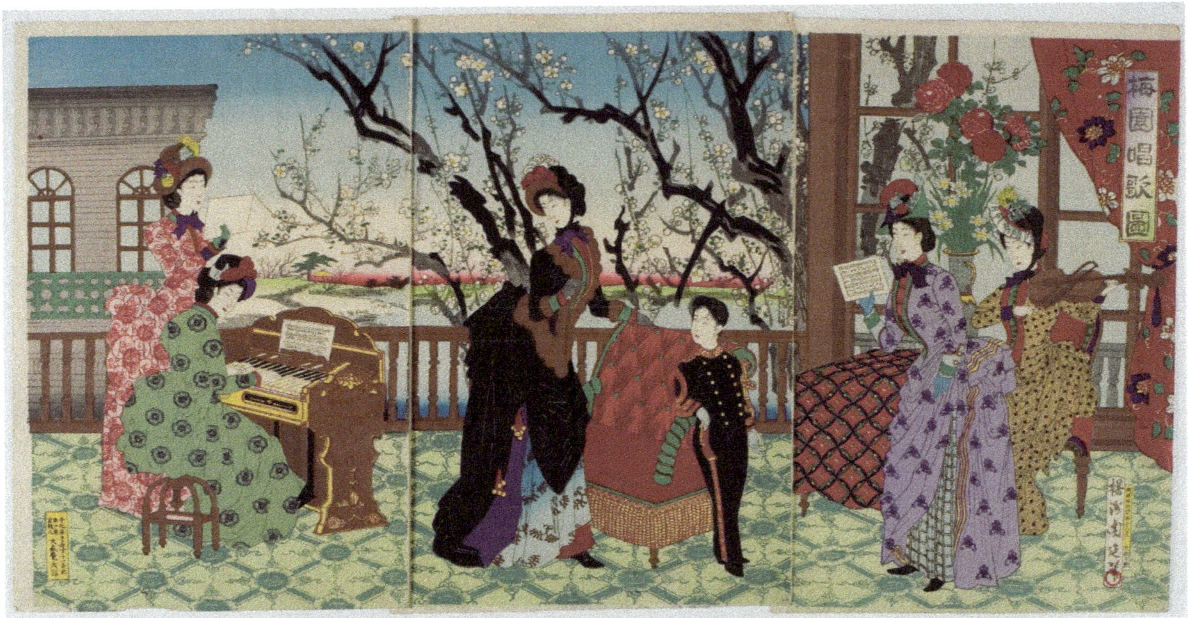

FIGURE 2.8 *Baien shōkazu* (Chorus in the Plum Garden), late nineteenth century, Toyohara (Yōshū) Chikanobu, multicolor woodblock print, Harvard Art Museums/Arthur M. Sackler Museum, Bequest of William S. Lieberman, Photo © President and Fellows of Harvard College, 2007.214.97.1–3

performances. European music was a means of entertainment and part of dinner table diplomacy, both in the private palace setting and in the more public-facing Rokumeikan, a European-style building utilized for formal state gatherings.[66] Seeing the empress' sponsorship of European musical performances would have validated music education for women, and combined with her benefaction of music at The Peeresses' School, prints such as *Chorus in the Plum Garden* visually encouraged participation in musical activity in the public forum.

Among Meiji empress prints the opulent interiors, fantastic patterns, and luxurious textiles all contribute to images that can at times be difficult to read, as the patterns and colors can in some instances make it difficult for the eye to rest or to easily discern the forms of the figures. In addition to the variety of conventional domestic activities Shōken was engaged with, such as viewing cherry blossoms, writing, or making music, court women and the empress participated in both palace and public diplomacy, new functions for noblewomen. In the September 20, 1877 Chikanobu print *Kagoshima zokuto chinsei ni yotte shoshō tenhai chōdai no zu* (Leaders of the Pacification of the Kagoshima Rebels Celebrating with Cups of Wine from the Emperor), Shōken and Meiji sit in the background at the far left, overseeing from a distance the presentation of sake to military leaders who were involved in suppressing the Satsuma Rebellion, a conflict which had very recently concluded.[67] Prime Minister Sanjō Sanetomi sits next to the emperor as attendants use their long-handled gold ladles to fill oversized red lacquer cups. The idea of an empress being present at a government- and military-themed event was a very new concept in the 1870s. Shōken did not frequently participate in military affairs, but on a handful of occasions she did attend ceremonial naval launchings and similar happenings. Visually, the focus of this print is on the court ritual as being performed primarily by women in religious or historically inspired dress for men in European-style military costumes. As was seen in the aforementioned examples, here Shōken sits as an equal with the emperor, and the palace and court environment is one that is largely feminine.

While early images such as the palace celebration from 1877 certainly exist, many of these images of governance are later, around the time of the Promulgation of the Constitution in 1889. When associated with the contemporary government, Shōken appears in supportive roles at the side of the composition, dressed in European fashions. Unlike the images of court life in the palace interior, images of government and government functions show a highly masculine environment. Created with the same spirit of nationalism and same didactic function as prints of factories and infrastructure that promoted the slogans of *shokusan kōgyō*, encourage new industry, or *bunmei kaika*, civilization and enlightenment, these prints were useful for and interesting to citizens who desired to learn about the new systems of government that were established in the 1880s.

Chikanobu's 1890 print *Kokkai kaigi no zu* (Session of the National Diet) (Figure 2.9) presents the empress as a focal point of the composition. Seated in plush, bright red chairs at the lower right corner of the triptych, the empress and three of her attendants are dressed in bright purples, greens, and blues as they oversee the activity of the legislature. In a similar style to other prints of the same subject the women stand out in their posh, colorful garments, set against a sea of men dressed

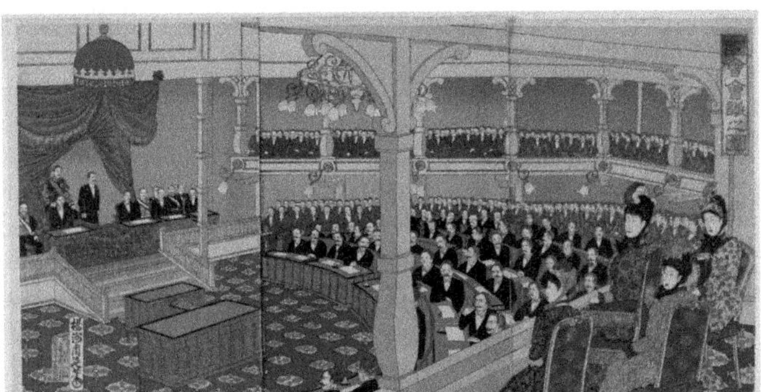

FIGURE 2.9 *Kokkai kaigi* (Session of the National Diet), 1890, Toyohara (Yōshū) Chikanobu, multicolor woodblock print, Harvard Art Museums/Arthur M. Sackler Museum, Bequest of William S. Lieberman, Photo © President and Fellows of Harvard College, 2007.214.98.1–3

in identical black suits. Emperor Meiji is placed opposite of the empress, his position beneath the red baldachin signifying his importance, which is visually contradicted by his small size and distant position. The print can be read in two ways: placing the women on the balcony removes them from the action of governance, yet the women are the largest figures in the print, the details of their clothing providing the most visual interest and their position implying power. Furthermore, as with the court images the women are the entry point to the image. It is through their gaze that the viewer gains access to the highest chamber of government—the women, and by extension the owner of the print—possess the panoptic position. The architectural features of the balcony railing and support column separate the women from the legislative body, with the composition opening the picture plane to the viewer, who can imagine themselves in the women's space. Thus, once again, and linked to larger queenship tropes, it is Shōken who provides entrée to the removed spaces of the emperor and, in this instance, the Diet.

In her book *Kōgō no shōzō*, art historian Wakakuwa Midori examines the impact of the visual component of the empress image produced in the Meiji period, arguing that with the image of Shōken the Meiji government attempted to project power over women's lives. Wakakuwa asserts that the empress image was used as a means of oppression, keeping women in domestic roles, and to promote a new model of the nuclear family in the nineteenth century. In the context of woodblock prints, the censorship system meant that imperial representations were controlled by the corporate monarchy, but it is unlikely that Shōken herself had any agency over her image in print. Wakakuwa uses the creation of the *koseki* (戸籍, family registration system), wherein all Japanese citizens are listed by their ancestry in government-held records in their hometown, as an example of population management, linking the *koseki* to the image of Shōken by stating that women were kept in the private domain, both visually and through public policy, and that the family unit as the foundation of government control was a means to regulate reproduction and thus population.[68] Wakakuwa astutely points out that even into the twentieth century Japanese law and culture worked to protect the male-dominated system, further asserting that the image of Shōken was a component in supporting the establishment of women's roles in the home. Wakakuwa's varied arguments and analyses of Shōken's image all support her larger point: that the empress image in the Meiji period was one component in the state's strategy to keep women out of positions of power.

While it is undoubtedly true that Shōken is often in a supporting position, as the images analyzed in this chapter show, she was highly visible and was frequently envisioned at central state events, often a visual equal. As evidenced by the prints themselves, even if Shōken was in a position that was manipulated by the patriarchal bureaucracy and represented in images created by male artists, a woman had an important and critical visual role to play in crafting the modern imperial family and thus familial ideas of the modern state. This in itself was dramatically different than in the previous eras. While there is undoubtedly a patriarchal component to these prints, it is critical to recognize that Shōken's image held a specific type of power: despite the fact that she did not hold religious or political authority as Emperor Meiji did and did not produce biological children, she remained a central component of the visual monarchy, espousing the virtues of education, charity, and work.[69]

In the realm of official public appearances, Yōsai (Watanabe) Nobukazu's (渡辺延一, 1872–1944) March 1890 *Daisankai Naikoku kangyō hakurankai* (The Third National Industrial Exposition) (Figure 2.10) is an image of a government function and government-sponsored public space. The print includes Empress Shōken, Crown Prince Haru, and a lady-in-waiting in the center, Emperor Meiji, and his entourage entering from the right. The interior of the exhibition space is decorated with textiles and flags, and the exhibition cases themselves are small details pushed to the background. The Meiji government invested heavily in domestic and international exhibitions as a means of advancing the state on the global stage of the World's Fairs. Once again, the empress is the center of the image, the recipient of the emperor's gaze, and the primary subject of the print. While ostensibly this triptych is about the exhibition, in reality it is a fantasy

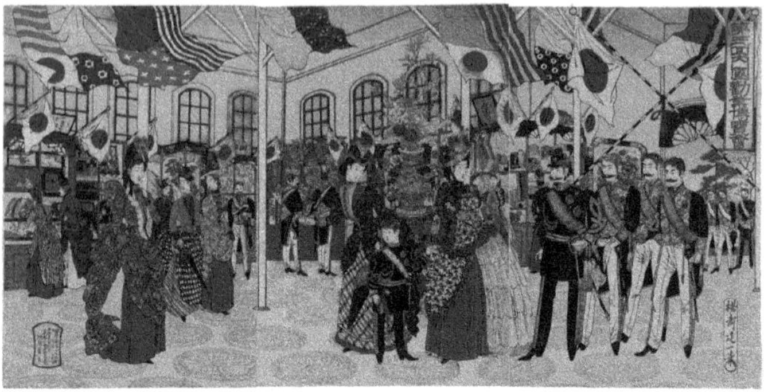

FIGURE 2.10 *Daisankai Naikoku kangyō hakurankai* (The Third National Industrial Exposition), March 7, 1890, Yōsai (Watanabe) Nobukazu, multicolor woodblock print, Collection of the Museum of Fine Arts, Boston

of fashion, maternity, and proper comportment and a fantastic show of government capability, in the form of the architecture, event, and all that it celebrated, as well as strong leadership, hinting at Japan's successful presence in the international forum of the World's Fairs. Unlike the interior scenes from the palace or the Diet building, the National Industrial Exposition was a space that was accessible to average citizens and a place where viewers could project themselves, further linking the imperial subject to their sovereigns in an imagined parasocial relationship but also allowing Shōken to act as a role model for how to comport oneself in the new environment of exhibition and museum spaces. Elegant and refined, the visuals of Empress Shōken in the court context show a corporate monarchy participating in cultured, modern activities in and around the new capital city.

The feminine sovereign image utilized the power of representation to exert domestic influence over women's activities and to connect to the citizenry through the flexible feminine side of the visual monarchy. The social and political impacts of the messaging from the Imperial Household Ministry, envisioned in disparate settings and sartorial selections, are difficult to measure, as there were many changes happening in the daily lives of Meiji women. Yet, as prints of the imperial family were produced in a market system, and therefore had to meet the sales criteria of publishers to continue to be selected as topics, we can conclude that they were popular. Publishers and artists utilized a variety of euphemisms for the imperial family in order to subvert censorship processes (thus the titles "picture of nobility" or "dignitaries of the empire"), which also informs us of the celebrity of the emperor and empress as subjects of print culture. With her established visibility, modeled dutiful charity, patriotism, and industriousness, and intimate glimpses of the fantasy of her court life, Shōken's image was a powerful form of a parasocial celebrity relationship. Her citizens were able to connect with her through the familiarity of reproduced multiples, viewing the emperor's gaze upon the empress and possessing a part of this gaze themselves. These prints included important topics for the Meiji national project, including maternity, charity and work, and court diplomacy. After the turn of the century, woodblock prints of Empress Shōken began to fade as the subsequent imperial couple was married in 1900, and attention turned to the Taishō monarchs and their children. The genre of woodblock prints also declined in popularity at the end of the Meiji period with the rise in lithography and photography, which is the subject of Chapter 3.

Although in the context of the broader culture some Meiji philosophers, writers, and intellectuals called for reforms that would promote women's equality, many felt that egalitarianism was not a desirable social goal. Nishimura Shigeki, a tutor to the emperor and educational policy maker, "emphasized women's unique characteristics and social roles" but maintained that men should enjoy rights over their wives.[70] Over time family policy, women's oppression through social attitudes, and the subjugation of women to horrific industrial conditions, not to mention the continuation of legal prostitution through the mid-twentieth century, meant that women's secondary social status was continued and reinforced. The complex situation of women as critical to the imperial lineage and surrounding the emperor, but outside of the primary positions of power, is evident throughout the visual culture of the modern empresses and imperial family.

The flexible roles of the imperial family in the media, as evidenced in a woman engaging in diplomatic or military affairs or a series of prints featuring *gon no tenji* alongside the empress, is often unrecognized but was utilized regularly throughout the modern era. In writing about Shōken's successor Empress Teimei, historian Hara Takeshi argues that the commonly held idea of the modern imperial family as organized in a fixed and static fashion is disproved in the early 1920s, evidence that there was not just one imperial system in the modern era, but rather the system adjusted to the needs of the day.[71] The prints investigated in this chapter are evidence that this is true in the Meiji period as well, that Shōken's image changed over the early Meiji decades in response to social and political events and evolving views of global monarchy. Images of the empresses are testaments to their activities and their roles in developing new understandings of the empress concept in the modern age. These images, and the women and corporate monarchy behind them, transformed the private women of the palace to something entirely new, blending centuries of imperial tradition with evolving values and new modern, international understandings of monarchy and queenship.

Notes

1 The term parasocial relationship was coined in 1956 by Horton and Wohl in reference to television personalities but can also be applied to the mediated, intimate multiplicity of empress prints. Daniel Chandler and Rod Munday, *A Dictionary of Media and Communication* (Oxford: Oxford University Press, 2011), www.oxfordreference.com/view/10.1093/oi/authority.20110803100305809.

2 Kunaichō, *Shōken kōtaigō jitsuroku* (Tokyo: Yoshikawa Kōbunkan, 2014); Kunaichō, *Meiji tennō ki* (Tokyo: Yoshikawa Kōbunkan, 1968–1977).

3 Kunaichō, *Shōwa tennō jittsuroku* (Tokyo: Tokyo Shoseki, 2014–2017). Archival sources documenting Empress Teimei's life are available at the Imperial Household Agency, but they are not compiled into a standard format as the published versions are.

4 Approximately three percent of Taishō's record was blackened out until 2015, but his record remains unpublished outside of the Archives, whereas the other records are reproduced and widely available from libraries and bookstores. "Taishō tennō jitsuroku

no kuroneri ōhaba kaijo, menkaisha nado kōkai," *Yomiuri Shinbun*, June 30, 2015, Tokyo morning edition, p. 13.

5 Theresa Earenfight, "Highly Visible Often Obscured: The Difficulty of Seeing Queens and Noble Women," *Medieval Feminist Forum: A Journal of Gender and Sexuality* 44, no. 1 (2008): 86–90.

6 Her name at birth was Tōka (桃花), but her name was changed six days later. Otabe Yūji, *Shōken kōtaigō Teimei kōgō: hitosuji ni makoto o mochite tsukaenaba* (Kyoto: Mineruva Nihon hyōdensen, 2010), 347.

7 Donald Keene, *Emperor of Japan: Meiji and His World, 1852–1912* (New York: Columbia University Press, 2002), 105.

8 For a complete history of the lineage of Japanese empresses: Shin Jinbutsu Ōraisha, *Rekidai kōgō jinbustsu keifu sōran* (Tokyo: Shin Jinbutsu Ōraisha, 2002). Beyond the scope of this book is the structure of the shogunal marital and sexual politics, which are a potential area for comparison.

9 The Japanese Red Cross (日本赤十字社, *Nihon sekijūjisha*) was founded in 1877 as the Philanthropic Society (博愛社, *Hakuaisha*) and in 1887 changed its name and was recognized by the International Committee of the Red Cross. *Japanese Red Cross Society*, "History," www.jrc.or.jp/english/about/history/.

10 *Empress Shōken Fund*, "Empress Shōken Fund," http://shokenfund.org/, and *International Federation of Red Cross and Red Crescent Societies*, "Empress Shoken Fund: Supporting Red Cross Red Crescent Work for 100 Years," www.ifrc.org/en/news-and-media/news-stories/asia-pacific/japan/empress-shoken-fund-supporting-red-cross-red-crescent-work-for-100-years/.

11 Her poetry is translated into English: Meiji Jingū, *Kenshō kōtaigō gyoka* (Tokyo: Meiji Jingū Shamusho, 1980).

12 "I hope you will observe/Moderation when drinking/From your sake cup/Amidst the springtime flowers/Or the crimson autumn leaves." As cited in Keene, *Emperor of Japan*, 174.

13 Harold Wright, *Meiji as Composed in Elegant Verse: 100 Poems by Empress Shōken* (Tokyo: Chuo Koron Shinsha, 2024).

14 Generally, English publications use *gon no tenji* when referring to the court ladies who served at the pleasure of the emperor; Japanese publications use 典侍 (*tenji*).

15 The 1868 change is often referred to as the Meiji Restoration; however, Meiji revolution is a more accurate term, as the events brought about change rather than a return to a previously established system. Robert Hellyer and Harald Fuess, eds.,

The Meiji Restoration: Japan as a Global Nation (Cambridge: Cambridge University Press, 2020).

16 Keene, *Emperor of Japan*, 157–159. Keene states that Iwakura Tomomi requested an officer of the Ministry of Shinto to "examine old records to determine authentically Japanese rituals," as he was "sure that most of what was considered to be traditional was in fact copied from Chinese models, and he believed that in a time of great changes, it was appropriate that the ceremony be revised so as to constitute a model for future coronations."

17 Keene, *Emperor of Japan*, 162–163.

18 Fujitani, *Splendid Monarchy*, 36–37.

19 Edmund T. Gilday, "Bodies of Evidence: Imperial Funeral Rites and the Meiji Restoration," *Japanese Journal of Religious Studies* 27, no. 3–4 (2000): 291–293.

20 Otabe, *Shōken kōtaigō Teimei kōgō*, 165–169.

21 Takashi Fujitani, *Splendid Monarchy: Power and Pageantry in Modern Japan* (Berkeley: University of California Press, 1996). For a discussion of Foucault and Bourdieu, see pages 102–103, and 138–143.

22 Gyewon Kim, "Tracing the Emperor: Photography, Famous Places, and the Imperial Progresses in Prewar Japan," *Representations* 120 (Fall 2012). For further discussion of the disciplinary regime of power, see: Michel Foucault, *Discipline and Punish: The Birth of the Prison*, trans. Alan Sheridan (New York: Vintage, 1977), 193.

23 Ozawa Asae, *Meiji no kōshitsu kenchiku: kokka ga motometa "wafū" zō* (Tokyo: Yoshikawa kōbunkan, 2008).

24 This image can be found at the Metropolitan Museum of Art, accession number JP3253a-c.

25 Sarah E. Thompson and H.D. Harootunian, *Undercurrents in the Floating World: Censorship and Japanese Prints* (New York: Asia Society Galleries, 1991), 88–90.

26 Bruce A. Coats, *Chikanobu: Modernity and Nostalgia in Japanese Prints* (Leiden: Brill, 2006), 18–19.

27 For one example of Meiji critique, see Kitamura Tōkoku, *Kokumin to shisō* (Tokyo: Aozora Bunko, 1893, reprinted 2004). For an analysis of *Kokumin to shisō* see, Kōji Makibayashi, "Hihyō no seisei: 'Kokumin to shisō' tameshikō," *Nihon bungaku* 40, no. 11 (1991): 1–11. Makibayashi states that Kitamura was attempting to confront Meiji monarchy through his cultural critique of the "superficial" Rokumeikan-Western culture and by analyzing the reaction to modernization, Westernization, and nationalism.

28 Wakakuwa Midori argues that Shōken personified the subordination of Japanese women, as her infertility was frequently discussed as a failure, and she was bound by Confucian tradition. Wakakuwa Midori, *Kōgō no shōzō: Shōken kōtaigō no kyōshō to josei no kokuminka* (Tokyo: Chikuma shobō, 2001), 334. In her recent study of women's education at court, Mamiko Suzuki added complexity to the situation stating that, "even if the empress' activities were Western in appearance and Confucian in their content, her position as subordinate and subject to the emperor and to the nation-state did not negate her authority." Mamiko C. Suzuki, *Gendered Power: Educated Women of the Meiji Empress' Court* (Ann Arbor: University of Michigan Press, 2019), 36.

29 That maternity brought power to royal women is true in a variety of historical and geographic contexts. For examples from other cultures, see: Elena Woodacre and Carey Fleiner, eds., *Royal Mothers and Their Ruling Children: Wielding Political Authority from Antiquity to the Early Modern Era* (New York: Palgrave Macmillan, 2015), and Carey Fleiner and Elena Woodacre, eds., *Virtuous or Villainess? The Image of the Royal Mother from the Early Medieval to the Early Modern Era* (New York: Palgrave Macmillan, 2016). For an overview of the Ōoku, the women's quarters of the shoguns which had parallel structures to the imperial family, see: Cecilia Segawa Seigle and Linda H. Chance, *Ōoku: The Secret World of the Shogun's Women* (Amherst, NY: Cambria Press, 2014).

30 The image is in a private collection but can be found at: www.miwajapaneseart.com/product/lady-naruko-and-prince-take-utagawa-kunitoshi/.

31 Coats, *Chikanobu*, 18–19. Coats translates the title as Parody of the Beauty of the Seven Nights, but in addition to the seven luminaries, *shichi yōsei* can also refer to the stars of the Big Dipper. The kanji for each are also the kanji for the seven days of the week.

32 Also in the title, Yoshitoshi switches the usual first kanji for *mitate-e*, or parody prints (見立絵) for the homonym kanji 美立, giving the series a double meaning of parody of beauty.

33 The print is in a private collection but can be found here: https://ukiyoe.yamabosi.jp/?p=44118.

34 Donald Keene, "Portraits of the Emperor Meiji," *Impressions* 21 (1999): 23.

35 The print can be found in the collection of the Tokyo Metropolitan Library (198-C1–3/東C198-C001–003) and reproduced

in: Segi Shinichi, ed., *Tsukioka Yoshitoshi gashū* (Tokyo: Kōdansha, 1978).

36 Kunaichō, *Shōken Kōtaigō jitsuroku* (Tokyo: Kunaichō, 2014), 196.

37 The print can be found in the Ruth Chandler Williamson Gallery, Scripps College, 2005.1.11.

38 Hayakawa Noriyo "The Formation of Modern Imperial Japan from the Perspective of Gender," trans. Leonie Stickland and Ulrike Wöhr, in *Gender, Nation and State in Modern Japan*, ed. Andrea Germer, Vera Mackie and Ulrike Wöhr (London: Routledge, 2014), 32.

39 Hayakawa Noriyo "The Formation of Modern Imperial Japan from the Perspective of Gender," 33.

40 Anne Walthall, ed., *Servants of the Dynasty: Palace Women in World History* (Berkeley: University of California Press, 2008).

41 Bruce A. Coats, *Chikanobu: Modernity and Nostalgia in Japanese Prints* (Leiden: Brill, 2006), 73–74.

42 Susan Kingsley Kent, *Queen Victoria: Gender and Empire* (Oxford: Oxford University Press, 2016), 105, 167–169.

43 Margaret Homans, *Royal Representations: Queen Victoria and British Culture, 1837–1876* (Chicago: University of Chicago Press, 1998).

44 Translation of Emperor's speech in: Charles Lanman, *The Japanese in America* (New York: University Publishing Company, 1872), 7.

45 Julia Meech-Pekarik, *The World of the Meiji Print* (New York: Weatherhill, 1986), 118.

46 Meech-Pekarik, *The World of the Meiji Print*, 119.

47 Rachel G. Fuchs and Victoria E. Thompson, *Women in Nineteenth-Century Europe* (New York: Palgrave Macmillan, 2005).

48 Julie Nelson-Davis, *Utamaro and the Spectacle of Beauty* (Honolulu: University of Hawai'i Press, 2008), 169–209.

49 Rebecca Copeland, "Fashioning the Feminine: Images of the Modern Girl Student in Meiji Japan," *U.S.-Japan Women's Journal*, no. 30/31 (2006): 13–35.

50 Sondra Wieland Howe, "Women Music Educators in Japan During the Meiji Period," *Bulletin of the Council for Research in Music Education*, no. 119, the 14th International Society for Music Education: ISME Research Seminar (Winter 1993/1994). Sondra Weiland Howe, "The Role of Women in the Introduction of Western Music in Japan," *The Bulletin of Historical Research in Music Education* 16, no. 2 (January 1995): 87.

51 Howe, "Women Music Educators in Japan During the Meiji Period," 105.
52 Alison J. Miller, "Imaging Industry: Woodblock Prints, Factory Women, and Sericulture in Meiji Japan," in *The Visual Culture of Meiji Japan: Negotiating the Transition to Modernity*, ed. Ayelet Zohar and Alison J. Miller (New York: Routledge, 2021).
53 Yi Jo-lan, "Gender and Sericulture Ritual Practice in Sixteenth-Century China," *Journal of Asian History* 48, no. 2 (2014): 281–302. Sin Myung-ho, *Joseon Royal Court Culture: Ceremonial and Daily Life*, trans. Timothy V. Atkinson (Gyeonggi-do: Dolbegae Publishers, 2004); Woo-young Lee, "The Making of a Joseon Queen: Exhibition highlights queens and concubines of Joseon," *The Korea Herald*, July 13, 2015.
54 The *Nihon Shoki* mentions silk production taking place in Japan as early as 462. *Nihongi, 697*, trans. W.G. Aston (London: Japan Society, 1896), 347.
55 This print can be found at the Nature and Science Museum, Tokyo University of Agriculture and Technology.
56 Vivian Li, ed., *The Kimono in Print: 300 Years of Japanese Design* (Worcester: Worcester Museum of Art, 2021).
57 Michael Como, *Weaving and Binding: Immigrant Gods and Female Immortals in Ancient Japan* (Honolulu: University of Hawai'i Press, 2009).
58 This image can be found at the Boston Museum of Fine Arts.
59 Coats, *Chikanobu*, 47. Sumiko Sekiguchi and Michael Burtscher, "Gender in the Meiji Renovation: Confucian 'Lessons for Women' and the Making of Modern Japan," *Social Science Japan Journal* 11, no. 2 (2008): 201–221.
60 Mara Patessio, *Women and Public Life in Early Meiji Japan: The Development of the Feminist Movement* (Ann Arbor: Michigan Monograph Series in Japanese Studies, 2011), 97–99.
61 Patessio, *Women and Public Life in Early Meiji Japan*, 98.
62 This image can be found at the Museum of Fine Arts Boston, 2000.380.27a-c.
63 Kunaichō, *Shōken kōtaigō jitsuroku* (Tokyo: Kunaichō, 2014), 685.
64 Jason G. Karlin, *Gender Nation and State in Meiji Japan: Modernity, Loss, and the Doing of History* (Honolulu: University of Hawai'i, 2014), 32.
65 Thanks to Dr. Geoffrey Ward and Dr. Hillary Dow Ward for their assistance in identifying the pump organ.
66 Mary Redfern, "Dinner Table Negotiations: Tableware and the Presentation of Japan at the Enryōkan," in *The Visual Culture of Meiji Japan: Negotiating the Transition to Modernity*,

ed. Ayelet Zohar and Alison J. Miller (New York: Routledge, 2021).

67 D. Colin Jaundrill, "Dress Rehearsal: The Satsuma Rebellion, 1877," in *Samurai to Soldier: Remaking Military Service in Nineteenth-Century Japan* (Cornell: Cornell University Press, 2016). The print can be found at the Metropolitan Museum of Art.

68 Midori, *Kōgō no shōzō*, 10–11.

69 Takashi Fujitani argues of the imperial women that, "The subordination of these women within the imperial family took place, then, not through their withdrawal from public view, but rather by their becoming more visible than any imperial consorts had ever been in all of previous Japanese history." Fujitani, *Splendid Monarchy*, 180. In his discussion of the emperor's gaze he also states that we should look to the empress' gaze, but a detailed analysis of this is outside of his scope.

70 Akiko Tokuza, *The Rise of the Feminist Movement in Japan* (Tokyo: Keio University Press, 1999), 46.

71 As Hara approaches the imperial family from the perspective of a historian, he uses the term image (像, *zō*) in the broad sense, encompassing the entirety of the impression conveyed to the public, not just the visual vestige. Hara Takeshi, " 'Kokutai' no shikakuka—Taishō • Shōwa shoki ni okeru tennōsei no saihen," in *Ō o meguru shisen*, ed. Yoshihiko Amino, vol. 10 of *Tennō to ōken o kangaeru* (Tokyo: Iwanami shoten, 2002).

3

THE OPTICS OF MODERNITY

Empress Teimei, Photography, Mass Media, and Gender in the Imperial Likeness

The early 1920s were a time of social mayhem: unpopular military campaigns, new rights for women in the public sphere, and the horrific loss of life and widespread damage experienced in the aftermath of the 1923 Great Kanto Earthquake led to tumultuous politics and public opinions. By extension, it was a perilous time for the imperial family in their visible role as a symbol of the state. The presence of the visual monarchy in the public eye was critical to maintaining the relevance of the imperial family at this time of upheaval. With Emperor Taishō's illness keeping him out of view, and the Crown Prince young and unproven, in the early 1920s it was Empress Teimei who made frequent media appearances, with the opaque apparatus of the Imperial Household Ministry ensuring that their photographs maintained an aura of respect while simultaneously providing the citizenry with the imagined connection of parasocial relationships that ensured the monarchy's significance in public life. The photographs analyzed in this chapter, such as *Kōgōheika hakurankai e gyōkei* (Her Majesty the Empress Visiting the Peace Exhibition), published in the magazine *Fujin gahō* (婦人画報) on July 1, 1922 (Figure 3.1), show the striking changes in the life and role of the empress, and by extension the presentation of the visual monarchy and how imperial images were crafted to fit the era of photomechanical reproduction.

Photographs, although readily available, were not easily reproduced by Japanese mass media outlets prior to 1906. However, with the advent of new technologies and changes in societal norms, the media presentation of the imperial couple changed

DOI: 10.4324/9781003376101-5

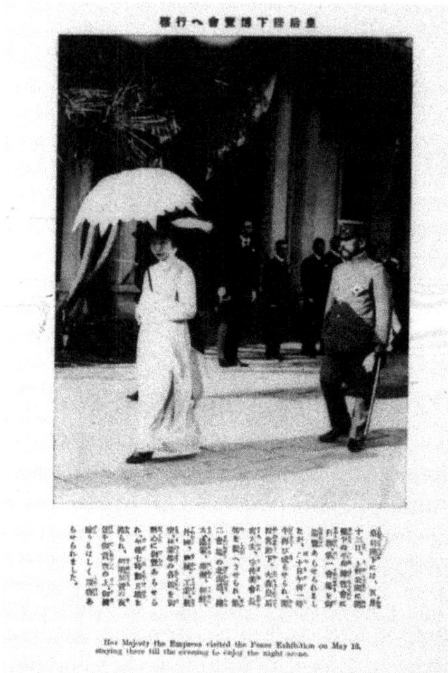

FIGURE 3.1 *Kōgōheika hakurankai e gyōkei* (Her Majesty the Empress Visiting the Peace Exhibition) *Fujin gahō*, July 1, 1922, page 9

quickly and dramatically within the decades marked by the start of the preparation for the Taishō imperial wedding in 1899 and the death of the Taishō emperor in 1926. This chapter focuses on photographs published in the women's magazine *Fujin gahō* in the first thirty years of the twentieth century, demonstrating how the strategic presence of the empresses in the media-oriented society of late Meiji and Taishō Japan represented nuanced changes in imperial gender politics between 1905 and 1928. Mass media images of the empresses show the connections between the visual monarchy and government ideologies in a specifically feminine media context and that Empress Teimei acted as an imperial proxy in the visual culture of the late Taishō period.[1]

By investigating themes of "proxy politics" and the "military mother role," this chapter considers issues of power, presence, the gendered gaze, and the imperial body in the context of both the empress' biography as well as imperial theories and government ideologies of the late nineteenth and early twentieth centuries. The first section provides biographical details of Empress Teimei and Emperor Taishō. Next, this chapter examines theories of gender and rulership in the Japanese imperial family and the proxy politics necessitated by the precarious position of global monarchy in the early twentieth century and Emperor Taishō's illness after 1920. The final section argues that Teimei's military mother image utilized these same tactics of media imaging to counterbalance unpopular political and military events.

These images were not an outright propaganda effort; rather there was a subtlety to their messaging. Most of the mass media photographs were created under the guise of royal celebrity culture: the empress envisioned as a cultural figure to admire. Because of the popularity of the empresses, their images could be used on select occasions to sway or influence cultural opinions. The opacity of the Imperial Household Ministry, and their famously congenial relationship with the media, means that the details and decisions behind the media publication choices remain a mystery. Photographs are generally attributed to anonymous photographers from the imperial household, and when images appear across publications, they are identical or nearly so. The concealed nature of the Imperial Household Ministry as the creator of these images potentially enhanced their success: citizens had no means of questioning the origins of the received imperial personae, no way of comparing different photographs, and no reason to believe that the images were anything but an accurate reflection of reality. Today what we can determine is that through the flexible function of the empresses, as contrasted with the more rigid roles taken on by the emperors, the visual monarchy of the royal women was intended to impact the behavior of average women at critical socio-cultural moments.

In the late Meiji and Taishō periods, photographs of the imperial family often appeared in newspapers and magazines, generally as an accompaniment to a narrative article documenting their activities or, in the case of popular illustrated magazines, as a photographic feature. In the years after 1906–7, with the technological innovations of the rotary press and offset printing, photomechanical reproduction became inexpensive, and image-heavy magazine publications became commonplace. Commemorative pictorial spreads of the imperial family were issued with regularity, generally in bi- or quad-fold inserts. Among these varied visual representations, the most accessible and commonly viewed images for the general public were newspaper photographs, with magazines a close second. Newspaper layouts prioritized text over image and were printed with lower resolution on thin newsprint. These mass media photographs served to link the imperial family to their subjects, providing the commoner with a sense of intimacy and familiarity with their rulers that they had come to expect.[2] This monarchical utilization of the media was commonplace in the globalized arena of the early twentieth century; from Thailand to England, the circulation of royal photographs as a means of power and legitimacy was accepted and expected by subjects and foreign observers alike.

Starting in the early Meiji period, mass media was part of the system of social control; for example, in the 1870s, newspapers played an integral part in educating the public about the role of the emperor in society and included didactic articles on proper behavior when viewing an imperial procession.[3] Newspaper, magazine, and book publishers were held to strict censorship laws, and most newspapers promoted imperial and state myths. As Richard H. Mitchell stated of Meiji publications, "Journalists, then, were foot soldiers in the state's battle to manipulate traditional values about authority and to expand the cult of the emperor."[4] These laws evolved during the early twentieth century, to the point of the Press Law of 1908, wherein anyone responsible for periodical publications which were interpreted to have defamed the imperial household could be punished with up to two years in prison and levied with steep fines.[5] It is difficult to exaggerate the severity of state media control in early twentieth-century Japan, as evidenced by these multifarious laws and publication standards. Simultaneously, these images were available for commercial sale; thus the photographs inform us about the self-perpetuating concept of the imperial family in the larger milieu of Japanese society—these photographs as they appeared in magazines were purchased out of the people's personal interest in the imperial family as celebrity figures, distinct from propaganda.

As discussed in previous chapters, visual representations of the preceding Meiji sovereigns and the succeeding Shōwa royals conveyed relatively conventional gender roles: the images of the emperors were visualized as masculine in the contemporary Euro-American sense, often associated with military costuming, and the empresses as feminine and frequently imaged in familial settings.[6] In contrast, the relationship between the emperor and empress was particularly complex during the Taishō period. Emperor Taishō was afflicted with illness, and midway through his reign passed along official imperial power to his son Hirohito, who was appointed regent in 1921. As a result of this change, Empress Teimei performed public roles otherwise reserved for the male members of the imperial household. This complexity was manifested in visual presentations of the couple. In surveying the image of Emperor Taishō, it was often his absence, rather than his presence, that defined him in the media of the regency period. Empress Teimei filled this void and together with the Imperial Household Ministry used new types of media to innovate unconventional empress roles in visual culture.

To what degree we can see Empress Teimei's agency in these images is difficult to discern. While photographs certainly allowed for a more realistic capture than the complete fantasies of woodblock prints or lithographs, they are still highly staged and censored images. Teimei's words as we are able to receive them today are similarly regulated by the Imperial Household Agency and the media. As with Chapter 2, this examination weds biography, image, and context in an attempt to get as close as we can to Teimei as a person while recognizing the opacity of the imperial institution in which she lived.

Imperial Events and Institutionality: Teimei and Taishō

The life stories of Empress Teimei and Emperor Taishō are well documented in Japanese literature but difficult to access in English publications. Many of the biographical publications on Empress Teimei were written by court ladies in the years after her death, and as with so many texts on the imperial family, there is a reverent tone to the majority of books devoted to telling the story of Teimei's life.

Born on June 27, 1884, Kujō Sadako (九条節子) was the fourth daughter of Duke Kujō Michitaka of the Northern Fujiwara lineage. She spent her infancy and early childhood away from her parents, living with a Quaker family near Tokyo. Teimei was removed from her foster family at age six and brought back to Tokyo, where she attended the Peeresses' School. At age thirteen she was selected to be Yoshihito's bride, after which she spent two years being instructed in court etiquette.

Yoshihito (嘉仁), or Crown Prince Haru, was born on August 31, 1879. He was the only surviving son of Emperor Meiji; ten of his fourteen siblings died during infancy or early childhood.[7] Born to an imperial concubine, Yanagihara Naruko (柳原愛子), Yoshihito was the third child Yanagihara and Meiji bore together, but as the birth of the young prince was so fraught with pain and difficulty, she was never again to share a bed with Emperor Meiji.[8] At age eight, the young prince was named heir apparent, and at age ten, Yoshihito was officially named Crown Prince.[9] From 1887 to 1895, he attended the Peers' School, for children of the aristocracy.

Teimei and Taishō were married on May 10, 1900, in a Shinto ceremony, the first of its kind for the imperial family. Shinto wedding ceremonies were an invention of the Meiji period, and just like the 1840 wedding of British monarchs Victoria and Albert impacted the matrimonial customs in Europe, Teimei and Taishō's wedding had a lasting influence on Japanese wedding culture. The wife of the Belgian ambassador was in attendance when the diplomatic corps visited the newlyweds in the afternoon of their wedding day and described the ceremony by stating:

> Their marriage took place in the Imperial shrine in the palace grounds at eight in the morning. Both bride and bridegroom were dressed in ancient court dress, but only Japanese were present and only two people outside the family witnessed the actual ceremony behind the curtain of the holy of holies. . . . [Then] they changed into Western-style court dress and decorations and presented themselves to the emperor and empress.[10]

The wedding was depicted in lithograph prints (Figures 3.2 and 3.3) and was an event watched with fascination by many in the

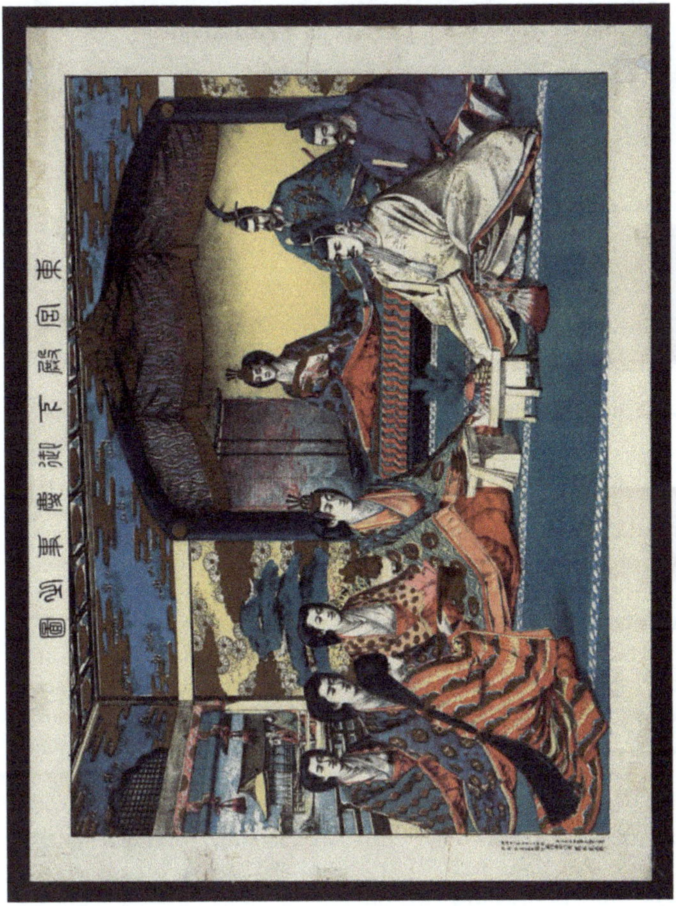

FIGURE 3.2 *Wedding of Crown Prince Yoshihito and Crown Princess Kujō Sadako*, May 1900, Kasai Torajirō, chromolithograph, U.S. Library of Congress

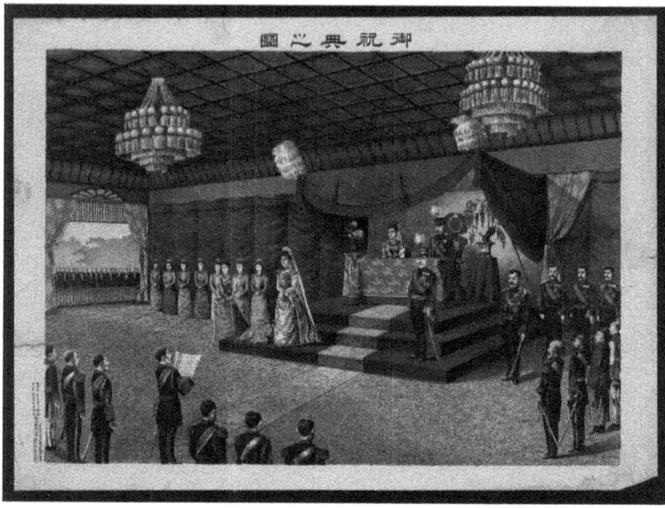

FIGURE 3.3 *Wedding Reception of Crown Prince Yoshihito and Princess Kujō Sadako* 1900, Kasai Torajirō, chromolithograph, U.S. Library of Congress

general citizenry. Wedding ceremonies were different by province in the pre-Meiji era but generally consisted of a gradual transition of the bride to the groom's home and a ceremony at the home with a celebration either at the home or at a nearby restaurant.[11] In the wake of the imperial wedding in 1900, weddings held at Shinto shrines became popular with the general public—a practice which remains fashionable to this day.[12] Following the ceremony, in late May and early June the newlyweds took a tour of the Kansai region, visiting the Ise Grand Shrine and the mausoleum of Emperor Jinmu, the legendary founding emperor of Japan, as well as observing students in Kyoto and touring temples and shrines in Nara.[13]

The lithographs show two sides of the monarchy—in historically inspired dress and in the latest European fashions. At first glance the images are starkly different, but closer investigation reveals that they are very similar in composition and presentation. Both of the images include Shōken and Meiji seated in a removed position behind Teimei and Taishō, a visual marker of the imperial lineage; both include opulent fine art objects, an indicator of both wealth and tradition; and both include an exterior view at the left with added figures. The interior spaces are opulent and detailed; the historic image includes gold painted screens with chrysanthemums and pine and fresh green tatami mats, and the contemporary image includes fanciful chandeliers and decorative arts in cloisonné and metal, the latter being objects that were desirable and acclaimed export goods. Luxurious textiles and imperial symbols abound in both. The prints, viewed separately or as a pair, alerted the public to the biographical event of the imperial wedding in all its opulence while establishing modern wedding customs in a public forum. This constructed conception of the imperial family as deploying visual ideas of both imagined tradition and aspirational modernity continues today.

During her years as Crown Princess, Teimei participated in a variety of state ceremonies and functions. One such example was her attendance at the dinner hosting the American delegation to Tokyo on July 26, 1905. As Empress Shōken was not in Tokyo during the visit, Teimei stood in, dining with Emperor Meiji, then-Secretary of War William Howard Taft, and Alice Roosevelt Longworth, daughter of President Theodore Roosevelt.[14]

Empress Teimei was influential in establishing a new court order and a new system for court ladies; specifically, her exclusive relations with the emperor were crucial in the general societal acceptance of marital monogamy. From the later Meiji period, policies surrounding *ippuippusei* (一夫一婦制, monogamy system) were encouraged and promoted by the government. With Empress Teimei and Emperor Taishō, a model of monogamy was created, and the government policy strengthened with the imperial couple as an example of marital policy.

Among Empress Teimei's feats was bearing four male heirs. The empress of Japan had not produced a male heir in nearly 150 years, with the bloodline of court succession passing through imperial court consorts.[15] The move to imperial monogamy created a risk for producing heirs, but in a parallel to medieval Europe, where the church promoted monogamy and desired for the royal couple to model this familial structure, the Japanese imperial family submitted to bureaucratic pressures to model monogamy and male primogeniture. Teimei gave birth to Michi on April 29, 1901 (Emperor Shōwa, or Hirohito, 昭和天皇, 裕仁); Atsu on June 25, 1902 (Prince Chichibu, or Yasuhito, 秩父宮, 雍仁); Teru on January 3, 1905 (Prince Takamatsu, or Nobuhito, 高松宮, 宣仁); and Sumi on December 2, 1915 (Prince Mikasa, or Takahito, 三笠宮, 崇仁). There is some rumor of a fifth child which cannot be verified. In 1984, journalist Kawahara Toshiaki published the book, *Higeki no kōjo: Mikasanomiya futagosetsu no shinsō* (The Tragic Imperial Princess), which investigated a possible hidden twin for Takahito, a girl who was kept in a Kyoto nunnery due to the inauspicious nature of twins in Shinto belief.[16] Although this child is undocumented outside of Kawahara's investigations, there is some evidence of a miscarriage in 1903–4 from the papers of Erwin von Bälz the German physician who cared for the imperial family in the early twentieth century.[17]

As was court custom in the past, the children of the imperial household were taken from the emperor and empress at birth, a convention of the Edo period that would keep the imperial family from banding together to overthrow the shogun. This practice and the accompanying court regulation was changed in the early twentieth century, with Teimei and Taishō taking custody of their children in March 1905, presumably under pressure from Empress Teimei, who desired to be near her children.[18] Furthermore, the practice was no longer necessary, as a familial bond among the imperial household no longer presented a threat to Japanese rulership and governance.

From 1909, Teimei and Taishō lived at the Ōmiya Palace (大宮御所, Ōmiya gosho) at Akasaka, Tokyo, also called the Tōgū Palace (東宮御所, Tōgū gosho, Crown Prince's Palace). Today the building is referred to as the Akasaka Detached Palace (赤坂離宮, Akasaka rikyū), and is used as a state guest house. Designed by the architect Katayama Tōkuma (片山東熊, 1854–1917) and constructed between 1899 and 1909, the building functioned as an Imperial Palace until the late 1920s, housing both Teimei and Taishō and later Hirohito and Kōjun. The building was constructed in an opulent neo-Baroque style and made Taishō and Teimei the first Japanese imperial couple to reside in European-style accommodations at such an early stage in their reign. During their time as emperor and empress, Teimei and Taishō lived at the Imperial Palace in the center of Tokyo.

As is standard for Japanese empresses, Teimei took on philanthropic activities during her time as monarch. In addition to her participation as the symbolic leader of the Red Cross, Teimei was drawn to helping those with Hansen's disease (leprosy). She donated money to various charities focused on eradicating the disease and helping suffering patients, supporting the efforts of English missionary Hannah Riddell in caring for the sick, and establishing the Tōfū Kyōkai (藤楓協会, Wisteria Maple Association), an organization dedicated to the prevention of leprosy. The organization was first established in 1931 as the Rai yobō kyōkai (癩予防協会, Leprosy Prevention Foundation), with the name change and a second large gift upon her death in 1951.[19] Teimei's other primary charity activity was to assist the keepers of lighthouses by providing radios to the lighthouses to allow them to have increased communication with the outside world.[20] Finally, Teimei undertook ritual sericulture activity at the Imperial Palace, a tradition for empresses that can be traced to the Nara period (710–796). Revitalized by Empress Shōken in 1871, sericulture connected the empresses to larger rituals in East Asian queenship (discussed in Chapter 2) and was a counterpart for the emperor's ceremonial rice cultivation.[21] These elements of her biography were cemented in magazine and newspaper photographs.

During her reign, Empress Teimei was a popular figure who was frequently in the public eye. Although the strict censorship on information regarding the imperial family makes it difficult to determine exactly how she was received by her public, the sheer number of publications on her, both during her reign and at the time of her death, prove that she was a popular celebrity. She is not, however, well remembered by historians. Empress Teimei's role in the imperial house may have been dismissed through the course of history for a variety of reasons. Foremost among these were her possible religious beliefs; although some biographers argue for her strong Shinto beliefs, others state that she may have been a Christian. Raised by Japanese Quakers in the countryside until age six, she surrounded herself with Quakers and other Christians in the palace and was said to have read the Bible daily and the New Testament with frequency. Christians were, and are, a small percentage of the Japanese population, and there is a long history of hidden Christianity and blended religious beliefs in Japan; however, the strong ties of the imperial family to the Shinto hierarchy and narrative preclude them from participating in religious practices other than Shinto. Furthermore, Prince Mikasa taught at a Christian university and Teimei selected a Quaker for her second son's wife. While none of these facts necessitate a label of "Christian," it must be remembered that she was operating in a time and place where the label could have worked to damage her reputation and position, and therefore any possible Christian religious activity had to be discreet and well-managed.[22] Additionally, the cultural memory of her husband is not one of strength for the monarchy; positioned between his highly masculine and military-oriented father and son, Taishō was often ill, and the collective memory of his eponymous era is usually associated with liberal democratic ideas and a loose cosmopolitan culture, not the emperor himself. Despite this historical oversight, she was a well-known and beloved figure in the first half of the twentieth century, even after the death of Emperor Taishō.

That Teimei was able to rise to a position of power in the palace was not particularly remarkable. She was the mother of Hirohito, the successive emperor, and the role and influence of the mother figure in Japanese culture is a powerful one, which should not be underestimated. It was the potential power and influence of the mother and the mother's family which led to many precautions with imperial children in the past. Practices such as raising children outside the palace compound or using imperial concubines diluted the power of the empress and imperial mother. Additionally, Teimei's strong personality and female status meant that she could not be influenced by the gift of concubines, as many male palace counterparts were. Finally, her Christian circle also gave her additional influence at court—the members of the Imperial Household Ministry and other palace bureaucracies that were selected by her from the Japanese Quaker community came from outside of the traditional Shinto and Buddhist groups.

These Christians were influential not for their religious beliefs but because they were outsiders and because they were loyal to Teimei for their placement, thus giving her additional power and an "expanded circle of influence."[23]

In the late 1910s, Taishō began to succumb to illness. His childhood bout with cerebral meningitis left him with compromised health, and complications from the disease grew increasingly worse until he had to turn over rule to his son, Crown Prince Hirohito, on November 25, 1921. The regency period began when Hirohito was unmarried, and quite young. He was twenty years old and had just had his Coming-of-Age ceremony two years prior.[24] As he was yet to take the throne, he traveled throughout this period, visiting Europe in 1921. Upon Hirohito's marriage to Princess Nagako (Empress Kōjun) on January 26, 1924, the younger imperial couple began to appear in the media and at public functions with greater regularity.

Emperor Taishō passed away on December 25, 1926, and Emperor Shōwa immediately took the throne, his coronation coming two years later. During Teimei's time as empress dowager, she took on a more private persona, appearing only occasionally with her grandsons or the larger imperial family. She was reticent during the height of the Pacific War. Emperor Taishō was the first member of the imperial family to be buried at the Musashino Imperial Mausoleum in Hachiōji, a city in the far western suburbs of Tokyo. The Edict on Imperial Household Mourning as passed in 1909 dictated the form of Emperor Meiji's funeral, but in 1911 a new imperial funerary edict was drafted (喪儀令草案, *Sōgi no rei no sōan*); this new edict was enacted into law as the Imperial Mortuary Rites Law (皇室喪儀令, *Kōshitsu sōgi rei*) in 1926, immediately before Taishō's funeral.[25]

Empress Teimei passed away on May 17, 1951. Hers was a state funeral, and various imperial funeral ceremonies were performed, including the *Rensō-no-gi* (斂葬の儀, Ceremony of the Funeral and Entombment), which took place on June 22.[26] Teimei was buried at the Musashino Imperial Mausoleum next to her husband. Like those of Emperor Meiji and Empress Shōken, the Taishō graves are in a style that is reminiscent of a Buddhist stupa, the same form that imperial graves took since the twelfth century. Their successors Emperor Shōwa and Empress Kōjun are also interred at Musashino in similar, slightly larger monuments. Emperor Akihito and Empress Michiko will be cremated and their ashes interred in significantly smaller mausoleums at the site, per their personal wishes.[27] With this general biographical background, this chapter now turns to an analysis of how Empress Teimei and her public image were distinctive in the expression of femininity and power, utilizing media outlets to communicate feminine imperial virtues that situated her in the milieu of global monarchy and supported government initiatives of the era.

Proxy Politics and the Strategic Presence of the Taishō Imperial Family

During most of the Meiji period, particularly in the years after 1885, the imperial family and the imperial institution were stable entities in Japanese society.[28] Yet during the final three years of the Meiji period and into the Taishō period, the court struggled to evolve with the times and to maintain holy inviolability in the face of both revolution in Europe and domestic political unrest. Global monarchy was in crisis in the 1910s: the Russian tsar fell in 1917; the deposition of Austrian Hapsburg ruler Charles I and abdication of Prussian King Wilhelm II both occurred in 1918; and after 1912, Puyi, the last emperor of China, underwent a complex loss of power and agency.[29] The empress and her handlers at the Imperial Household Ministry were undoubtedly apprehensive about the stability of the monarchy in light of these global events as well as potential perceived weaknesses in the Japanese imperial family. In the years after 1920, Emperor Taishō's illness prevented him from participating in public life, leading to concerns with maintaining the male axis of imperial authority in the face of external pressures. Near the end of his reign, Emperor Meiji, for the most part, retreated from public view, and in the years after the Promulgation of the Constitution in 1889, his outings from the palace decreased dramatically.[30] Yet his public presence was maintained through images, news stories, and participation in major public ceremonial events such as the imperial wedding of 1900, as well as processions marking major civic anniversaries, holidays, and military and cultural events.[31]

As Taishō was physically unwell, his retreat was total and therefore his visual public presence decreased dramatically. Additionally, while Taishō made public appearances at the end of Meiji's reign, Crown Prince Hirohito was unmarried, only twenty years old, and did not yet possess the deportment and presence of a mature leader when his father fell ill. He spent much of the regency period traveling, both domestically and internationally, and while he was an important part of the visual monarchy between 1920 and 1926, he had not yet received the *daijosai*, or rites which would eventually make him emperor.[32] In the case of unforeseen events, the succession of the imperial line could have gone to another of Emperor Taishō's sons, making an investment in Hirohito as an imperial proxy an imprudent choice during the regency period. Furthermore, Hirohito and Kōjun's engagement was announced in 1919, but they were not wed until 1924, leaving Hirohito as an incomplete imperial unit in the first four years of the regency. Absence is, of course, a relatively common phenomenon in the history of monarchy both in Japan and globally, and there were many models available for how to manage the regency period.[33] In the face of this instability, the imperial family, together with the Imperial Household Ministry and their allies in the press, responded with a heretofore unseen flexibility in the use of the empress image, one that filled the void of the emperor and worked as a strategic presence to secure the position of the imperial family in Japanese society.

In terms of mass media representations, the adaptability of the visual monarchy meant the occasional re-publication of formal emperor photographs from years past, purposeful placement of the empress in new situations, and using images of other nations' monarchs to validate the imperial family in a larger milieu of global royalty.[34] These varied tactics of visual concealment and promotion provided for bureaucratic hegemony over the imperial image in an age of uncertainty, thus allowing for the imaged monarchy to play a role in the maintenance of *kokutai*, or national polity. For the purposes of explicating the politics of vision during the regency period, I employ a new term for Taishō period imperial visual culture, "proxy politics." This term refers to the strategic promotion or restraint in the use of the image of various imperial household members for political purposes, specifically the use of images of the empress for the express aim of sustaining centralized imperial power in the 1910s and 1920s.

A photograph published in the *Asahi shinbun* on March 28, 1922, of Teimei appearing on the deck of the ship Tenryū, a light cruiser of the Imperial Navy, provides an example of how the empress acted as an imperial envoy during the regency period (Figure 3.4). Allowing for the maintenance of imperial visibility and demonstrating proxy politics, the image shows Teimei investigating military equipment and presumably listening to an explanation from a military official. Although the poor printing quality precludes a close examination of details, the image is clear

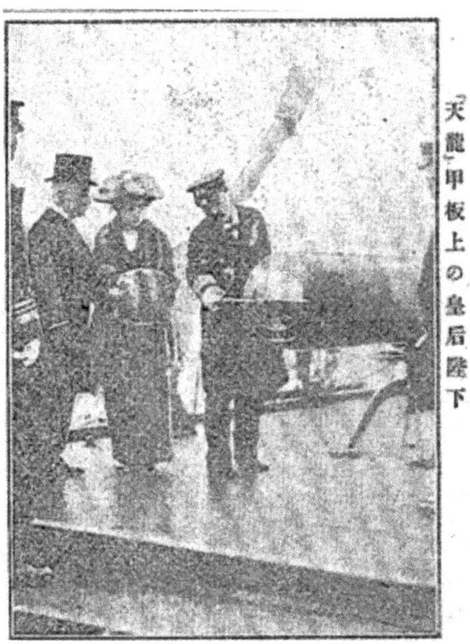

FIGURE 3.4 "*Tenryū*" *kanpan jō no kōgōheika* (Her Majesty the Empress on the Deck of the "Tenryū") *Asahi shinbun*, March 28, 1922, page 7, Tokyo morning edition

in presenting the empress, dressed in fine winter attire including a large decorative hat and fur muff, as a military official points to the smooth metal weaponry that dominates the right half of the photograph. The space around them indicates the open air of the ship deck, and the presence of military officers at either margin of the composition remind the viewer of the location and the martial nature of the photograph. Published during a week when suffrage legislation and military reports filled the newspaper, this image shows Teimei supporting state aims in an active political role, something that was unconventional for the female members of the imperial household and which was unprecedented in representations of the modern empresses.[35]

Coinciding with the publication of this photograph, the Imperial Army was involved in the Siberian Intervention, a military maneuver which was highly unpopular with the Japanese public. Undertaken by the Allied Powers in an effort to support White Russian forces in their conflict with the Bolshevik Red Army in the Russian Civil War, the Siberian Intervention lasted from 1918 to 1920, with the Japanese maintaining military outposts in Siberia through 1922. This photograph also corresponds directly with Navy Minister Katō Tomosaburō's return from meetings with United States military officials at the Washington Naval Conference, an event which was widely covered in the media.[36] Upon returning to Japan in March of 1922, the minister was involved in public lobbying for the adoption of negotiated treaties and the reduction of the military budget.[37] This reduction in spending was part of a larger international agreement to limit arms; Katō believed that by curtailing the size of the Imperial Navy, and thus creating an accord with the United States that included proscriptions on U.S. forces in the Pacific, that the overall Japanese naval position would be strengthened.[38] Both of these news events were widely reported on and would have been topics of public discussion, debate, and concern at the time.[39] By appearing in a naval setting, Teimei as imperial proxy conveyed her popularity and influence to state matters.

Moreover, in addition to military concerns, in early 1922 the government was dispelling civil unrest over the defeat of the Adult Suffrage Bill in February. The day after the Tenryū photograph appeared in the *Asahi,* the newspaper ran a photograph of Empress Teimei leaving the Rokumeikan, a space for diplomatic and social events. The article directly above the Rokumeikan image was titled "Gunjijō yori mita fusen" (The View of Universal Suffrage From the Military) and was written by a member of the Rikugunshō (Army Ministry) in opposition to women's suffrage.[40] The contrast of the article and the photograph, which show a woman as imperial proxy next to text that denies women's rights, combined with the Tenryū image being published only one day earlier, suggests the importance of Teimei's image in a time of political tumult.

In 1922, Empress Teimei's image received the most media visibility, coinciding with this was the revision of Article Five in the Diet, allowing for women to participate in and sponsor political activities.[41] In light of these various political events, the Tenryū photograph represents not only an attempt on behalf of the Imperial Household Ministry to counter the unpopularity of military affairs but also shows the empress as an active stand-in for her husband at a time when women were slowly gaining political rights. The photograph exemplifies proxy politics: Taishō was not able to make physical appearances, but Teimei needed to do so in a way that balanced conventional femininity with political aims. In both of these ways, through the association of a female member of the imperial household with the military, and through the use of the empress as a surrogate imperial figure in a situation of national political importance, this photograph demonstrates how strict imperial gender roles which were established in the recent past were relaxed in the early 1920s.[42] The visual culture of the modern imperial family was the primary means of communicating the imperial presence, yet, in the regency period, the newly absent emperor necessitated the use of alternative imperial symbols. In the era of the visual monarchy, an invisible emperor was simply too great a risk; by 1920 the citizenry was accustomed to imperial imagery, and imagery was crucial in justifying and maintaining imperial rule.

The flexibility of the imperial family is often unrecognized, but has been utilized on regular occasions throughout the modern era. Hara Takeshi argues that the commonly held idea of the modern imperial family as organized in a fixed and static fashion is disproved by the regency period and that the use of Crown Prince Hirohito as a major national symbol is evidence that there was not just one imperial system in the modern era but rather a system that adjusted to the needs of the day.[43] Furthermore, he suggests that this increase in the public activities of members of the imperial family other than the emperor led to the mobilization of domestic suffrage movements in Japan: the increased visibility of the women of the imperial family, combined with ideas of social equality, strengthened the movement for expanded rights of citizenship.[44] The analysis of *Asahi* photographs from March 1922 adds nuance to Hara's position and shows that these changes were not linear. In the Tenryū image, we can see the increased visibility of women and their new social positions, yet the very next day Teimei's Rokumeikan photograph, exhibiting a more conventional gender role, was juxtaposed with the words of a powerful anti-suffrage male figure. There are many ways to interpret these differing images and articles, and the readers of the time would likewise have had varied responses and understandings of corporate media.

The repositioning of family members in the absence of the emperor or king is a common strategy to maintain royal power, one which has had mixed results. Certainly the Qing dynasty succession crisis that led to Empress Dowager Cixi's de facto rule over China for over forty years was closely watched by the Japanese imperial family, as Cixi and her image were alternatingly successful and controversial in the midst of multiple regencies and a chaotic political atmosphere.[45] While she was not a regent, Empress Myeongseong's 1895 assassination by Japanese agents is attributed to her influential position at court, often said to be more powerful than her husband. The removal of a formidable Korean queen is evidence that Japanese leaders in the late Meiji era were aware of royal women's power and concerned with controlling it.[46] Examples abound of earlier regency eras outside of Asia when in the midst of disorder family members were held up in the public forum to maintain royal stability.[47] What is evident is that the use of proxy politics, combined with the visibility of global royal women, as well as the shift in imperial etiquette and new public image of the imperial family, led to a myriad of changes in the gendered social and political milieu, changes that contributed to advancing new roles for women and which would impact women's social standing in the late Taishō period.

While Taishō-era news media photographs exhibit visual innovations, the intellectual underpinnings of the Japanese monarchy primed the royal apparatus and the public for monarchical flexibility. The malleable nature of the dual royal roles was necessitated by the conditions of the regency, but justified by theories of the king's two bodies, which arose from philosophical writings of the day, and which were introduced in Chapter 1. Taishō, and the emperor as institution, maintained power vis-à-vis his concealed status, while Teimei acted as a visual place holder, or an imperial vessel, channeling the imperial gaze and acting as a visual reminder of the imperial household in the mass media, but without threatening the traditional gendered imperial order. This role as imperial proxy allowed her to maintain her status as an elevated cultural symbol and as a royal celebrity paragon of femininity and female decorum, yet did not diminish her husband's role as the absolute center of imperial power. By balancing her role as imperial proxy, Empress Teimei was able to appear in the masculine field, yet still be conventionally feminine, indeed her conspicuously feminine fashions amidst masculine settings continually grounded her as empress. She was represented as a political symbol in her appearances on imperial tours and in the context of the military photograph on the deck of the Tenryū, yet she maintained her motherly and nurturing role in other instances. As a figure whose femininity was essential to the success of her image, she could not take on overtly masculine roles, yet the circumstances of the regency necessitated her moving beyond the confines of the type of traditional feminine imperial duties that were established in the late nineteenth century. Concurrently, her image was used to promote a new type of women's role, and one which also redefined gendered expectations, that of the military mother.

The Military Mother: Maternity as Imperial Virtue

While many of the *Fujin gahō* photographs represented Teimei as a feminine celebrity empress, visiting exhibitions and Red Cross meetings, or taking garden strolls, occasionally her role as an exemplar of the *ryōsai kenbo* ideology (the "good wife, wise mother," further examined in Chapter Five) turned to more political concerns, as with the Tenryū photograph. Within the pages of *Fujin gahō* Empress Teimei also took on the nuanced role of a "military mother," appearing with young cadets in a military context with subtle differences from the images seen in the newspapers. In the 1910s and 20s it was common for royals to visit troops during World War I, or to support nursing efforts, as with Queen Alexandra's Royal Army Nursing Corps, of which the Queen was president during her reign.[48] One such example of this appeared in the publication on July 1, 1923 (Figure 3.5). As part of a two-page,

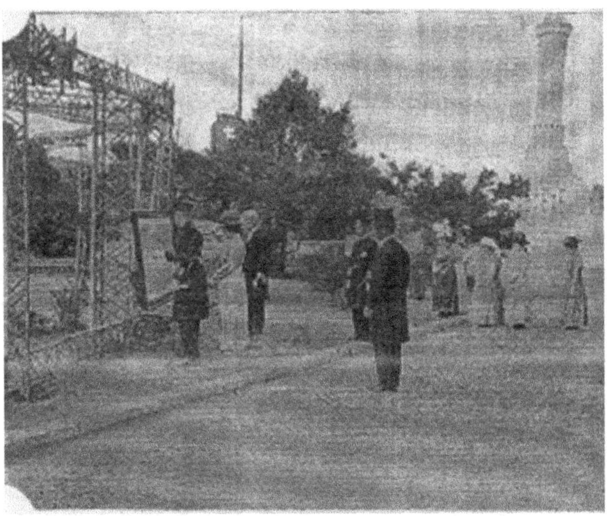

FIGURE 3.5 *Kōgō heika gyōkei* (Attendances of Her Royal Highness the Empress), *Fujin gahō*, July 1, 1923, page 8

three-photograph layout titled *Kōgō heika gyōkei* (Attendances of Her Royal Highness the Empress), Empress Teimei appears with four male officials and four ladies-in-waiting at the Naval Institute at Tsukiji. In the image she is looking at a large framed picture, unseen to the viewer of the photograph.

The naval training facility was part of a well-known officers training program popular with educated cadets.[49] Depicted in Meiji-era woodblock prints as well as early twentieth-century photograph postcards, the Naval Institute was familiar to the Japanese public of the time.[50] This image depicts the sovereign in her capacity as a ruler and as she related to the military, but with a soft power element that goes beyond proxy politics. As these images of her as interacting with the naval forces on what may be read as a political level were rare, that they were widely published in the early 1920s helps deepen our understanding of Teimei as an imperial proxy. Teimei's interactions with the military went further than those of her predecessor. While Empress Shōken was envisioned as a caretaker, images of Shōken and the military were limited to field hospitals. In contrast, Teimei was involved in training and more active military maneuvers. The military-oriented photographs also suggest the complexity and flexibility of imperial gender roles in the Taishō period. Here, as with the Tenryū photograph, we see an empress who is involved with state affairs, yet who in other photographs, and with her progressive fashions, maintains an element of feminine style and comportment.

Additionally, this photograph shows Teimei at an educational training facility, thus tempering her involvement with the military by affiliating her with the feminine, motherly concern over education. This was a particularly poignant detail when considering that the photograph was published in the context of a women's magazine, a venue in which exhibiting the *ryōsai kenbo* value of women's support for their military-involved sons was of critical importance. Furthermore, while the Naval Institute was decidedly a masculine military institution, placing Empress Teimei at a location associated with young cadets and their instructors, rather than established active military men, softens her involvement in hard military affairs, as do the other two images appearing on the two-page spread: that of her at a Red Cross meeting and that of a crowd of Red Cross volunteer women awaiting her arrival. Owing to the complex nature of women's status in Taishō Japan, Teimei's maternal image was more nuanced than that of her successor or her predecessor.

In the months and years following the Russo-Japanese War (1904–5) and World War I, the role of women within Japanese society was reevaluated out of necessity. In the instance of the post-Russo-Japanese War, the position of war widows and their children in the social order required an assessment of the purely domestic position of women under the previous *ryōsai kenbo* ideology, leading to discussions of wage-based employment for women outside of the home and vocational courses for girls, among other issues.[51] Women who had no skills beyond those of a housewife had no means to support themselves or their orphaned children if their husbands died while in military service. In the first decade of the twentieth century, stories of war widows and orphans with no long-term financial support led to public anxieties over a purely domestic model of femininity. In the context of World War I, officials held greater concern for strategic military issues. Specifically, there was a worry that

> a purely domestic role for women would impede future military success. With the defense of the nation and empire at stake, even conservatives who were loath to endorse a public role for women had to grapple with the relationship between women's work and their social participation and national progress.[52]

This apprehension over the expanding empire led to the promotion of what I term the "military mother," a role within the *ryōsai kenbo* framework which Empress Teimei exemplified in the pages of *Fujin gahō*.

During the course of these early twentieth century conflicts, the metropole was unscathed by direct military battles, and as a result, the inclusion of women in the expanding Japanese Empire did not go as far in changing gender roles as the same conflict (WWI) did in Europe, where mass casualties led to reconsiderations of women's positions in the private and public spheres.[53] Women's roles in Japan did, however, change, and Empress Teimei's image was part of that shift. In the context of women's magazines such as *Fujin gahō* Teimei's image was used to involve women in the training of their sons as imperial soldiers. The support of women was crucial to maintaining a conscripted military; as mothers they needed to encourage their sons to respond to calls for patriotic duty, and as wives they needed to maintain the home front without protesting their husbands being sent into battle. Enacting the role of military mother allowed women to maintain their feminine roles within the home and provided an active outlet for patriotic activity without conceding too much social influence and clout. Government officials also fretted about the involvement of women in the rice riots of the late 1910s and over backlash against unpopular military campaigns in the early 1920s. By the mid-Taishō period it was understood that women, as wives and mothers as well as citizens, needed to be included in the greater national project of imperial expansion in order to achieve the aims of the government.[54] Imperial images were one means of promoting these values.

In the May, 1922 edition of *Fujin gahō* Teimei was represented in a two-page, four-photograph spread. Three of the images are shrine visits from her tour of Western Japan; she is shown exiting the Daizufu Shrine in Fukuoka and inspecting a tree planted there by the Crown Prince. Known as the resting place of Sugawara no Michizane (845–903), regarded as the *kami* of learning (Tenjin), and therefore associated with education, the combination of a familial link and the conventional feminine concern of education made Daizufu a logical stop for the empress. In the two photographs the empress is viewed at a distance, her fashionable white dress providing contrast with both her surroundings and the black clothing of her attendants and her large hat drawing the eye to her. A third photograph shows her visit to Kashii-gu, a Fukuoka shrine with close ties to the imperial family. Kashii-gu is dedicated to Emperor Chūai and Empress Jingū, mythical rulers of the second and third century, and houses a tree reportedly planted by Jingū. The fourth photograph shows Teimei as she visited naval cadets at the Etajima Naval Academy on March 24, 1922. Located near Hiroshima, Etajima is known for the red brick architecture of its primary building, designed by an English architect in 1893, and in the photograph the main facade frames Teimei as she proceeds through the Academy grounds with four men accompanying her in a line. In the Etajima photograph she wears black, and the focal point of the photograph is the building itself, the white pillars mirroring the rhythm of the figures as they proceed through the school yard. These four photographs, as placed in a single layout, inform the viewer of orthodox ideas of women's propriety—Teimei views her son's work and worships her ancestors but is also involved with a modern military institution.

A similar image of Empress Teimei is seen in the *Fujin gahō* photograph series captioned, *Kōgōheika shikangakkō e gyōkei* (Her Majesty the Empress Visiting the Military Academy, Figure 3.6). Dating from July 1, 1922, in these images Empress

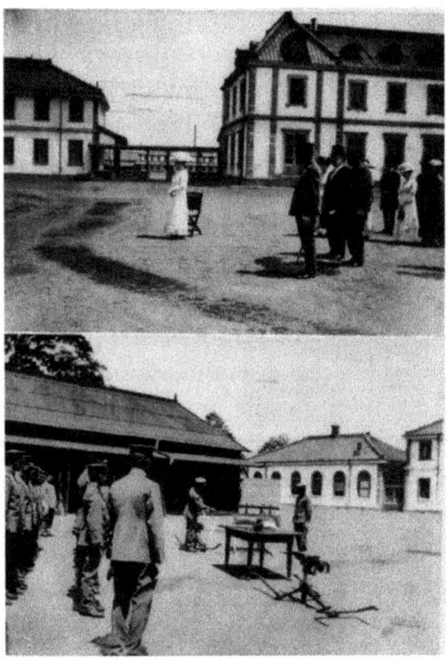

FIGURE 3.6 *Kōgōheika shikangakkō e gyōkei* (Her Majesty the Empress Visiting the Military Academy) *Fujin gahō*, July 1, 1922, page 10

Teimei is shown standing in front of a folding chair in the midst of a dirt yard, stately European-style buildings in the background, and a small crowd of officials gathered at the right. The photograph in which Teimei appears fills the top half of the page, with a separate photograph of military cadets observing tactical lessons comprising the bottom half of the page. The lower image depicts the scene which Empress Teimei was gazing upon; the buildings in the background of the two images show a continuation of architectural features, and in the layout the figures in each photograph turn to face each other, thus providing visual cues for the viewer to understand the unbroken nature of the scene. Among the military cadets pictured is Prince Chichibu, Empress Teimei's second son, as viewers are informed by the caption at the right of the page. The Military Academy students stand in straight, tight formation while they observe two superiors instructing them with mounted weaponry and other tactical paraphernalia.

Two points about this image reinforce the message of the Naval Academy photograph and are worthy of note here: that Teimei as an empress was associated with military training activities and that she is pictured as a mother. First, that a Japanese empress was associated with the military was unusual. Empress Shōken appeared in paintings and prints as she visited military hospitals but was never depicted as directly communicating with military leaders or soldiers, as her husband was present and able to do so. The context of Empress Teimei's appearance on the ship Tenryū as published in the *Asahi shinbun,* was connected to a larger government interest in popularizing an unpopular military campaign and to Teimei's role as an imperial proxy, but in the military images published in *Fujin gahō*, there is a subtext of military mother at work which differentiates these photographs from those marketed to the larger *Asahi* audience.

Throughout the course of the Taishō period, and in investigating the body of images of Empress Teimei which were distributed prior to 1926, there is an absence of photographic evidence of the imperial household as a domestic, familial unit. Pictures of the imperial family envisioned in the context of a family tree or in lithographs as a nuclear family were popular in the years just after 1900, but photographs of the monarchs in a state of domesticity were not available to the public until the Shōwa period.[55] This notable absence of imagery depicting Empress Teimei as a mother to her own four sons is particularly significant in light of Teimei's status as the first empress to birth the successive emperor in the modern period. Additionally, as issues of imperial primogeniture were, and are, a recurring issue with the modern Japanese monarchy, that Teimei biologically mothered four healthy boys is of relevance to her biography and her high status in the twentieth-century imperial lineage.

Despite these key historical facts, Teimei is rarely seen as a maternal figure to her own children. As shown in Chapter 2, maternity is a central virtue and role for empresses and queens; globally it is very common to see the family unit represented together in the past and today. Empress Shōken was frequently represented in the same space as her adopted son, images of her maternity were a means of cementing her imperial role, and Empress Kōjun was frequently photographed with a baby in her arms in the first decades of her husband's reign. Yet, for both Shōken and Kōjun, their roles as progenitor of the lineage were not always fixed; Shōken did not have biological children, and Kōjun did not give birth to a male heir until 1933, almost ten years after her marriage and seven years after ascending the throne. Teimei's maternity, however, was on sound footing, for she bore a male heir just one year after her marriage and eleven years prior to becoming empress. For Teimei, the Military Academy photographs of her observing the military training of her second son are an exception to her generally un-imaged maternity. In the photograph, Teimei and Prince Chichibu, who was the second-in-line to the Japanese throne, are seen together, and the Empress performs the role of *ryōsai kenbo*, astutely observing her son and acting as a military mother but with a few key points which remind the viewer of her exalted status.

In the photographs, her familial connection to Prince Chichibu is not immediately apparent; in fact, it is difficult to discern which of the young cadets the young monarch is. Furthermore, her isolated position as an overseer of the training process is visually similar to other images, such as her appearances before the Red Cross, where she views a crowd or group from a distant space. From analyzing this photograph, we see a monarch who is involved with the lives of her children but in an indirect, distant fashion. Indeed, rather than being envisioned as a nurturing birth mother to Crown Prince Chichibu, Teimei is constructed as a removed maternal presence; she watches over her son with interest but also pays attention to the other cadets. The mother-son relationship is not singled out, but Teimei is rather pictured as a guiding figure for all of the military youths. She is not, as her successor Empress Kōjun would later be, depicted with a baby carriage or in physical contact with her offspring, nor is she engaged with her son on a personal level. In fact, if the caption did not inform the viewer that she was observing her child, the image could be easily read as a ruler observing the general activity of her subjects.

The *ryōsai kenbo* that Teimei exemplifies here is one which was produced for the upper classes to emulate, but which provided universal lessons. The institutions which Teimei visited were not for the enlisted men of the lower classes or rural areas but for officers-in-training, young men who mostly came from well-off, urban family backgrounds, yet Teimei was promoting the *ryōsai kenbo* core values of education and military readiness in these photographs, concepts which could be implemented in differing ways at many levels of society. By promoting Empress Teimei as a military mother, common women would possibly have had an easier time accepting the conscription of their sons into the military. In showing the imperial family as making the same sacrifices for the national good as was being asked of the citizenry, Teimei was modeling *ryōsai kenbo* and the role of the military mother for her subjects by promoting lofty imperial goals of military participation and national service through motherhood.

The vision of Teimei as *ryōsai kenbo* in the late 1910s and early 1920s was less about a conventionally feminine, caring maternal model and more about the conflation of the nuclear and imperial family. By exemplifying the distant motherly figure who willingly sacrifices her sons for the greater national cause, Teimei models a new Taishō gender politics, that of strong women in the public sphere who maintain their femininity while serving the nation with their domestic skills. Teimei's representation in photographs published in women's magazines showed a savvy, independent, and cosmopolitan empress and one who was also involved with issues of concern to Taishō women, such as household economy and national service. This military mother role was not to last, however, as the calamity of the 1923 earthquake altered the course of imperial responsibilities.

Transitions to a New Era: Distant Charity and Imperial Piousness

In the years after the 1923 Great Kantō Earthquake, Empress Teimei's role as an exemplar of Taishō *ryōsai kenbo* values shifted to reflect the importance of feminine care-giving in the post-earthquake weeks. Media coverage of the earthquake was strictly state censored, and in the months after the disaster, a moralizing impulse arose across Japanese society. The Ministry of Education published a series for use in the national school curriculum titled *Shinsai ni kansuru kyōiku shiryō* (Education Materials Related to the Earthquake), which emphasized loyalty to the emperor, sacrifice, and bravery as critical social values.[56] Teimei's appearances as a devoted public servant were crucial in promoting these morals, particularly in the context of women's magazines. Her appearances with survivors, however, are photographed as philanthropic visits of distant encouragement rather than the staged hands-on labor that often accompanies such visits today, be they by Japanese, British, or other monarchs visiting disaster sites. This conservative turn was reflected in many of the photographs of Empress Teimei which appeared in the final years of the Taishō period, particularly as published in *Fujin gahō*.

In the three years after the earthquake and prior to the start of the Shōwa period, the use of Empress Teimei's image in the press decreased, as that of the next generation of royals grew. Much of the imperial family press coverage in early 1924 addressed the wedding of Crown Prince Hirohito (Shōwa) and Crown Princess Nagako (Kōjun), which took place on January 26, 1924, in a ceremony that was delayed due to the 1923 calamity. On December 6, 1925, the young couple bore their first of seven children, Princess Shigeko. Thus, the crown prince and princess dominated news of the imperial family until the passing of Emperor Taishō on December 25, 1926.

In these waning years of Taishō reign, Empress Teimei's image grew to be conservative in nature; she was imaged as frequenting religious institutions and praying for the health of her husband or in photographs that worked to transition the monarchy to the crown prince and princess. In the years after the earthquake, Teimei's image never returned to the active imperial proxy of the early regency period. The crown princess, on the other hand, together with other women of the nobility, transitioned to a visual monarchy that was more approachable and modern than their predecessors and which competed with the contemporary, stylish feel of the front matter of *Fujin gahō*. It was around the start of the Shōwa era that the magazine's front matter photography took an increasingly modern turn and simultaneously began to read like society pages featuring increasing coverage of garden parties and engagements and fewer reprinted formal portraits. The combination of the return to convention in Teimei's image and the concurrent move for Kōjun's image to appear soft, feminine, and approachable presented an overall turn to tradition in the late 1920s, representing the final stages of significant imperial coverage in *Fujin gahō*.

Late in the Taishō period, a full-page single image of Empress Teimei at Daitokuji appeared on page six of the February 1, 1925, edition of *Fujin gahō*. In this image Empress Teimei is smiling and appears engaged in conversation with a gentleman who is turned away from the camera, while a monk leads the empress and two accompanying men through the forested grounds of the temple. The large trees in the background and the low horizon ground the photograph and emphasize the natural beauty of the temple site. These visual elements also serve to express how expansive the grounds of the temple are and, combined with the monk's traditional clothing, place the empress' Kansai visit in history and tradition. In the photographs of her visit to the ancient capital region Empress Teimei maintained her confident demeanor but turned away from events where she intermingled with military officials or acted as an imperial proxy.

In the context of photographs published in *Fujin gahō*, Teimei visited predominantly religious institutions in these final Taishō years, praying and emphasizing traditional Japanese religious practices, showing the common queenly virtue of piousness that links Teimei to woman royals through time and space. This return to conservative *ryōsai kenbo* values was indicative of the cultural climate in the mid-1920s. In the latter half of 1920s Taiwan and Korea were already annexed as colonies (in 1895 and 1911, respectively), and in 1924 the United States banned Japanese immigration, adding insult to what Japan viewed as poor outcomes of the Treaty of Versailles in 1919.[57] Furthermore, the Japanese economy in the 1920s was in a period of deflation, which generally leads to political conservativism.[58] Each of these events, combined with many others, pushed Japan further down the road to imperialism and led to a dismantling of the open, liberal mores of the late 1910s and early 1920s. In the context of photographs published in women's magazines, this conservative turn in imagery reflects political changes which occurred between the early 1920s and the early 1930s.

The photographs from *Fujin gahō* as published in the final years of Taishō and first years of early Shōwa show the transition of the monarchy not just to the successive period but to a new mediascape, wherein the moving image would play a significant role. The images also show a conservative turn in gender politics, imaging women in supportive roles and as the keepers of tradition. Empress Teimei grew to act as a more conventional empress in the final days of Taishō, appearing as a carrier of tradition and working to ease the transition to her son's rule. In the Shōwa period Teimei faded to the background of imperial imagery, making infrequent public appearances throughout her reign as empress dowager, while Kōjun's image came to the fore as a soft, feminine empress, eventually turning to a motherly figure.

This chapter investigated the proxy politics of Empress Teimei as an alternate imperial symbol by examining the ways in which photographic representations of the empresses in the mass media responded to current events in Japan in the first three decades of the twentieth century. The duality of the imperial body formed the philosophical and theoretical milieu in which Teimei's image as an alternative imperial symbol was produced, and her image was at times that of a military mother, a national mother, and a wife. In many ways the empresses mirrored the broader trends for women to play increasingly important roles outside the home, yet these roles, as seen in the pages of *Fujin gahō,* were always kept within the confines of appropriate feminine comportment. Women's roles may have been expanding, but they continued to be kept in check. Investigating contradictory concerns over women's roles in society and the home as well as reactions to events such as military expansion, shows the nuances of early twentieth century gender politics as seen in the images of the empress.

Thus, while Taishō's concealed image had precedent in history, and was justified by imperial rescripts and ties to religious beliefs, it was Teimei's appearance and image that was truly something new. While female rulers appeared sporadically throughout Japanese history, and Empress Shōken had a public role in the Meiji period, Teimei's strong and independent visual presence was markedly different than that of her predecessor. Her appearance acted as a surrogate for her husband in his absence, something that can be attributed to not just ideas of the dualistic imperial body but also to her personal character and the changing cultural norms regarding women and appropriate feminine behaviors. Changes in the way women were perceived and modifications in accepted modes of femininity were inevitable in light of the woman problem. Yet these adjustments were never drastic and generally maintained an element of political conservatism. In images where Teimei is involved with her son's military training we see her strong, feminine aura as part of the complex phenomenon of imperial gender representation in the 1920s, but in the early years of the magazine and again in the early Shōwa years, the empresses projected a more conventionally feminine role, which both impacted and reflected social concerns over women's positions in the home. In experimenting with how the various new roles for women could fit Japanese society and what types of roles were appropriate for women to play, the concept of serving the nation was never distant, for either the average woman or for the empress.

Although the axis of imperial power remained in the hands of the male members of the imperial household, this chapter traced a change in Teimei's image, one with possible implications for the future lineage of the imperial household. As debates swirl around the succession of the Chrysanthemum Throne in the twenty-first century, Teimei stands historically as an example of a strong female imperial presence in an age of regency, one in which she pushed the acceptable limits for what was appropriate and acceptable for an empress, and one where she reflected the changing culture that surrounded her and her family.

Notes

1 1905 marks the start of *Fujin gahō*'s publication and 1928 the coronation of Hirohito. In the early 1930s the practice of showing royals at the start of *Fujin gahō* ceased, and the practice of showing the imperial family in film reels started in the mid-1920s, thus changing their visual representation and reception.
2 Amy Bliss Marshall, *Magazines and the Making of Mass Culture in Japan* (Toronto: University of Toronto Press, 2019), 6–10; Marilyn Ivy, *Discourses of the Vanishing: Modernity, Phantasm, Japan* (Chicago: University of Chicago Press, 1995), 195.
3 Yamada Shunji, *Taishū shinbun ga tsukuru Meiji no "Nihon"* (Tokyo: Nihon Hōsō Shuppan Kyōkai, 2002); Richard H. Mitchell, *Censorship in Imperial Japan* (Princeton: Princeton University Press, 1983), 40–52.
4 Mitchell, *Censorship in Imperial Japan*, 43.
5 After the High Treason Incident of 1910–11, an incident where twelve people were hanged for a failed plot to assassinate the emperor, public debate and critique of the emperor system completely cooled. Mitchell, *Censorship in Imperial Japan*, 143, 145–146.
6 The construction of gender roles in the imperial family from Meiji through Shōwa is discussed by Kawamura Kunimitsu, who focuses on the imperial family's relationship with and impact on the public vis-à-vis mass media representations. See: Kawamura Kunimitsu, "Tennōke no konin to shussan," in *Ō o meguru shisen*, ed. Yoshihiko Amino, vol. 10 of *Tennō to ōken o kangaeru* (Tokyo: Iwanami shoten, 2002), 161–182.
7 Ben-Ami Shillony, *The Emperors of Japan* (Leiden: Brill, 2008), 317.
8 Keene, *Emperor of Japan*, 251. The footnote cites a recounting of the birth by an attendant, who stated that Yanagihara was so distressed that the women of the court and the nurses ran from her bedside, unsure of what to do.

9 See Julia Meech-Pekarik, *The World of the Meiji Print: Impressions of a New Civilization* (New York: Weatherhill, 1986), 126–127 for a full description of the Crown Prince's official reception.
10 As cited in Leonard Mosley, *Hirohito: Emperor of Japan* (London: Weidenfeld and Nicolson, 1966), 1–2.
11 Walter Edwards, *Modern Japan Through Its Weddings: Gender, Person, and Society in Ritual Portrayal* (Stanford: Stanford University Press, 1989), 36–41.
12 Edwards, *Modern Japan Through Its Weddings*, 41.
13 Katano Masako, *Kōgō no kindai* (Tokyo: Kodansha, 2003), 83–84.
14 David Hogge, "Alice in Asia: The 1905 Taft Mission to Asia," *Freer Sackler Galleries, Smithsonian Institution*, www.asia.si.edu/research/archives/alice/.
15 The last emperor to have a child with the empress was Go-Momozono (r. 1770–1779). Peter Martin, *The Chrysanthemum Throne: A History of the Emperors of Japan* (Honolulu: University of Hawai'i Press, 1997), 133.
16 Kawahara Toshiaki, *Higeki no kōjo: Mikasanomiya futagosetsu no shinsō* (Tokyo: Dainamiku-sarazu, 1984), 1–4.
17 Toku Baelz, ed., *Awakening Japan: The Diary of a German Doctor* (Bloomington: Indiana University Press, 1974), 329.
18 Sterling Seagrave and Peggy Seagrave, *The Yamato Dynasty: The Secret History of Japan's Imperial Family* (New York: Broadway Books, 1999), 77.
19 Ichiro Kikuchi, "Hansen's Disease in Japan: A Brief History," *International Journal of Dermatology* 36 (1997): 629–633, 630, and Toyoda Maho, "State, Sterilization, and Reproductive Rights: Japan as Occupier and Occupied," in *Japan as the Occupier and Occupied*, ed. Christine de Matos and Mark E. Caprio (New York: Palgrave MacMillan, 2015), 48.
20 Kudō Miyoko, *Hahamiya Teimei kōgō to sono jidai: Mikasa nomiya ryōdenka ga kataru omoide* (Tokyo: Chuokoron shinsha, 2010), 114–122.
21 Sannomaru Shōzōkan, *Kōgō heika no goyōsan to Shōsōin-gire no fukugen: Kōgō heika koki kinen tokubetsuten* (Tokyo: Kunaichō, 2005).
22 Seagrave and Seagrave, *The Yamato Dynasty*, 12, 83.
23 Seagrave and Seagrave, *The Yamato Dynasty*, 82–83.
24 Kunaichō, "Emperor Shōwa and Empress Kōjun," www.kunaicho.go.jp/e-about/history/history11.html. The ceremony takes place at age eighteen.

25 Gilday, "Bodies of Evidence," n. 29, 293. See also: Robert J. Smith, "Wedding and Funeral Ritual: Analyzing a Moving Target," in *Ceremony and Ritual in Japan: Religious Practices in an Industrialized Society*, ed. Jan van Bremen and D.P Martinez (New York: Routledge, 2005).
26 Kunaichō, "Imperial Funerals, Accession to the Throne, Weddings, and other Events," www.kunaicho.go.jp/e-about/seido/seido10.html.
27 *The Asahi Shinbun*, "Mausoleum, Cremation Plans Revealed for Emperor, Empress," November 15, 2013, http://ajw.asahi.com/article/behind_news/social_affairs/AJ201311150060.
28 David Ansun Titus, *Palace and Politics in Prewar Japan* (New York: Columbia University Press, 1974), 111–129.
29 Puyi's case is particularly interesting, as he ruled from 1908 to 1912, was restored as a figurehead by a warlord briefly in 1917, and was placed back on the throne by the Japanese as the Emperor of Manchuria during the 1930s and 1940s.
30 Titus details the imperial excursions from 1868 to 1910, both within and outside of Tokyo, dividing them by purpose. The height of imperial excursions was in 1880, with 163, most of which were in Tokyo. After 1890, which saw 47 excursions, Emperor Meiji averaged 16 excursions per year from 1891–1910, with as few as 4 tours in the year 1897. Titus, *Palace and Politics in Prewar Japan*, 48.
31 See Titus, *Palace and Politics*, 48–49 for a more detailed list of the purposes of imperial excursions.
32 Hirohito's 1921 trip to Europe was documented in film reels that were widely distributed and viewed in both the metropole and the colonies. Recent scholarship tells us that the 1921 films were based on 1905 film of Prince Arisugawa's European travels. Kamiya Makiko, "Saishoki no 'Kōshitsu eiga' ni kansuru kōsatsu: Kakusareru/sarasareru 'karada'," *Eizōgaku* 100 (2018).
33 Frédérique Lachaud and Michael Penman, *Absentee Authority across Medieval Europe* (Rochester, NY: Boydell & Brewer, 2017).
34 Alice Y. Tseng, "Imperial Portraiture and Popular Print Media in Early Twentieth-Century Japan," *Journal of Japanese Studies* 46, no. 2 (2020).
35 In 1888, Teimei's predecessor Empress Shōken appeared at the ceremonial launching of an imperial ship in Yokosuka when Emperor Meiji fell unexpectedly and suddenly ill. This incident, however, was not visually reproduced in the media and did not coincide with military controversy. The visit is mentioned in: Julia Meech-Pekarik, *The World of the Meiji*

Print: Impressions of a New Civilization (New York: Weatherhill, 1986), 129.

36 Paul E. Dunscomb, *Japan's Siberian Intervention, 1918–1922* (Lanham, MD: Rowman & Littlefield, 2011), 181. Dunscomb provides a highly detailed study of the Intervention, the policies that led to the historical moment of the Intervention, and the aftermath of the conflict.

37 Dunscomb, *Japan's Siberian Intervention*, 181.

38 J. Charles Schencking, *Making Waves: Politics, Propaganda, and the Emergence of the Imperial Japanese Navy, 1868–1912* (Stanford: Stanford University Press, 2005), 217–221.

39 Showing this widespread interest in the conflict, Izao Tomio analyzed newspaper articles about the Siberian Intervention in Yamaguchi Prefecture, many of which honored the war dead and included anti-Russian bias. Izao Tomio, "Shinbun no naka no Shiberia shuppei," *Yamaguchi kenritsu daigaku kokusai bunka gakubu kiyō* 12 (2006): 1–12.

40 "Gunjijyō yori mita fusen," *Asahi shinbun*, March 29, 1922, 3, Tokyo morning edition. Japanese men over the age of 25 were afforded universal suffrage in 1925.

41 Women were not afforded suffrage in Japan until 1945. For a more in-depth discussion of the debates surrounding Article Five in the late teens and early twenties, as well as a description of the original Article from 1900. Sheldon Garon, *Molding Japanese Minds: The State in Everyday Life* (Princeton: Princeton University Press, 1997), 123–126. For data showing the increase in Teimei's image at this time see: Alison J. Miller, "Imperial Images: The Japanese Empress Teimei in Early Twentieth-Century Newspaper Photography," *Trans Asia Photography* 7, no. 1 (October 1, 2016), n/p.

42 It is of interest to note that Empress Teimei later spoke out against Japan's role in the Pacific War. In her position as the Empress Dowager, she controversially expressed her distaste for military activities in the 1930s and 1940s.

43 As Hara approaches the Imperial Family from the perspective of a historian, he uses the term image (像, *zō*) in the broad sense, encompassing the entirety of the impression conveyed to the public, not just the visual vestige. Hara Takeshi, "'Kokutai' no shikakuka—Taishō • Shōwa shoki ni okeru tennōsei no saihen," in *Ō o meguru shisen*, ed. Yoshihiko Amino, vol. 10 of *Tennō to ōken o kangaeru* (Tokyo: Iwanami shoten, 2002).

44 Hara argues that the theory of constitutional authority, or one ruler with no discrimination or distinction amongst social

classes, led to the generation of the theory of universal suffrage and that the expanded and newly visible roles of the imperial family led to the strength of suffrage movements in popular society. Hara, "'Kokutai' no shikakuka," 147.

45 Ying-chen Peng, *Artful Subversion: Empress Dowager Cixi's Image Making* (New Haven: Yale University Press, 2023).

46 Frank Jacob, "Queen Min, Foreign Policy and the Role of Female Leadership in Late Nineteenth-Century Korea," in *The Routledge History of Monarchy*, ed. Elena Woodacre, Lucinda H.S. Dean, et al. (London: Routledge, 2019); Danny Orbach, *Curse on This Country: The Rebellious Army of Imperial Japan* (Cornell: Cornell University Press, 2017).

47 The regency of George III of England similarly took place amidst turmoil, and he was likewise of ill health, though his son George, Prince of Wales, was able to publicly act as leader. M. da Mota Gomes, Lucio Lage Goncalves, et al. "King George III of England and Queen Maria I of Portugal: Bipolar Disorder and Prince Regents as Common Features of Their Reigns," *Trends in Psychiatry and Psychotherapy*, March 19, 2023. https://doi.org/10.47626/2237-6089-2021-0315.

48 Juliet Piggott, *Queen Alexandra's Royal Army Nursing Corps* (London: Leo Cooper Ltd., 1975).

49 Schencking, *Making Waves*, 23.

50 For an example of these images, see: *The Naval Institute at Tsukiji* (Tsukiji kaigunshō), from the series "Famous Places in Tokyo" (Tōkyō meisho zue), Utagawa Hiroshige III, published by Maruya Tetsujirō, February 1873, collection of the Museum of Fine Arts Boston, 2000.272.

51 Kathleen Uno, "Womanhood, War, and Empire: Transmutations of 'Good Wife, Wise Mother' before 1931," in *Gendering Modern Japanese History*, ed. Barbara Molony and Kathleen Uno (Cambridge: Harvard University Asia Center, 2005), 492–519, 504.

52 Uno, "Womanhood, War, and Empire," 506.

53 Christa Hämmerle, Oswald Überegger and Birgitta Bader Zaar, *Gender and the First World War* (Basingstoke, Hampshire: Palgrave Macmillan, 2014).

54 During the First Sino-Japanese War (1894–1895), Japanese leaders grew to understand that women needed to be mobilized for success in modern warfare. See Uno, "Womanhood, War, and Empire," 500–501.

55 A few photographs of Emperor Taishō together with his sons were published in the media, and photographs of the Shōwa

monarchy as a family unit were widespread in popular media sources, starting with the Shōwa Emperor and Empress as Crown Prince and Princess in the late Taishō period. The lithographs of the Imperial Family from the time around the 1900 wedding of Taishō and Teimei were fictional. The previous statement, that domestic photographs were not widely available until the Shōwa period, is true across publication types.

56 Sharon H. Nolte and Sally Ann Hastings, "The Meiji State's Policy Toward Women, 1890–1910," in *Recreating Japanese Women, 1600–1945*, ed. Gail Lee Bernstein (Berkeley: University of California Press, 1991), 187.

57 Japan did not receive territory at Versailles, as was expected, and there was no clause on racial equality at the League of Nations, also an insult to Japan.

58 For an analysis of the inter-war economy, see: Masato Shizume, "The Japanese Economy during the Interwar Period: Instability in the Financial System and the Impact of the World Depression," *Institute for Monetary and Economic Studies*, May 2009, www.boj.or.jp/en/research/wps_rev/rev_2009/data/rev09e02.pdf. The period under consideration here, the mid-1920s, was the start of a slide toward conservativism, which would reach full fruition in the 1930s and 40s. The poor economy would reach crisis points in 1927 and 1931, immediately before the invasion of Manchuria. This move from economic crisis to right-leaning politics is part of a larger modern, global pattern. Manuel Funke, Moritz Schularick and Christoph Trebesch, "Going to Extremes: Politics after Financial Crises, 1870–2014" (October 2015). CEPR Discussion Paper No. DP10884. CEPR Press, Paris and London. https://cepr.org/publications/dp10884.

PART II

4

TOWARD THE SACRED AND THE STANDARD

Formality, Lineage, and Decorum in the Modern Japanese Imperial Portrait

In the spring of 1900, at the time of their marriage, Crown Prince Yoshihito and Crown Princess Sadako, the future Emperor Taishō and Empress Teimei, posed for two commemorative photographic studio portraits. Dressed in layers of robes reminiscent of the fashions of the Heian period (794–1185), the imperial couple was represented in a way that imagined how their distant ancestors appeared. Crown Princess Sadako stands with her body enveloped in thick, dark-colored textiles, a small fan folded and held in her hand, disguised beneath the abundance of silk (Figure 4.1). Attached to her hair is the same style of crown that her predecessor, Empress Shōken, wore the first time she was photographed, a circular metal coronet with five adornments on the front and three metal plumes at the top. The Crown Princess gazes off into the distance, with her facial expression appearing neutral. The Crown Prince's companion portrait has a similar feeling, one of constructed timelessness and one in which the individual personalities of the monarchs recede to an eternal aura of the imperial lineage. The backgrounds of both photographs are minimally arranged—aside from the central figures, the viewer only sees a floral-patterned rug—and the sovereigns are shot at eye level.

Although lithograph reproductions and copies abound, the original images stand as rare photographic examples of Empress Teimei and Emperor Taishō in historically inspired clothing. As

DOI: 10.4324/9781003376101-7

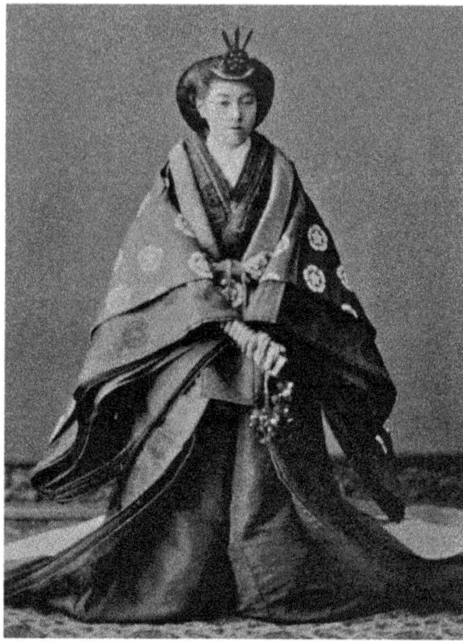

FIGURE 4.1 Crown Princess Sadako, 1900, photograph published in *The Sphere*, September 7, 1912, p. 213

with all imagery of the Japanese imperial family, studio portrait photography of the emperor and empress was, and remains to this day, highly controlled and staged. Studio portraits of the emperor and empress in both the Meiji and Taishō periods were few in number and were generally in European-style dress. Although photographs in traditional court costume were published in magazines and newspapers, and the sacred *goshinei* had significant visibility, the portraits which received the widest vernacular reproduction and distribution were of the monarchs in European-style dress.[1] Four of the five modern Japanese monarchical couples participated in the custom of taking wedding photographs in historically inspired robes, but these images are only occasionally seen—published upon the change of imperial era, the photographs subsequently faded to the background.[2] This ubiquitous use of contemporary European fashion harkens back to the concern from the late nineteenth century that the emperor in traditional Japanese costume would present a problematic, exotic impression to other nations; it was crucial for Japanese royalty to be presented as a modernized, cosmopolitan monarchy, not a relic of the past.

By the time Emperor Taishō and Empress Teimei came to the throne, the practices of production, distribution, and display of imperial portraits were well established and were codified in the Japanese legal code. This was not so for the earliest modern imperial portraits. When Emperor Meiji was first photographed in 1872, it was in an unsanctioned image captured by a foreigner.[3] When Japan opened their borders just over a decade earlier, they found a global culture of royal image circulation and quickly realized that a response was needed.[4] Yet the Japanese visual monarchy, while devised in a seemingly European way, was fashioned with distinct domestic meanings. By the early 1940s, photographic imperial portraits were developed in water which was purified by means of Shinto rites and drawn from a well which was adorned with *shimenawa* (しめ縄), ropes and papers which are usually seen at Shinto shrine altars.[5] This systemization of invented ritual occurred within a time span of less than seventy-five years, the majority of which transpired in the late Meiji to early Taishō periods.

This chapter examines modern Japanese imperial portraiture, demonstrating how the images evolved between the Meiji, Taishō, and early Shōwa eras. Simultaneously with the schematization of laws and norms surrounding the distribution and exhibition of imperial portraiture in the late nineteenth and early twentieth centuries, images of the empresses moved from auxiliary roles to central figures, as the women became gradually more visible and "modern." Concurrently, images of the emperor were progressively standardized and increasingly carried an augmented aura of sacredness. To analyze these changes, this chapter first interrogates the initial construct of the modern empress portrait in the Meiji period, turning to the fully articulated modern empress portrait in the Taishō period. In addition to investigating studio portraits and their reproductions, the chapter concludes with an examination of the *hōanden* and *hōankura*, small structures that housed the sacred *goshinei* in the early Shōwa period. Throughout each stage of modern Japanese history, imperial portraiture grew to be more regulated and regimented, with increasingly complex messages embedded in paintings, prints, and photographs. These portraits worked to legitimize the empress and emperor vis-à-vis European-style portraiture and the simultaneous visualization of their place as the rightful heirs of the sacred lineage of the Japanese imperial family. Modern imperial portraits became an unchanging visual standard against which casual images such as woodblock prints and mass media photographs operated. Between 1870 and 1930, imperial portraits took on meanings of performed monogamy, the normalization of the nuclear family, and the escalation of authority, yet their appearances remained stable. The empress' visible presence in portraiture as half of the imperial couple points to women's centrality in the legitimacy and lineage of the visual monarchy, core concepts that were promoted through these formal photographs.

The Initial Meiji Imperial Portrait Construct

The official reaction to the illicit 1872 image of Emperor Meiji (see Chapter 1) was swift and evolved quickly.[6] The response included the first official portrait photographs of the sovereign dressed in clothing that referenced historic Heian styles (*sokutai* 束帯 and *nōshi* 直衣) and followed soon thereafter with a photograph in European-style military garb. These three official studio photographs of the emperor, produced by artist Uchida Kūichi (内田九一, 1844–1875) in 1872 and 1873, were to form the basis for the public representation of Emperor Meiji for the remainder of his lifetime, with the 1873 military portrait receiving the most circulation (Figure 4.2).[7] The photograph shows that both the emperor and his handlers understood the power of the visual monarchy: his body position shows the details of his military uniform, which was the global standard clothing style for male royal portraits in the late nineteenth century, and his pose exudes a calm confidence. A seated, relaxed pose could indicate passivity or weakness, but the careful positioning of his left foot and conspicuous placement of his sword are evidence of the staging

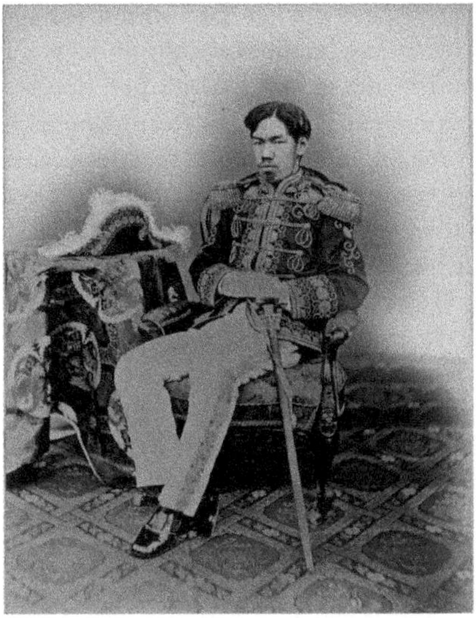

FIGURE 4.2 Emperor Meiji, October 8, 1873, Uchida Kūichi, albumen silver print from glass negative with applied color, Metropolitan Museum of Art

efforts; both of these elements are different than historic Japanese portraits where the feet, for example, are hardly visible. Meiji's bent right foot, though, which reads as weak in the context of European body language, demonstrates to viewers that the development of the visual monarchy as a hybrid of European royal signs and Japanese imperial symbols was still in its nascent stages. Although the earliest images of the emperor were not controlled, post-1875 photographs and subsequent images in lithograph, oil, and woodblock formats would receive the attention of censorship authorities. In 1874 Uchida Kūichi was denied access to the negatives of the imperial photographs he took, and the commercial sale of imperial photographs was banned from the start.[8] In addition to the carefully distributed image of the emperor, the empress also began to be envisioned in the pictorial realm, which denoted a revolutionary change in how both the imperial household and women generally were represented in public.

In the late 1870s, early images of Empress Shōken and Emperor Meiji with widespread public distribution were generally woodblock prints and did not feature realistic portraiture. Often, in early prints, symbols such as palanquins were a common aniconic representation of the imperial presence; therefore censorship of these images was not a priority for the government.[9] Formal censorship of the imperial image did not commence until 1875, with a move to standardize images in order to promote the emperor as a strong national icon.[10] Concurrently, in the 1870s, officials and bureaucrats were developing a visual strategy that envisioned Emperor Meiji as exhibiting the mature qualities of a world leader.[11] Tied up with this strategy were the first government-sanctioned photographs of the imperial family, which were partially based on the perceived need to emulate the visual characteristics of European leadership to gain global respect.

On the same occasion as Emperor Meiji's 1872 photographs in historic dress, Empress Shōken's portrait was captured by Uchida Kūichi (Figure 4.3). Like the emperor, the empress was depicted in Heian-style court clothing, but unlike her husband, the image of her in these costumes was not updated with a photograph in European-style costume the following year. In fact, it was not until 1889 that Shōken was photographed in European dress. While the political circumstances of the 1870s led to the reimaging of Emperor Meiji in the masculine ideal of European monarchs, the empress, as the preeminent woman of the realm, was to act as an exemplar of femininity, and in this instance, part of the ideal of femininity was to be the keeper of tradition. While the new modern men were active in industry, politics, and military concerns, women acted as the *ryōsai kenbo*, or "good wife, wise mother," an ideal of domesticity that I will return to in Chapter 5.[12] In the immediate instance of the 1872 photograph, Empress Shōken was exemplifying the highest standards for women's appearance in the aftermath of the ban on short hair for women which was instituted in the same year: her hair was long, her eyebrows natural, and her teeth white, exemplifying new beauty standards that contrasted with historic Japanese ideals.[13] Thus, while she remains in historically inspired costume, her physical characteristics, the medium of photography, and the revolutionary act of her public portrayal, were nods to modernity.

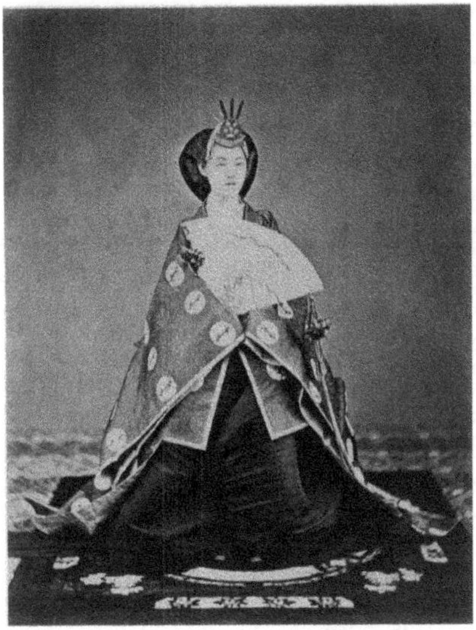

FIGURE 4.3 Empress Shōken, 1872, Uchida Kūichi, photographic print, National Museum of Asian Art Archives, Smithsonian Institution, The Henry and Nancy Rosin Collection of Early Photography of Japan, FSA_A1999.35_032

The 1872 Uchida Kūichi photograph portrait of Empress Shōken is similar to the accompanying photographs of her husband in that it is an image of the monarch in traditional, Heian-style clothing, *kōchiki* (小袿) in this instance. Like with Emperor Meiji, she stands upon a decorative carpet in an otherwise unidentifiable studio space. The empress, however, stands upon an additional rug, one which is square in shape with a circular pattern at the center. She stands on this circle, her body enveloped in many layers of robes and holding an open fan which is tucked among the strata of dress, her hands unseen. One small sprig of flowers is also placed in the folds of the fabric, and another posy is attached to the fan at her proper left, cascading down the outer layer of cloth with a collection of ribbons. Neither bouquet is easily identifiable. Her hair is gathered at her neck, highly styled, and she has a small crown atop her forehead.

In a similar style to the emperor's *nōshi* photograph, her physical form is completely hidden beneath the large conical shape of her luxurious outfit. Her facial expression is blank; she gazes off to the side of the camera. She appears confident in her position, and her expression does not expose any discomfort or uncertainty that she may have had in being photographed. This level of ease with the camera and Uchida Kuichi's skillful use of light, positioning, and composition make Shōken's 1872 photograph a match for Meiji's of the next year. This pair of images—representing the imperial couple as Japan's global leaders for their day and balancing masculine modernity and feminine tradition—contrasts with the two 1872 photographs of Emperor Meiji in *nōshi* and *sokutai* dress. In the earlier photographs Meiji is cramped in the frame of the image, hunched in posture, and dwarfed by his clothing, appearing solo as the single sovereign. By 1873, the emperor was linked with the empress, and the set of images presents a regal pair for the world stage.

Based upon this photograph, Italian artist Giuseppe Ugolini (1826–1897) completed an oil painting of Empress Shōken in 1875, commissioned by the Japanese authorities and undertaken in Milan.[14] This portrait was again copied by Goseda Yoshimatsu (五姓田義松, 1855–1915) in 1879 on a commission from the *genrō* (元老, imperial advisers) to create three portraits for the legislative building depicting Emperor Meiji, Empress Shōken, and Empress Dowager Eishō.[15] While the empress' pose and costume are ostensibly the same in the photograph and the painting, the painting provides the viewer with a closer-cropped image, the luxury of color, and added representations of texture. The changes are small: Shōken's crown is in the shape of a phoenix rather than an abstract design, her fan shows the details of a plum blossom motif, her facial expression slightly tighter, her outer robe exhibiting the same pattern, but with different colors. Yet contours of the oil paint create an image that appears softer and more elegant than the photograph. That there were close connections between representations in photographs and oil paintings is unsurprising; during the early Meiji period the two genres were closely linked for their ability to represent reality. Photographers and oil painters in mid-nineteenth century Japan were part of a continuum of interest in mimesis, which was considered desirable for the sacred representations of the heads of both religion and state.[16] Much as with the developing field of photography, the oil paintings of the imperial family led to the furthering of the nascent field of *yōga* (洋画, Western-style painting) in Meiji Japan, and the artists of the Goseda school were closely linked with this process.[17]

Throughout the 1870s and into the 1880s, while the negatives for the Uchida photographs were kept under state control and the sale of reprints of the photographs was maintained as illegal, woodblock prints and lithographs of the empress and emperor were sold on the commercial market. Around the turn of the decade in 1880, realistic imperial portraiture grew to increasing popularity, leading to a ban on sales of the imperial image in 1881, although many publishers evaded the law by not using the official title of the emperor, empress, and empress dowager.[18] In creating prints that envisioned the imperial heads of state, but which did not label them as such in the titles, printmakers and sellers could capitalize on the growing popularity of the monarchy while still staying within legal boundaries. During this time, a plethora of lithograph and woodblock prints were published and sold, with many including increasingly realistic portraits, some based upon the 1873 photographs.[19]

One such example is the January 1881 woodblock print *Imayō bijin shashinkyō* (Realistic mirror of today's beauty), by Toyohara Kunichika (豊原国周, 1835–1900) (Figure 4.4). The iconography of the crown, robes, and fan, combined with the angle of the face and similarity of the visage clearly indicate that the woman in the print is Empress Shōken, just as the companion print visually signifies that the represented figure is Emperor Meiji.[20] The simple, framed style is respectful but familiar. At a time when photographs were still limited in distribution, this print and others like it could be sold on the vernacular market to citizens interested in their nascent celebrity empress. The print is part of a series of actor portraits, which use the term *haiyū* (actor) instead of *bijin* (beauty). The slight title change allowed the artist to evade censorship issues, but by including portraits of the emperor and empress in the series, there was potential for a mutually beneficial sales boost. That the empress was included in a series depicting actors, obvious stars,

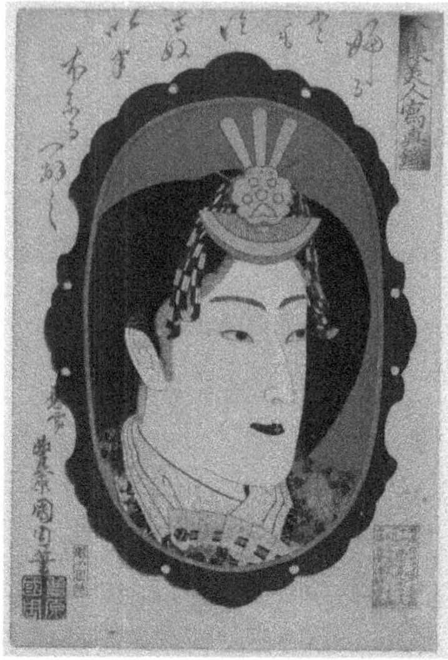

FIGURE 4.4 *Imayō bijin shashinkyō* (Realistic mirror of today's beauty), 1881, Toyohara Kunichika, color woodblock print, National Museum of Asian Art, Smithsonian Institution, Arthur M. Sackler Collection, Robert O. Muller Collection, S2003.8.2698

reinforces her celebrity status and function. The emperor and empress attended kabuki performances, and the ancient imperial family were occasionally represented as fictional kabuki characters, but in this instance Meiji and Shōken are included for their social and economic cache. The reproduction of the 1873 photograph in oil and in woodcut shows that from the early Meiji period there was a spectrum of visual access to the imperial family across media and in diverse public and private forums.

Lithographs began to corner the market on imperial portraiture in the 1880s and were the dominant media for imperial images by 1890.[21] The technological development and spread of lithography, with its photograph-like aesthetic, led to changes in how prints, both woodblock and lithograph, were conceived and produced, pushing the genre towards a higher degree of naturalism in terms of line, color, and composition.[22] By 1887, the rules would once again change with increased censorship standards being issued as part of the Press Ordinance and Publication Ordinance, both of which dictated the treatment of the imperial image and which remained in place for the following fifty years.[23]

Although she appeared in myriad woodblock and lithograph images throughout the 1870s and 1880s, it was not until 1889 that Empress Shōken was photographed again (Figure 4.5). In this later image, captured by Suzuki Shinichi (鈴木真一, 1835–1918) and Maruki Riyō (丸木利陽, 1850–1923), the empress is in a dramatically different studio setting and wears an elaborate costume

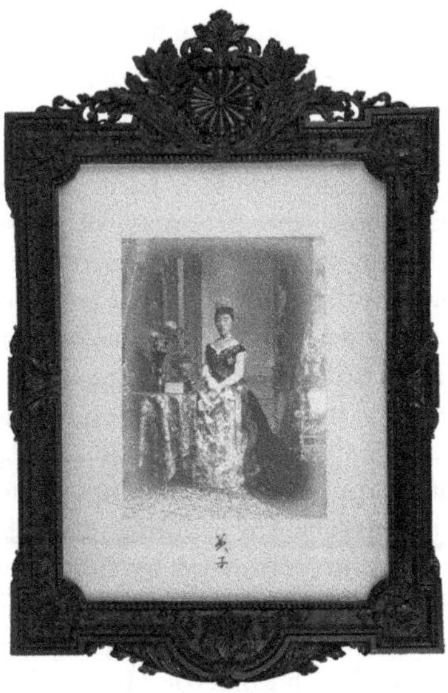

FIGURE 4.5 Empress Shōken, 1889, Suzuki Shinichi and Maruki Riyō, gelatin silver print in wood frame, National Museum of Asian Art Archives, Smithsonian Institution, the Alice Roosevelt Longworth Collection of Photographs from the 1905 Taft Mission to Asia, FSA_A2009.02_05b

similar to those worn by European monarchs. She stands clad in a red velvet dress with a silk embroidered frontispiece, a sash across her torso, and imperial medallion on her chest.[24] Wearing a three-strand jeweled necklace, and a European-style crown, her hair is pulled up, and she holds a folded fan and handkerchief in her gloved hands. Behind her is a painted backdrop, intended to look like a posh European-style interior, and next to her is a table covered in opulent fabric and topped with a rose-filled vase and a large book bound in the Japanese style. Advances in technology also mean that this photograph is crisper than the earlier one. Sixteen years after the photograph was taken, it was reproduced, signed by the empress, framed, and gifted to Alice Roosevelt Longworth, daughter of then U.S. President Theodore Roosevelt, when she accompanied the 1905 Taft Mission to Asia. The image, exhibiting a visual monarchy that over the past seventeen years transformed alongside the Japanese nation, was also reproduced on cartes de visite and postcards in the decades after it was produced.

Beginning in the late 1880s, a variety of imperial officials were concerned about the propriety of presenting a nearly twenty-year-old photograph of the emperor to dignitaries, officials, and foreign royals. The nation was on the cusp of codifying many of political modernization projects, such as the Promulgation of the Constitution (1889), the first general election (1890), and the release of the Imperial Rescript on Education (1890), the last of which cemented the emperor's role as the patriarchal head of the Japanese nation. With the Rescript came the need for a new image of the emperor. The resulting image, a composite photograph of a conte crayon drawing by European artist Edoardo Chiossone (1833–1898) termed the *goshinei* (御真影, imperial portrait), was a specific category of Japanese imperial portraiture which originated with Emperor Meiji and was actively used through the end of the Second World War. The *goshinei* was treated as a sacred object, the ritual creation, handling, and display of which was standardized in imperial law.[25]

At the time of the *goshinei*'s production in the late 1880s, Emperor Meiji was not interested in sitting for a photographic portrait, but the government officials involved in the project of procuring an image of the monarch were concerned with having a realistic photograph-like representation. It was with these dual concerns that Edoardo Chiossone, an Italian artist in the employ of the Japanese Printing Bureau was commissioned to create a likeness of the emperor by the Minister of Imperial Affairs, Hijikata Hisamoto.[26] As Emperor Meiji refused to participate in a sitting, Hijikata and Chiossone conspired to create the image stealthily; in January of 1888, the painter was provided with a space next to the emperor's dining room, from where he sketched the visage of the monarch. Chiossone proceeded to costume himself in a military uniform and have his appearance photographed. From these two images, the sketch of the emperor and the photograph of himself, Chiossone created a composite portrait; the resulting image was the model for the emperor's figure in the *goshinei*.[27] The completed portrait was a drawing produced in conte crayon. Upon being shown the portrait of himself by Hijikata, Emperor Meiji neither approved nor disapproved of the image, but soon thereafter signed over permission for copies of the image to be presented to foreign dignitaries.[28]

Chiossone's drawing was reproduced in photograph form in 1889 by Maruki Toshihiro.[29] Although the original distribution records of the *goshinei* are not open to the public, it is estimated that over 20,000 copies of the image were distributed to schools throughout the country in 1889.[30] The image, although a compilation of two different bodies and two different mediums, was treated as the most authentic image of the emperor. The art historian Mikiko Hirayama argues that the *goshinei*, "successfully perpetuated an eternally youthful, masculine emperor. . . . The state needed the illusion of authentic reality that photography created. Thus, it was always treated as a photographic image even though it was actually a drawing."[31]

Meiji's *goshinei* is highly idealized. In the portrait, the emperor was aged thirty-six, and he is envisioned as a mature, confident leader. Although there are few appropriate contemporaneous photographic images to compare Chiossone's drawing to, in contrasting the *goshinei* with the 1872 photographs by Uchida Kūichi, the idealized nature of the later drawing is apparent. In the *goshinei*, Emperor Meiji's jaw is softened, and his head shape perfected. The piercing, serious eyes and distinctive upturned eyebrows that distinguish the emperor's face remain the same as in photographs, but the drawing allowed Chiossone to polish and enhance the countenance of Emperor Meiji. The physique of the emperor, which was actually modeled on Chiossone's own body, closely resembles the photograph that the artist took of himself; the frame is expanded in the chest, and the torso bulges beneath the highly adorned military uniform. The emperor's posture is stiff and upright, with his right arm resting on the table beside him, and his left holding a sword.[32] From the neck down, the portrait is based on the artist's appearance and not the emperor's, leading us to understand that the attributes and gestures of the *goshinei* provide few cues to the actual appearance of Emperor Meiji in the period when he was at the height of his power, in the years immediately before the Promulgation of the Constitution and the Imperial Rescript on Education. Rather, the image provides more information on the politics of the imperial image in the late 1880s and early 1890s than the genuine look of the monarch. The circumstances of its creation and later distribution are a window into the control and construction of the modern imperial symbol in its early days.

The 1889 photograph of Empress Shōken was, like the *goshinei* of Emperor Meiji, taken in response to the Promulgation of the Constitution and the subsequent desire to distribute imperial portraits to schools and government buildings. Art historian Wakakuwa Midori addresses the creation of this image, citing the Italian royal portraits that influenced the style of the Shōken image, including that of Queen Margarita of Italy from 1878.[33] Italian artists were working in the Japanese capital in the early Meiji years as part of the *oyatoi gaikokujin* (御雇い外国人, hired foreigners) system, wherein foreign experts were brought to Japan to assist with instruction in a variety of fields, from art to education, military to manufacturing. Wakakuwa traces the visual inspiration for the early Meiji Japanese imperial images to the Italian artists working in the Japanese capital, including Edoardo Chiossone, the creator of Emperor Meiji's *goshinei*. Wakakuwa also attributes the creation of what she refers to as the *kōgō goshinei* (皇后御真影, empress *goshinei*) to developments in gender politics in the mid-Meiji period. She cites the continuing need for Japan to be viewed as a peer to the European and American powers and the necessity of altered, Euro-American style roles for women in Japan's pursuit of a position in international society. From this change in women's roles, out of the historic Confucian system and into a hybrid modern system, arose the Meiji ideology of *ippuippusei* (一夫一婦制, one man, one woman policy), and with it came the need for the empress to be envisioned in Euro-American clothes, in the same fashion as her husband.[34] The 1889 portrait photograph was taken only two years after Empress Shōken appeared in public in European-style dress for the first time, and two years after she issued her edict on Western-dress, in which she encouraged Japanese women to don European-style garments made with Japanese textiles.[35] This consensus decision to adapt the visuals of European queenly models for the modern Japanese empresses shows the sense of continuity with wider practices of global queenship.

The varied images of Empress Shōken, including those in photograph, print, and oil form, had an outsized impact on the public acceptance and understanding of portraiture as a concept in the modern era, particularly in reference to women's portraiture. Because of the legacy of the *bijin* (美人, beautiful women) as a category of *ukiyo-e* (pictures of the floating world, or Edo period woodblock prints), it was controversial to represent middle- and upper-class women who worked outside of the realm of entertainment in portrait form in the late nineteenth century. The *bijin* were generally of a low social status and worked as courtesans, shop girls, or other famous entertainers of the pleasure quarters of Edo. The idea of women's portraiture, particularly in the public realm, as a marketing tool for brothels or shops of the red-light districts was not overcome until the mid to late-Meiji period. The public images of the empress and other women of the imperial family were a catalyst in this change; with the female leadership of the nation appearing frequently in visual form, the public grew accustomed to seeing respectable women in public images.[36] As happened with other monarchical women, including Marie Antoinette or Queen Alexandra and their contemporary public imaging, the modern Japanese empress image would eventually impact the way that middle- and upper-class women in the late Meiji and later eras represented themselves, meaning the visual monarchy led the way in women's images across society.

In the aftermath of the 1889 photograph of Empress Shōken, the ban on the commercial sale of imperial imagery was lifted in 1891, allowing for a wider distribution of imperial portraiture in more established sources, such as magazines and newspapers.[37] Further permissions to reproduce and distribute the imperial likeness were given to the media in 1898 and 1900, immediately prior to the Taishō wedding.[38] This relaxing of the censorship laws was a response to the heightened public interest in the upcoming nuptials and to the widespread desire for more imperial imagery in an age when there was a keen interest in national culture and an excitement surrounding the expansion of printed visual materials created with new technologies. It is this expansion and proliferation of imperial imagery in the Taishō period which will be examined presently.

Teimei and Taishō: The Fully Articulated Imperial Portrait

Throughout the Meiji period the numerous government institutions with a vested interest in the imperial portrait worked to construct a standardized image of the modern imperial family. Yet the rites and rituals that would come to surround the imperial images were not fully established as universal activities for the citizenry until the early twentieth century—in the Taishō period. Erwin von Bälz, a doctor serving in Meiji Japan, recorded the progression of imperial activities in his diary, noting that police intimidation was needed to convince citizens to fly the Japanese flag on new holidays in 1880, general awareness of imperial rites did not occur until after 1900, and it was not truly until after 1910 that the holidays were widely observed.[39] In the last two decades of Meiji rule, with the Imperial Rescript on Education, the Promulgation of the Constitution, and eventual switch to the Taishō monarchy, the systems put in place by the Rescript and Promulgation were absorbed and normalized in the daily practices of the common people. Thus, upon the change to Taishō rule in 1912, imperial norms and guidelines were in place for the first monarchial shift in modern Japanese history. In relation to the visual strategy of the modern Japanese imperial family, the Meiji period was defined by the establishment of imperial visual culture, while the Taishō period was characterized by the application of said culture. Furthermore, wide social shifts between the Meiji and Taishō periods led to a differing focus for the imperial icon, moving from the Meiji emphasis on establishing a global reputation to the Taishō focus on building the metropole as the power center of the budding Japanese empire.[40] In other words, Teimei and Taishō were primarily domestic figures, as contrasted with the more international characters of Shōken and Meiji.[41] This difference in the perceived and intended audience for the imperial image had a great impact on the visual strategy in the 1910s and 1920s. It is this Taishō implementation of imperial visual strategy that this section will examine.

Empress Teimei was visibly known from the beginning; she first appeared in the mass media in 1899, one year before she married into the imperial family, and as the first Japanese sovereign to grow up in the public eye, Emperor Taishō was also a familiar sight. Although image technology changed dramatically between Taishō's birth in 1879 and the imperial couple's ascension to the throne in 1912, the Japanese public was fairly familiar with their images in the early twentieth century. In Taishō's youth, he was frequently represented in woodblock prints, as well as photographs in lesser numbers. However, the year before the imperial wedding in 1900 saw a dramatic increase in widely distributed images of the crown prince and soon-to-be princess, represented as the upcoming imperial couple. While Emperor Meiji had the benefit of testing his leadership without the watchful eye of the camera and the international media, Taishō was thrust into the media immediately, with no opportunity to rehearse his public persona in an undocumented fashion. Even though the censorship of the Imperial Household Ministry assisted in controlling the imperial public image, the margin for error was slim, and threats to rule both from within and without the imperial palace were a constant concern. Balancing the visual monarchy with images of the well-liked crown princess was a means of popularizing the institution to maintain its relevance.

The Imperial Household Ministry, and the imperial family themselves, learned a great deal between the Meiji and Taishō monarchies. The continual growth and spread of monarchical images as well as the increased circulation of publications between nations meant that the members of the corporate Japanese monarchy had a savvier understanding of image craft. They also observed the lessons of Chinese Empress Dowager Cixi, whose slow acceptance of European hegemonic ideas of monarchy cost her in the international press. Although Cixi played with painted and photographed portraiture, the minimal circulation meant that the foreign press was able to create the image for her that they desired, not that which she and her handlers produced. In the aftermath of racist caricatures of her that were published in the European press, Cixi eventually agreed to portraits that would be exhibited overseas, for as Ying-Chen Peng states, "she had realized that conforming to Western ways of presenting monarchy, including having a public presence, was inevitable."[42]

There are four frequently published studio portraits of Teimei. The earliest of these images was that of her in childhood, although it was not published until the 1910s (Figure 4.6).[43] The image appeared in the women's magazine *Fujin gahō* in the first and fourteenth years of the Taishō period (1912 and 1926, respectively) and *Fujyosei* in Taishō 13 (1925), among other publications. The portrait shows Sadako as a child, before she was selected to be crown princess, standing in a *hakama* (袴), and wearing heavy makeup, making her appear older than her age. She holds a small fan in her hands, and her expression is serious, with her lips pursed as she gazes off into the distance. The background is a studio setting with a painted European-style interior. In publications from the Taishō era, the photograph is often paired with the childhood studio portrait of Yoshihito (Taishō) in military-style dress. Through her confident, straight posture, with shoulders back and head held high in a regal position, and her strong gaze, combined with makeup that makes her appear more mature than her years, the photograph attempts to show that Sadako had the comportment of an empress long before her selection and rise to the role. It also acts as evidence of her preparations for a position within the monarchy and reminds the viewer

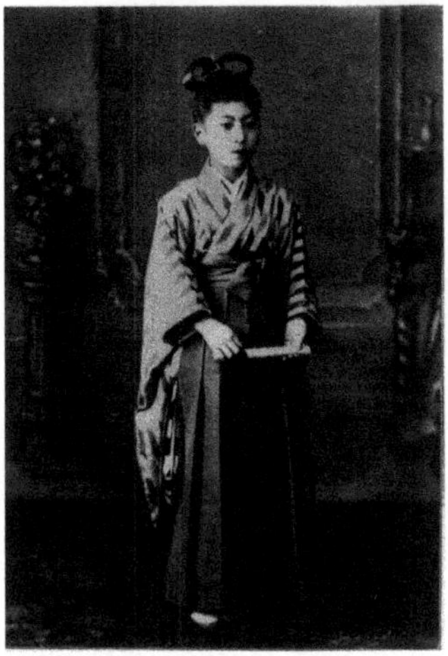

FIGURE 4.6 Kujō Sadako (Empress Teimei), photograph reproduced in *Fujin gahō*, September 1, 1912

of her noble birth as a daughter of the Fujiwara lineage, thus legitimizing her place within the imperial family. Furthermore, by pairing her childhood portrait with that of the young Crown Prince Yoshihito, it links the two monarchs as having a common upbringing, giving their union a sense of destiny.

Among the most widely viewed portraits of Empress Teimei was the studio photograph in European-style dress taken upon her wedding in 1900 (Figure 4.7). This image was published in a variety of magazines at the start of the Taishō period in September of 1912. In addition to gracing the pages of women's magazines such as *Fujin gahō* (1912, September 1, and 1914, January 15), *Shōjo gaho* (1912, September), and *Fujin no tomo* (1912, September), the portrait appeared in the nationalist publication *Daikokumin* (1912 September) and in specialist business, industrial, and agricultural publications such as *Nōji shinhō* (1912, September), *Kōgyō no Nihon* (1912, August), and *Nihon jutsugyō shinhō* (1912, August), among other examples.[44] It was also published in newspapers in the same year. In this photograph,

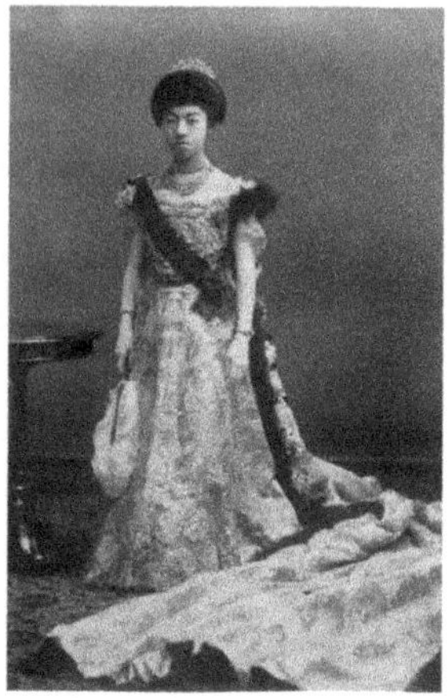

FIGURE 4.7 Crown Princess Sadako, 1900, photograph reproduced in *Fujin gahō*, September 1, 1912

Empress Teimei appears in the style of European monarchs with outward signs of nobility. Her clothing, luxurious fabrics with a train, and plentiful jewelry in the latest Parisian style, indicate her high status, and the sash, crown, and medal she wears remind the viewer of her position as the future empress. Although the public was by this time familiar with her image from the various lithographs and other images that were disseminated around the time of the Taishō wedding, this photograph marks her rise to the role of empress. In the photograph, Teimei appears very young and does not exhibit the comportment of royalty or regality. Her shoulders are slumped, and at this point she seems somewhat unaware of the power of the camera in conveying an image of imperial authority. When the photograph was taken, Teimei was only sixteen years old, and the distribution of photomechanical imperial images was not as widespread as it would be a mere twelve years later, when this photograph was widely published upon her taking the role of empress. Her facial expression is neutral, yet also slightly pouty; in this image she has yet to become comfortable with her position of power: Teimei still appears as a princess, not yet an empress. This lack of regal presence is likely why this image was distributed mostly in the year that Teimei and Taishō ascended the throne and not much in the years thereafter.

Although less popular, an additional early photograph which is noteworthy as a step in the development of imperial imagery is that of Empress Teimei in Heian-style robes at the time of her marriage (Figure 4.1). This image, as described at the beginning of this chapter, was published predominantly in women's magazines and shows Teimei in a studio portrait setting with very minimal markers surrounding her—only a small drapery at the right and the carpet on which she stands. Her robes indicate the lengthy imperial tradition which she is inheriting with her rise to the throne. This image was published in a *Fujin gahō* photo spread in 1912 together with a similarly styled photograph of Emperor Taishō and a small inset photograph from her childhood. It was also published in 1912 the women's magazine *Shōjo sekai* with Taishō's companion portrait and the *Asahi shinbun* in 1915, upon the occasion of the formal imperial ascension rituals, and reproduced on the *Coronation of the Emperor Taishō* scroll (Figure 4.9). Later, the photograph was published in the women's magazine *Fujyosei* in 1925, together with a small grouping of photographs, including Teimei's childhood portrait and her later imperial studio photograph, a matching montage of Emperor Taishō's photographs on the opposite page.

Commemorating major milestones with this style of portrait, in which the emperor and empress are portrayed in Heian-style robes, was a Meiji-period innovation that is still practiced today. That the images of Taishō and Teimei in the traditional-style costumes were published in greater numbers in women's magazines is important to note, as it informs us about one of the key factors of Japanese gender politics throughout the modern era: women were viewed as the keepers of tradition, while men were the driving force of modernity. Images of the imperial family reflected these widespread societal beliefs and how they evolved between the late nineteenth and mid-twentieth centuries. While Empress Shōken was frequently represented in traditional clothing alongside her husband in European-style garb, Empress Teimei's sartorial selections generally matched those of her spouse. As a result, during the Taishō period, although women as an audience still received a greater amount of traditional-style imagery, the imperial family as a unit was promoted on a more equitable level than they were in the preceding era.[45] This discourse of the image was happening within the images themselves, rather than in textual treatises, thus making the examination of the distribution and reproduction of imperial imagery critical to our understanding of both the visual monarchy and the modern imperial institution as a whole.

When the Taishō imperial couple took the throne, conventional portraiture was necessary for exhibiting their authority. The death of Emperor Meiji in 1912 and Empress Dowager Shōken in 1914 necessitated a more mature image of Taishō and Teimei as global heads of state and as the pinnacle of the imperial household and the nation. This development of the imperial couple as subject occurred simultaneously with the advent of new technologies in photography and its reproduction, which would provide innovative possibilities for imperial imagery in the early twentieth century. Photography grew to be an increasingly important component of portraiture in general, and the imperial image in specific, in the years immediately after the Russo-Japanese War (1904–1905), when new reproduction technologies allowed for more widespread, inexpensive distribution of photomechanical images. Formal studio portrait photography of the emperor and empress—that in which they are seen in a staged full or half-length portrait and in a formal, composed studio context—was now readily viewed by the masses in the pages of popular magazines or newspapers. Over the course of the Taishō period, formal, photographic studio portraits were the most commonly viewed images of Empress Teimei and Emperor Taishō, as contrasted with the vernacular woodblock prints and lithographs of their predecessors. Distributed to schools and government buildings throughout the nation, as well as reproduced on postcards and in newspapers and mass-market magazines, these photographs—limited in number yet expansive in reproduction, distribution, and use—formed the core of the public image of Empress Teimei during the Taishō period and beyond.

The final studio portrait that received wide distribution in Taishō-period media is that of 1916 (Figure 4.8), her *goshinei*.

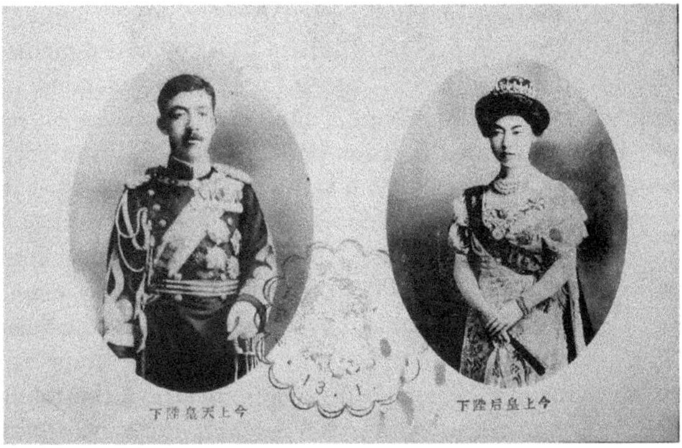

FIGURE 4.8 Postcard of Emperor Taishō and Empress Teimei, postmarked 1924, collection of the author

This portrait is the most recognizable and widely distributed image of Empress Teimei. The photograph was widely published in magazines, newspapers, on postcards and, like the *goshinei* of Emperor Taishō, and of Emperor Meiji and Empress Shōken before them, received widespread distribution to schools and government buildings, as well as to individuals as an imperial gift on select occasions. This portrait shows Empress Teimei as having risen to the role of monarch: unlike the earlier studio photograph wherein she appeared young and unsure of her position, in this image she is the model of royal comportment. Her shoulders are positioned back, giving her an aura of regal authority, and her crown, sash, robes, and medal are clearly visible signs of her status. Her facial expression is still neutral but projects an element of confidence not seen in the earlier portrait. She is mature and beautiful, a regal symbol of the nation.

As with Shōken's copied 1873 portrait, Teimei's *goshinei* was also copied as an oil painting. Portraits in oil were not widely viewed by the Japanese public; there was not a tradition of the public portrait gallery or other permanent established forum for the social viewing of these works, nor was there a tradition of adorning royal palaces with portraiture.[46] The

European tradition of public statuary of political figures was also non-existent in pre-Meiji Japan; thus the two-dimensional media covered in this book had a larger significance in Japan than similar media in Europe.[47] One example of an oil painting of Empress Teimei is from 1920, painted by John Wycliffe Lowes Forster (1850–1938), a Canadian artist who specialized in portraits and who was commissioned by the World Sunday School Association to paint the images for their eighth convention, held in Tokyo in October of the same year. The image has rarely been seen by the public but is a clear copy of the *goshinei* of Empress Teimei. The artist only glimpsed the empress and used mechanically reproduced images to create the painting, which took him six weeks' time.[48] As such, the viewer sees the same confident, regal empress as in the photograph, but with the addition of color. The artist added further expression to Teimei's face as well, giving her a slight upturn of the lips that reads as a small smile, and makes her appear more approachable to the viewer. He additionally rendered her clothing in a flattering fashion, using the oils to create more nuance of light than in the contrast of the black-and-white photograph.

Two photographs of Emperor Taishō in military-style dress were often published, distributed, and exhibited in the 1910s. These images, one from 1900 and the other from 1915, taken by Imperial Household Artist Maruki Riyō are very similar in pose, costume, and composition. The latter image acted as Taishō's *goshinei* and was also reproduced in newspapers, magazines, and postcards (Figure 4.8).[49] Only a few details mark the difference between the two images and other, similar photographs of Emperor Taishō which received less distribution.[50] Just over a decade later, Emperor Shōwa was photographed in a nearly identical military uniform and in an indiscernibly different studio setting upon his rise to the throne in the mid-1920s. These photographs, beginning with the *goshinei* of Emperor Meiji, and continuing through to that of Emperor Shōwa, represent the increasingly removed and sacred emperor; imaged in nearly identical poses, dress, and comportment; the *goshinei* of Emperor Taishō, as well as the similar photographs in military dress, show an emperor that was progressively being revered for both military leadership and his sacred role within the Shinto structure, roles which were slowly being conflated in the midst of imperial expansion.

When the Taishō imperial couple came into public prominence in 1900, they began the process of succession. By the time they ascended the throne as established monarchs in 1915, they had reinterpreted the visual legacy of their predecessors, transforming the imperial image into one which was savvier and more nuanced than in the past. During the Taishō period, images of the emperor and empress were standardized in form, distribution, and display. Laws and guidelines that were invented and established during the late Meiji period were put into practice with Teimei and Taishō. A fully articulated visual strategy of the imperial family, something which the bureaucrats and officials surrounding the monarchs desired since the first days of the Imperial Restoration, came to fruition with Teimei and Taishō.

Utilizing Portraits for Legitimacy and Lineage

In their years as crown princess and prince, Teimei and Taishō were known to be more independent, direct, and casual than their predecessors. For the public to readily accept the transition from the charismatic and regal Emperor Meiji to his more casual and free-spirited son, some effort on behalf of the Imperial Household Ministry and by extension the media was necessary.[51] Much of what was popularly understood to be the modern imperial institution and modern imperial state was intertwined with Emperor Meiji personally. As Natsume Sōseki famously stated on the passing of Meiji in his novel *Kokoro*, "And then, at the height of the summer, Emperor Meiji passed away. I felt that as the spirit of the Meiji era had begun with him, so it had ended with his death."[52] If the "spirit of the Meiji era" was equated with the public notion of modernity, this quotation exemplifies the crisis in national confidence that occurred at the end of the Meiji period, and explains why the proliferation of images showing the imperial family as a unit and as part of a lineage became so important in the years between 1900 and 1915.[53] Formal portraiture was the genre best suited to promote the unity and lineage of the imperial family—it imparted a quality of respect, worldliness, and aristocratic class and removed traces of individual personalities or expressions. As such, the portraits presented to this point were reproduced not just in their original form, as individuals, but in composite lithographs, scrolls, and postcards that drew the portraits together into singular objects representing the imperial lineage.

Images such as the lithograph *Kiken gosonei* (Venerable Portraits of Aristocrats) of 1900 show bust portraits of the Crown Princess Sadako and Crown Prince Yoshihito in small roundels, together with portraits of Empress Shōken and Emperor Meiji.[54] Printed and sold around the time of the imperial wedding, by depicting the well-established and respected Emperor Meiji and Empress Shōken together with their future successors Crown Prince Yoshihito (Taishō) and Crown Princess Sadako (Teimei), these portrayals allowed the citizenry to become accustomed to the crown prince and princess as upcoming rulers and cemented the image of the unbroken lineage of the Japanese imperial family in the public eye. As the Japanese citizenry was quite familiar with the visages of Empress Shōken and Emperor Meiji, images such as *Kiken gosonei*, and many other lithographs from the last decade of Meiji, were key in aiding the transition between Meiji and Taishō; this is particularly true as Emperor Meiji began to limit public appearances in the years after 1900 due to declining health. In the lithograph Meiji and Shōken appear in the background, their bodies partially fading away as the new generation of royals is featured at the center of the image, pronounced by a darker color background within their foregrounded roundels. Teimei and Taishō's portraits are bound together, the unity of which produces a sprig of chrysanthemum blooms, providing a literal illustration of fecundity and the future branches of the imperial lineage that they will produce. This lithograph, and the many similar images that were produced in the early twentieth century, inform the viewer not just of the imperial lineage but also of the performed monogamy of the throne and the nuclear family values that would be promoted by Teimei and Taishō. The *gon no tenji*, or imperial concubines, that were the biological mothers of Meiji's children are nowhere to be seen in the varied family lithographs of this era; rather these images promote monogamous marriage and the imagined motherhood of the empresses.

Chapter 1 addressed theories of the king's two bodies, the duality of gender and rule, and how concepts of the immortal and physical bodies of the emperor impacted the gendering of the throne, allowing for the empresses to act in the secular realm to compliment the position of the emperors in the sacred realm. Formal portraiture tells the story of how the roles of the imperial family were conceptualized for vernacular media: the empress' presence as half of the visual monarchy points to her centrality in the institution. Kanō Mikiyo addresses the duality of imperial gender in the *goshinei*, terming Meiji's image as the "strict father" (厳父, *genpu*) and Shōken as the "better half" (ベターハーフ, *betāhāfu*) who could appeal to the public.[55] Within this theory, both the emperor and empress are critical to the institution, and the lineage lithographs imagine the visual monarchy as such: the cosmopolitan and fashionable empresses compliment the strong emperors in military dress.[56] Theresa Earenfight complicates definitions of queenship and the gendered monarchy, arguing that they are dynamic, "best understood as a repertoire of collective norms, institutional structures, and strategies for women's participation in the public political sphere of monarchy."[57] In other publications Earenfight argues for the study of queens and kings together, in order to better understand the relational aspect of monarchy, which is explicitly on display in the imperial portraits.[58]

The 1915 collotype scroll *The Coronation of the Emperor Taishō* (Figure 4.9) is another example in which we see the portrait of Empress Teimei in print media and as part of the promotion of the lineage and tradition of imperial history. This scroll was produced upon the occasion of the emperor's ascension and coronation ceremonies, the *sokuirei* (即位礼) and *daijōsai* (大嘗祭), likely as a commemorative memento.[59] Although most of the narrative of the scroll relates to the ceremonies themselves and is therefore populated with a majority of male participants, Teimei appears in a full-length portrait in a small roundel at the start of the scroll, which unfolds right to left at the leisure of the viewer. She is opposite Emperor Taishō, dressed in Heian-style costume.

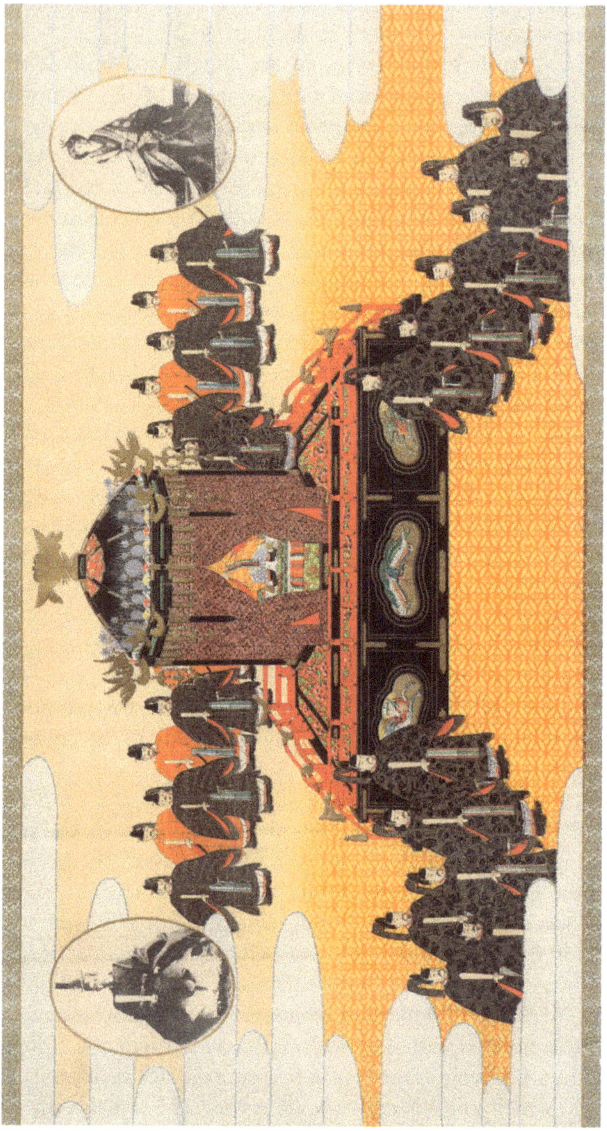

FIGURE 4.9 *Coronation of Emperor Taishō*, November 10, 1915, unknown artist, relief printing, halftone, collotype on paper, Spencer Museum of Art, University of Kansas, Gift of Dr. and Mrs. William L. Mundy, 1991.0051

Her image and his frame the temporary structure, the *takamikura* (高御座), wherein the *sokuirei* was performed.

The *sokuirei* was detailed in the 1909 Edict of Imperial Accession; in the instance of Emperor Taishō, the ceremony took place in early November 1915 and was the official public announcement of the emperor's ascension to the Chrysanthemum Throne.[60] It is inside the *takamikura* where the emperor sits when the ascension ceremonies occur. Following the historic ceremonial precedent for the *sokuirei*, which was loosely based on Chinese rituals, the *takamikura* exhibits Chinese and Korean style painting and metalwork. Within twenty minutes of Emperor Meiji's death in 1912, Emperor Taishō inherited the three imperial regalia—the sword, the jewel, and the mirror—in a ceremony termed the *senso* (践祚), or inheritance of the divine objects, officially giving him rule of the nation. Yet, the *sokuirei* and *daijōsai* were to take place two years later to allow time for Emperor Meiji's funerary rites and for the extensive planning that the two later ceremonies required. Due to the death of Empress Dowager Shōken, the ceremonies were delayed for an additional year to allow for an appropriate period of mourning.

The *Coronation of the Emperor Taishō* scroll uses a variety of imagery and symbols, both historic and modern, to represent the sacred events of imperial ascension. The angular style of perspective and the use of flat areas of color were indicative of artistic tradition and acted as pictorial reminders of both pre-modern times and the revival of traditional visual forms.[61] The architecture and ritual structures shown in the scroll were also reminders of the ceremony's location in the ancient capital city of Kyoto, where the imperial family resided from the ninth through the nineteenth century. Additionally, the use of the handscroll format itself emphasized Japanese tradition. By the early twentieth century most Japanese were accustomed to modern visual culture such as newspapers, magazines, and cinemas. The handscroll, a format used for calligraphy and painting in the pre-modern period, which hinted at the elite status of those who accessed these objects, was reminiscent of historic painting practices. Furthermore, the large, angular robes and multiple layers of colorful clothing that the emperor, empress, and their attendants wear in the scroll is in the style of the Heian period (794–1185). The use of historic costume gives an air of authenticity and legitimacy to the ceremony, performed publicly for the first time, and works to establish the validity of the monarchy as the modern incarnation of a lengthy and distinguished lineage. The collotype reproductions of photographs of the sovereigns that grace the scroll provide a counterpoint to the traditional format, style, and costuming and provide a reminder that this is a modern object. The small roundels also create a hybrid of tradition and modernity, presenting the viewer with a monarchy rooted in historic legitimacy but contemporary in technological savvy.

A final note: the inclusion of the empress in the imagery of the imperial coronation rituals was revolutionary but also false. Empress Teimei was pregnant with the couple's fourth child in 1915 and did not travel to Kyoto to attend the ceremonies; her role would have been as a distant observer, not as an active participant.[62] This scroll, as with the collotype portraits of the imperial family in the last decade of the Meiji period, acted to establish the Emperor Taishō and Empress Teimei as the inheritors of imperial lineage. The invented ceremonies of imperial ascension and rule were to link Emperor Taishō to the past, even if that past was partially imagined, and this scroll works to cement that link visually.

Another example of female centrality and imperial links to tradition by means of portraiture is evident in an early Taishō hanging scroll with the *Gunjin chokuyū* (Imperial Rescript to Soldiers and Sailors) (Figure 4.10). The bottom half of the scroll includes a lithograph reproduction of Teimei and Taishō in historically inspired dress, and the top half of the image is loaded with imperial symbolism: a chrysanthemum seal and two phoenixes frame the summary of the rescript, issued in 1882. The text was officially presented by Emperor Meiji, linking the imperial institution to the military. Meiji's portrait is at the upper right of the scroll, his gaze fixed upon the text. Above the text is Amaterasu, light shining from behind her as she floats down upon a cloud. At the upper left is the legendary first Emperor Jinmu, holding a bow and arrows. Chrysanthemum flowers and flags decorate the remaining area around the rescript. Although the provenance of

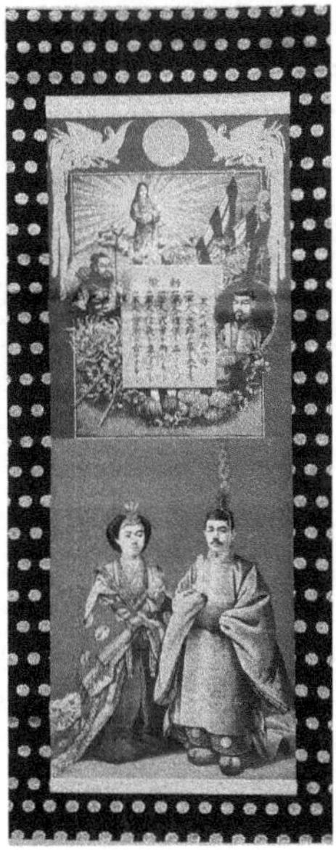

FIGURE 4.10 *Gunjin chokuyū* (Imperial Rescript to Soldiers and Sailors), c. 1915, lithograph scroll, collection of author

this scroll is uncertain, the imagined lineage of Amaterasu, Jinmu, Meiji, and Teimei and Taishō is clear, as is the connection to the military with the featured text. Other scrolls with similar messages of authenticity and tradition were distributed in the early Taishō period, some of which visualize Ise, Nijubashi, the Promulgation of the Constitution, and the modern and historic imperial lineage all in one composite lithograph.[63]

In regard to the many images which secured the concept of the imperial lineage in the mind of the public, it must be recalled that all of the ceremonies and events surrounding the Taishō wedding and ascension were performed in the public arena for the first time with Taishō and Teimei. These images, therefore, worked not just to demarcate the lineage but also to introduce the citizenry to imperial rites and ceremonies. When Emperor Meiji came to the throne in the 1860s, it was prior to the advent and spread of mass media outlets. As such, the early days of his reign were not a part of public awareness. Additionally, the laws that detailed the imperial wedding customs were adopted in the 1890s, and those for the ascension ceremonies were put in place in the early 1900s, both in anticipation of the Taishō transition. This multiplicity of new ceremonial observances, combined with the fact that the move from Meiji to Taishō was the first modern changeover in imperial power, created a fertile environment for picturing the imperial subjects. The representations of the monarchs and the newly constructed ceremonials was a learning process for all involved.

Finally, representations of imperial women were not limited to contemporary empresses, princesses, or the secular sphere but were also projected back into an imagined Japanese history. In the imperial milieu, the semi-legendary Empress Jingū, who ruled in the third century, enjoyed a renaissance in popularity in the late Meiji and Taishō periods. She was added to banknotes in the early twentieth century and was an important figure in newly created narrative histories of Japan, and as such, her image was well known amongst the populace.[64] According to legend, Jingū ruled Japan for nearly seventy years, living to be over two hundred years old, and may be the same figure as Queen Himiko, a strong shaman queen who is documented in Chinese records of Japan in the second century.[65] The mythological Jingū was an imperial consort and shaman who, according to legend, conveyed the desires of the gods to the emperor; his subsequent dismissal of the gods' desires led to his untimely death.[66] After the death of the emperor, Jingū allegedly ruled Japan in her own right—her exploits are documented in the legendary text of the *Nihon shoki* (日本書紀, The Chronicles of Japan), wherein she conquered the three kingdoms of Korea, delayed the birth of her baby by placing a stone in her groin, quelled domestic rebellions, and wore masculine attire.[67] Jingū's narrative provides a model of a strong female military leader; the rise of her popularity in the Taishō period, as coinciding with the rise in the political and visual power of Empress Shōken and Empress Teimei, should not be overlooked. Jingū was historic, legendary, and military oriented, making for a sharp contrast against the modern, globally oriented, and visually reproduced modern femininity of Shōken and Teimei.[68] In the late Taishō period, there was even a popular movement to include Empress Jingū in the official lineage of emperors, proving that there was a certain openness towards women being included in the imperial line, despite contemporary bans on regnant empresses and female-line descent.[69]

Teimei and Taishō were the first imperial couple to fully live their reign in the public eye, the first to have a fully developed Imperial Household Law for the entirety of their time on the throne, and the first to perform public ceremonies such as marriages and ascension rites. The imperial rituals that were new in the Taishō period would continue on in the early Shōwa years, as would the increasing standardization of the imperial image.

1930s Innovations: Family Portraits, Hōanden, and Hōankura

The visual representation of the imperial family in the early Shōwa era was different from that of their predecessors in significant ways. Emperor Shōwa and Empress Kōjun were frequently depicted with their children as a nuclear family in photographs, a distinct departure from earlier imperial imagery. As the Japanese public generally grew more comfortable with private, domestic life being exhibited in public, and as the empire expanded, leading to the promotion of the concept of Japanese nationals as a family beneath the emperor, the nuclear imperial family became a suitable role model image. In the realm of imperial media, this meant that casual family portraits were preferred to formal studio portraits of individuals. Yet the *goshinei* and formal portraiture continued in both commemorative publications and in the regulated environment of public buildings, where the authority of the monarchy was appropriate for exhibition.

With the change to the Shōwa imperial family came a return to the conventional imperial gender roles as established under Empress Shōken and Emperor Meiji. Three days after succeeding to the throne, on December 28, 1926, Hirohito issued a series of imperial edicts, mainly to establish the primacy of the military in the social order and also to inform the public of political continuity. Within his message, Hirohito promised to, "abide by the constitution, 'cultivate inherited virtue and . . . maintain intact the glorious tradition set by our ancestors,' starting with 'Our imperial grandfather,' whose 'educational developments' and 'military achievements' had 'enhanced the grandeur of the empire.'"[70] With this address, he immediately connected himself to the strong historic figure of Emperor Meiji, rather than his own father, who was plagued by illness for the last six years of his life, and who, while popular, never took on the strong masculine presence that Meiji and Hirohito did. In these edicts, and in the successive imagery of the Shōwa imperial family, we see an emperor who is affiliated with military affairs and an empress who is associated with domestic concerns, particularly childrearing.[71] This return to conventional gender roles in the late 1920s and early 1930s was related to the upturn in conservatism and the expansion of empire and the military, both of which were related to calls for more traditional gender norms. As the growing Japanese empire fashioned itself as a strong, modern, masculine state in opposition to the weak, feudal, feminized colonies of Korea and China, and as the need for conscripted male soldiers and their female support system grew, physical bodies and familial roles were molded into a standardized, conservative gender binary to best serve state needs.

A resulting change in the display of the imperial image in the 1930s was the large-scale expansion of the *hōanden* (奉安殿) and *hōankura* (奉安庫), Taishō-era innovations that grew in popularity during the Shōwa period. These structures were small safe enclosures that were part of schools or government buildings, either built as a room within extant architecture or in a small, shrine-like independent building, with the intended purpose of both safely housing and creating a more sacred aura for the *goshinei*. Developed in the 1910s and 1920s and lasting until the end of the Second World War, the style of the structures had religious overtones, either in the form of neo-classical European-style or Shinto-style architecture, lending to a message of the holy inviolability of the emperor and empress, whose sacred images were housed within.

Both structures were originally built as a means of protecting the *goshinei* from destructive mishaps or accidents. *Hōanden* were independent structures that were typically built in the style of Shinto shrines or Greek temples, while *hōankura* were safe-like structures placed inside of municipal buildings. A booklet published in 1937 to commemorate typhoon victims included a list of the twenty-eight people who died as a result of protecting the *goshinei* since 1872. The commemorated were primarily educators, both in the metropole and the colonies, and the dead received praise for their loyalty to the emperor.[72] This extreme form of veneration for the imperial portraits was an extension of the varied rituals that surrounded the images starting in the late nineteenth century. The woodblock print diptych *Shintomichōtoza shichigatsu kōgyō daikaishō* (Great Tsunami: Action from July, capitol seat of Shintomi) shows school principal Tochinai Taikichi of Hakozaki Jinjō Elementary School in Iwate Prefecture rescuing the Meiji *goshinei* from the Sanriku Daikaishō tsunami in July 1896.[73] Tochinai was found dead on the beach the day after the tsunami, still clutching the portrait. In the print, his fierce, brave gaze falls upon Shōken's portrait as he works to uphold the framed image, about to be overtaken by a menacing wave. In the aftermath of the incident, Tochinai's actions were debated in the newspapers, but the end result was widespread recognition of the sacred, embodied nature of the portrait and the acceptance of extreme actions to save it from harm.[74]

When the *goshinei* began to be held by schools and government offices in the late Meiji period ritual salutes, recitations of government proclamations, and ceremonial care of the portraits became standard.[75] The *hōanden* and *hōankura* were developed as a response to incidents of ruin but were also part of a larger attempt to formalize and standardize the rituals surrounding the *goshinei*. Most of these structures were purposefully destroyed in the weeks and months following the end of the Second World War, but a handful survive today.[76] The majority of the surviving *hōankura* were built between 1910 and 1935 and were moved in 1946 from schools to shrine complexes. This move allowed the structures to be preserved while keeping local governments in compliance with the *Shinto shirei* (Shinto Directive). This directive, issued to the Japanese government on December 10, 1945, by the occupying General Headquarters (GHQ), mandated the separation of Shinto and state and led to the destruction of not just the *hōanden* and *hōankura* but the *goshinei* housed inside.[77] The remaining *hōanden* and *hōankura*, as well as those that are documented in photographs, show structures that utilized both the visual language of Shinto shrines, as well as neo-classical Greek architecture. The ties between the imperial family and the Shinto complex are easily understood, and the reception of ancient Greece in Japan was part of a complex aesthetic and intellectual movement in the Meiji era.[78]

During their primary period of use in the early Shōwa period, the treatment of the *goshinei* and the use of the *hōanden* and *hōankura* differed by prefecture.[79] As such, it is impossible to discern broad, national trends in the reception and veneration of these images in the Taishō and early Shōwa periods—the practices of display, viewing, and ritual were simply too diverse, and the records are too dispersed, concealed, and vast to provide a complete picture. Furthermore, the structures were also built in the colonies, where some remain today, and where the ritual use of the *goshinei* and structures would have had dramatically different impacts on the citizens who were compelled to use them. For example, Migita Hiroki cites a 1938 survey of middle-school girls in Nagano Prefecture in which less than one percent of those surveyed thought that the veneration of the *goshinei* instilled the importance of *kokutai* values.[80] This disregard for the *goshinei* as a sacred national symbol shows that at least among this group of students the image was not internalized as was intended by the offices that distributed it. It is easy to imagine that there were many others who participated in imperial rituals but like the girls in Nagano did not fully embrace the intended message of the *goshinei*.

What is known is that the *hōanden*, which were generally built on the grounds of elementary schools, were used regularly in military simulation exercises in the 1930s and 1940s.[81] The Shinto style of architecture, combined with the rhetoric of *tennōsei* (天皇制, the ideology of the emperor) and the military exercises, were fully in support of the nationalist propaganda which began to saturate all aspects of Japanese life in the imperial age. Although the doors to the *hōanden* were often closed, the students who gathered before the structures were familiar with the *goshinei* images housed inside and were highly aware of the symbolism of the structure, which embodied the sacred presence of the emperor as the head of the religious and political establishments. Japanese citizens were trained to bow before the *goshinei*, as well as prior to the emperor's appearances in newsreels. The *Nippon News*, which was from June 1940 the only wartime newsreel, one which was mandatory to screen prior to any feature-length film, preceded the emperor's appearance with a title image that instructed viewers to remove their hats. Hikari Hori argues that this practice of veneration in newsreels reflected the practice of *goshinei* worship and is evidence of the widespread static and photographic portrayal of Hirohito in the early 1940s.[82] What is often left out of discussions of these structures and portraits is that the *goshinei* as housed in the *hoanden* and *hoankura* was that of the emperor and empress as a set pair. Even in this masculine military setting, the empress was a visible, critical presence.

In the arc of imperial imagery from early Meiji to the wartime years of Shōwa, the empress image changed alongside that of the emperor, was central to the institution and to the visual monarchy, and evolved from ad hoc creations in the early Meiji years to ritualized visual culture in the 1930s. Throughout the Meiji and Taishō eras, the imperial image held a connotation of modernity but embedded with domestic messages of lineage, authenticity, and legitimacy. Beginning with the earliest official studio portraits of Shōken and Meiji, continuing through Teimei and Taishō as the first imperial couple to entirely live in the public eye, and finishing with the ritualized *hōanden* and *hōankura*, the Japanese imperial image grew increasingly sacred, removed, and modern over the late nineteenth and early twentieth centuries. Portraits are globally read, and foreign artists had a distinct impact on the evolution of the official imperial portraits, as did the models of the European monarchs, but these were always imbued with domestic philosophies and meanings. Government policies were also greatly influenced by models from abroad; the aim of the visual monarchy was not just to increase domestic reverence for the imperial family but also to increase respect for the Japanese royals overseas. By creating a visible imperial family, something that was unprecedented in Japanese history, the bureaucrats of the Meiji and Taishō eras achieved their ambitions to see the Japanese sovereigns included in the ranks of the global monarchs but also to achieve reverence and respect at home. Formal portraits were critical in achieving both of these aims.

The images examined in this chapter display the performed monogamy of the imperial family as well as the importance of exhibiting legitimacy and lineage for the modern imperial household. Throughout this survey of portraiture, the empresses were central figures in the visual monarchy, providing a relatable element for women and for the general public, balancing the sacred functions of the emperors in the public forum. As the office of the empress evolved in the modern period and images crafted in a global milieu of monarchy made up the public understanding of modern Japanese queenship, formal portraits formed the unchanging visual standard of the imperial household against which casual images were able to operate. It is these informal images which are the topics of the next two chapters.

Notes

1 For the purposes of this chapter, I am using the term studio portrait as defined in the Getty Art and Architecture Thesaurus, "portraits taken in a professional photographer's studio, often making use of backdrops of props." Getty Art and Architecture Thesaurus, "Portraits," www.getty.edu/vow/AATFullDisplay?find=portrait&logic=AND&note=&english=N&prev_page=1&subjectid=300223022.

2 Empress Shōken and Emperor Meiji were photographed in historic costume but on separate occasions four and three years after their wedding, respectively.

3 Luke Gartlan, "A Chronology of Baron Raimund von Stillfried-Ratenicz," in *Japanese Exchanges in Art 1850s–1930s*, ed. John Clark (Sydney: Power Publications, 2001), 131.

4 Stephanie E. Koscak, *Monarchy, Print Culture, and Reverence in Early Modern England: Picturing Royal Subjects* (New York: Routledge Studies in Eighteenth-Century Cultures and Societies, 2021), 5. Koscak's examination of late seventeenth- and early eighteenth-century royal images in England shows the modern "fantasy of intimate access to the royal family" that

mass produced images provided. While she argues that widespread reproductions removed the sacredness of the monarchy while allowing them to be revered, in Japan the sacred qualities of the emperor remained; it was the empress who was venerated in vernacular culture, and always with a degree of respect.

5 Sebastian Dobson, "Frederick William Sutton, 1832–1883: Photographer of the Last Shogun," in *Britain and Japan: Biographical Portraits*, ed. Hugh Cortazzi, vol. 4 (London: Japan Society, 1994), 297.

6 Kuramochi Motoi, "Meiji tennō shashin hiroku," *Rekishi yomihon* 54, no. 3 (2009).

7 There are a variety of portraits of Emperor Meiji outside of the realm of photography, many of which were based upon the official photographs. Some of these additional portraits are official commissions, such as the Takahashi Yuichi oil painting of 1879. The image can be found in: Kyoto kokuritsu kindai bijutsukan, *Kōshitsu no meihin: kindai Nihon bijutsu no iki* (Kyoto: Kyoto kokuritsu kindai bijutsukan, 2013), 252.

8 Mikiko Hirayama, "The Emperor's New Clothes: Japanese Visuality and Imperial Portrait Photography," *History of Photography* 33, no. 2 (2009): 165–184, 173.

9 For samples of early Meiji images: Kanagawa kenritsu hakubutsukan, *Oke no shōzō: Meiji kōshitsu arubamu no hajimari* (Yokohama: Kanagawa kenritsu rekishi hakubutsukan, 2001); Taki Kōji, *Tennō no shōzō* (Tokyo: Iwanami, 2002).

10 Taki, *Tennō no shōzō*, 11. Sarah E. Thompson and H.D. Harootunian, *Undercurrents in the Floating World: Censorship and Japanese Prints* (New York: The Asia Society Galleries, 1991), 85–91.

11 Taki, *Tennō no shōzō*, 2–7. John Breen, "Ornamental Diplomacy: Emperor Meiji and the Monarchs of the Modern World," in *The Meiji Restoration: Japan as a Global Nation*, ed. Robert Hellyer and Harald Fuess (Cambridge: Cambridge University Press, 2020), 232–248.

12 The term *ryōsai kenbo* was first coined in November of 1875 by Nakamura Masanao, writing in the *Meiji Six Journal*. The nationalist ideal of women as patriotic caretakers and educators of the next generation, however, began to develop a few years prior. Sharon Sievers, *Flowers in Salt: The Beginnings of Feminist Consciousness in Modern Japan* (Stanford: Stanford University Press, 1983), 22. As will be examined in Chapter 5, *ryōsai kenbo* ideology evolved throughout the over seventy-year period during which it was promoted as an ideal. At this early

stage, the ideology encouraged women to bear many children and to be educated so as to take an active role in the education of their children, who as the next generation were crucial to the success of the empire. Women were also to maintain Japanese traditions in the home, all in patriotic, nationalist service.

13 In addition to the law banning short hair, there were informal proclamations against blackened teeth and shaved eyebrows for married women. Sievers, *Flowers in Salt*, 14–15. Prior to the Meiji period, the custom of traditional appearance included the latter two, shaved eyebrows and blackened teeth, as common beauty standards.

14 The Ugolini portrait, and a catalogue entry on the painting, can be found in: Meiji Jingū, *Meiji no kōgō: Meiji tennō to ayumareta Shōken kōtaigō* (Tokyo: Meiji Jingū, 2014), 11.

15 Kyoto kokuritsu kindai bijutsukan, *Kōshitsu no meihin*, 329.

16 The links between photography and oil painting in their pursuit of realism are detailed by Doris Croissant, "In Quest of the Real: Portrayal and Photography in Japanese Painting Theory," in *Challenging Past and Present: The Metamorphosis of Nineteenth-Century Japanese Art*, ed. Ellen P. Conant (Honolulu: University of Hawai'i Press, 2006), 153–176. The concepts are also discussed at length in: Maki Fukuoka, *The Premise of Fidelity: Science, Visuality, and Representing the Real in Nineteenth-Century Japan* (Stanford: Stanford University Press, 2012). Hirayama also connects the interest in "accuracy of vision" to imperial portraits in her article. Hirayama, "The Emperor's New Clothes."

17 Kyoto kokuritsu kindai bijutsukan, *Kōshitsu no meihin*, 329–330. Meiji Jingū, *Nisei Goseda Hōryū to kindai yoga no keifu: kindai no rekishiga no kaitakusha: Meiji Jingū kyōgaku kenkyū sentā* (Tokyo: Meiji Jingu, 2006).

18 These bans included images of the emperor and empress if they were defined with their official titles. By not labeling the images with text, printmakers and sellers were able to evade the laws. Hirayama, "The Emperor's New Clothes," 174–175, and Tōyama Shigeki, ed., *Nihon kindai shisōshi taikei: Tennō to kazoku* (Tokyo: Iwanami Shoten, 1988).

19 Migita Hiroki, "'Kōshitsu gurabia' to 'goshinei': senzenki shinbun zasshi ni okeru kōshitsu shashin no tsūjiteki bunseki," *Kyōtō shakaigaku nenpō* (2001): 94–96.

20 The companion print can also be found at the National Museum of Asian Art. https://asia.si.edu/object/S2003.8.2697/. Accessed June, 2021.

21 Mashino Keiko, "Meiji Tennō imeji no hensen ni tsuite: sekihanga ni miidaseru tennōzō," *Bijutsushi kenkyū* 38 (2000).
22 Sasaki Suguru, "Kindai tennō no imeji to zuzō," in *Hyōchō to geinō*, ed. Ōtsuka Shinichi, vol. 6 of *Tennō to ōken o kangaeru* (Tokyo: Iwanami shoten, 2002), 139–163, 145–146.
23 Richard Mitchell, *Censorship in Imperial Japan* (Princeton: Princeton University Press, 1983).
24 A detailed history of this dress, along with the imperial medallions and costume of Emperor Meiji, can be found in: Bunka Gakuen Fukushoku hakubutsukan, *Meiji, Taishō, Shōwa senzenki no kyūteifuku—yōsō to shōzoku* (Tokyo: Bunka Gakuen Fukushoku hakubutsukan, 2013).
25 The term *goshinei*, or honorable true shadow, was first used in 1888, sixteen years after the first formal portrait of Emperor Meiji was created. See: Hirayama, "The Emperor's New Clothes," 166. Hirase Reita, *"Shōzō" bunkakō* (Tokyo: Shunjusha, 2014), 33–57.
26 Kunaichō, *Meiji tennō ki* 7 (Tokyo: Yoshikawa Kōbunkan, 1972), 7–8.
27 Hirayama, "The Emperor's New Clothes," 167.
28 Keene, "Portraits of the Emperor Meiji," 21–22.
29 Kunaichō, *Meiji tennō ki* 7, 336–337. Interestingly, Hirayama cites this incident, stating in a footnote that Maruki later wrote that he worked on the *goshinei*, "after bathing and a period of abstinence, just like Shinto priests." Hirayama, "The Emperor's New Clothes," 180.
30 Kanagawa kenritsu rekishi hakubutsukan, *Oke no shōzō*, 21–22.
31 Hirayama, "The Emperor's New Clothes," 181.
32 For further analysis of the visual characteristics and iconography of the emperor's portrait, see: Wakakuwa Midori, *Kōgō no shōzō: Shōken kōtaigō no kyōshō to josei no kokuminka* (Tokyo: Chikuma Shobō, 2001), 38–48.
33 Wakakuwa, *Kōgō no shōzō*, 50–52.
34 Wakakuwa, *Kōgō no shōzō*, 112–113.
35 Wakakuwa cites this first appearance in European costume as July 30, 1887, Wakakuwa, *Kōgō no shōzō*, 56. The empress' proclamation was published in the *Chōya shinbun* on January 17, 1887. For an English translation, see: Julia Meech-Pakarik, *The World of the Meiji Print: Impressions of a New Civilization* (New York: Weatherhill, 1986), 129–130.
36 Karen Fraser details this change, along with the increasing visual use of *bijin* for nationalist and political purposes on

the international stage in the early twentieth century. Karen Fraser, "Beauty Battle: Politics and Portraiture in Late Meiji Japan," in *Visualizing Beauty: Gender and Ideology in Modern East Asia*, ed. Aida Yuen Wong (Hong Kong: Hong Kong University Press, 2012). The resulting change in public portraiture of women, particularly in the context of newspapers, is discussed in: Yoshimoto Hiroko, "Taishō shoki no shinbun ni miru kazoku shashin: Yomiuri shinbun, Tokyo Asahi shinbun o jirei toshite," *Matsuyama shinonome jyoshi daigaku jinbunkagaku bukiyou* 10 (2002–2003): 91–101. Yoshimoto discusses the difference in photographic treatment by gender in different Japanese newspapers of the Taishō period.

37 Migita, "Kōshitsu gurabia," 93–114, 98.

38 Migita, "Kōshitsu gurabia," 98.

39 Helen Hardacre, *Shintō and the State, 1868–1988* (Princeton: Princeton University Press, 1989), 33. Hardacre also states of the period between 1905 and 1930 that Shinto "priests were a great asset in universalizing such practices as formal veneration of the imperial portrait and the Imperial Rescript on Education," 23.

40 Regarding this change, philosopher and literary critic Kōjin Karatani states that the Meiji philosophers Uchimura and Okakura "were not unpatriotic, but their patriotism was revealed only to Westerners and was not directed internally. . . . The Taisho discursive space came into being with the eradication of the transcendent otherness and exteriority maintained by Uchimura Kanzo and Okakura Tenshin. . . . The Taisho discursive space emerged as an affirmation of 'Japanese nature,' and the eradication of the West and Asia as Other." Kojin Karatani and Seiji M. Lippit, "The Discursive Space of Modern Japan," *boundary 2* 18 (1991): 203–204.

41 Karatani and Lippit, "The Discursive Space of Modern Japan," 207.

42 Ying-chen Peng, *Artful Subversion: Empress Dowager Cixi's Image Making* (New Haven: Yale University Press, 2023), 51.

43 The image is not published with a date; rather it states "in adolescence" or "in childhood." I estimate her age to be approximately ten to twelve years old.

44 For more information on *Daikokumin*, and its stance as an anti-Christian nationalist publication, see Gregory Adam Scott, "Finding Aid for Daikokumin Records," *The Burke Library Archives*, Columbia University Libraries, Union Theological Seminary, New York, 2009, updated 2014, http://

library.columbia.edu/content/dam/libraryweb/locations/burke/fa/mrl/ldpd_4492622.pdf

45 For further analysis of the concept of women as the "receptacles of tradition" and the contrasting "symbol of mass culture" within the modern discourse, see: Rita Felski, *The Gender of Modernity* (Cambridge, MA: Harvard University Press, 1995). Also, Sarah Frederrick discusses a variety of gender issues surrounding women's magazines in the early twentieth century, including the mostly male editorial staffs and that many men read women's magazines—perhaps up to one-third of the readership of women's magazines in the Taishō period were male. Sarah Frederick, *Turning Pages: Reading and Writing Women's Magazines in Interwar Japan* (Honolulu: University of Hawai'i Press, 2006), 31–33.

46 On the development of British royal portraits, see: Jennifer Scott, *The Royal Portrait: Image and Impact* (London: The Royal Collection Trust, 2010).

47 Public sculpture of secular figures grew between 1880 and 1940 but was still relatively small in number compared to Euro-American spaces. Sven Saaler, *Men in Metal: A Topography of Public Bronze Statuary in Modern Japan* (Leiden: Brill, 2020).

48 Kyoto kokuritsu kindai bijutsukan, *Kōshitsu no meihin* 265, 332. A companion image of Emperor Taishō was also created in oil.

49 Alice Y. Tseng, "Imperial Portraiture and Popular Print Media in Early Twentieth-Century Japan," *Journal of Japanese Studies* 46, no. 2 (2020): 305–344.

50 The *goshinei* of Emperor Taishō was not only distributed to government buildings and schools but was also published in newspapers and magazines. The *goshinei* was distributed upon the occasion of the ascension to the throne in 1915. For an example of the distribution of the *goshinei* of Meiji and Taishō as compared within a single prefecture, see: Aoki Shōji, "Goshinei chokugo tōhon "hōan"no jissō: Yamagataken no jirei," in *Yamagataken hakubutsukan kenkyū hōkoku* 26 (2006): 13–38. Maruki Riyō served as an Imperial Household Artist, or Teishitsu gigei-in (帝室技芸員); a brief biography of the artist can be found in: Terry Bennett, *Photography in Japan, 1853–1912* (Tokyo: Tuttle Publishing, 2006), 317.

51 For further discussion of the personality and antics of Emperor Taishō, see: Hara Takeshi, "Emperor Taishō—Image vs. Reality," *Japan Quarterly* 48 (2001).

52 Natsume Sōseki, *Kokoro* (Tokyo: Kadokawa, 1952), 231.
53 Large printed hanging scrolls showing portraits of the entirety of the imperial lineage also became popular at this time. For examples, see Kanagawa kenritsu rekishi hakubutsukan, *Oke no shōzō*, Illustration 114, p. 73. This scroll shows portrait rounds of every emperor with Emperor Taishō at the bottom center as the rightful inheritor of 2,000 years of imperial history.
54 For further examples of these types of lithographs of the Imperial Family from the years surrounding 1900, see: Kanagawa kenritsu rekishi hakubutsukan, *Oke no shōzō*.
55 Kanō Mikiyo, *Tennōsei to gendā* (Tokyo: Inpakuto, 2002), 193–200.
56 Other scholars have chosen to focus on the patriarchal aspects of the lineage visible in the prints. For example, Mashino Keiko, "Meiji tennō imeji no hensen ni tsuite: sekihanga ni miidaseru tennōzō," *Bijutsushi kenkyū* 38 (2000): 52–53.
57 Theresa Earenfight, *The King's Other Body: Maria of Castile and the Crown of Aragon* (Philadelphia: University of Pennsylvania Press, 2009), 4.
58 Theresa Earenfight. "Without the Persona of the Prince: Kings, Queens and the Idea of Monarchy in Late Medieval Europe," *Gender and History* 19, no. 1 (2007): 1–21.
59 A similar scroll is published in: Mainichi Shinbunsha, *Tennō yondai no shōzō: Meiji Taishō Shōwa Heisei* (Tokyo: Mainichi Shinbunsha, 1999), 41–43. For further information on the emperor's image in this print, see: Alison J. Miller, "Coronation of Emperor Taishō," in *Divine Inspiration in Japanese Prints*, Spencer Museum of Art, 2012, www.spencerart.ku.edu/exhibitions/divine-inspiration/miller-taisho.shtml
60 Adrian C. Mayer, "Recent Succession Ceremonies of the Emperor of Japan," *Japan Review* 2 (1991).
61 The angular, top-down perspective used in the scroll was a common pictorial convention of the Heian period (794–1185), as was the use of flat areas of color without three-dimensional contouring and shadows. These techniques were popular in the nineteenth century among artists practicing *nihonga*, or neo-traditional Japanese painting. Traditional perspective and modeling was also present in the early twentieth-century revival of printmaking, known as *shinhanga*.
62 Her pregnancy is likely the reason that her *goshinei* was produced in 1916 as well. Tseng, "Imperial Portraiture and Popular Print Media in Early Twentieth-Century Japan." As of the Reiwa ascension, the women of the imperial household remain unable to attend the enthronement rituals.

63 Kanagawa kenritsu rekishi hakubutsukan, *Oke no shōzō*, 74–75.
64 Melanie Trede, "Banknote Design as a Battlefield of Gender Politics and National Representation in Meiji Japan," in *Performing "Nation": Gender Politics in Literature, Theater, and the Visual Arts of China and Japan, 1880–1940*, ed. Doris Croissant, Catherine Vance Yeh and Joshua Mostow (Leiden: Brill, 2008), 55–104.
65 The full text of the *Wei zhi*, or history of the Wei Dynasty, attributes societal order to the female ruler Himiko, who "occupied herself with magic and sorcery, bewitching the people." See: Ryusaku Tsunoda and L.C. Goodrich, eds., *Japan in the Chinese Dynastic Histories* (Pasadena: P.D. and Ione Perkins, 1951), 13–16.
66 Ben-Ami Shillony, *Enigma of the Emperors: Sacred Subservience in Japanese History* (Kent: Global Oriental, 2005), 36.
67 *Nihon shoki*, trans. Hideo Yamada (Tokyo: Kyōikusha, 1979).
68 The increased interest in popular female figures was part of a larger trend of nostalgia. Carol Gluck, "The Invention of Edo," in *Mirror of Modernity: Invented Traditions of Modern Japan*, ed. Stephen Vlastos (Berkeley: University of California Press, 1998); Itō Kimio, "The Invention of Wa and the Transformation of the Image of Prince Shōtoku in Modern Japan," in *Mirror of Modernity: Invented Traditions of Modern Japan*, ed. Stephen Vlastos (Berkeley: University of California Press, 1998).
69 "Jingū kōgō o dai 15dai on-rekidai ni kuwae," *Yomiuri Shinbun*, May 30, 1924.
70 Herbert P. Bix, *Hirohito and the Making of Modern Japan* (New York: Perennial, 2001), 182.
71 Emperor Shōwa and Empress Kōjun had seven children, two sons and five daughters six of the children lived to adulthood. Princess Sachiko passed away in 1928 at six months of age.
72 Hikari Hori, *Promiscuous Media: Film and Visual Culture in Imperial Japan, 1926–1945* (Cornell: Cornell University Press, 2017), 57.
73 Iwamoto Tsutomu, *Goshinei ni junijita kyōshitachi* (Tokyo: Ōtsuki shoten, 1989), 40–45.
74 Yuki Morishima, "Political and Ritual Usages of Portraits of Japanese Emperors in Eighteenth and Nineteenth Centuries" (PhD diss., University of Pittsburgh, 2014), 218–223.
75 Morishima, "Political and Ritual Usages of Portraits of Japanese Emperors in Eighteenth and Nineteenth Centuries," 191–207.

76 The Kunishite bunkazai tō dētabēsu [国指定文化財等データベース, Designated Cultural Properties Database], as managed by the Agency for Cultural Affairs, includes fifteen listed properties under the search *hōanden* [奉安殿]. https://kunishitei.bunka.go.jp/bsys/index_pc.asp, accessed July 3, 2019.
77 Ōhara Yasuo, "Shinto shirei [The Shinto Directive]," *Encyclopedia of Shinto*, Kokugakuin University, http://k-amc.kokugakuin.ac.jp/DM/dbTop.do?class_name=col_eos.
78 Michael Lucken, "Classical Greece in Japan. Why It Matters. A Postcolonial Perspective," in *The Visual Culture of Meiji Japan: Negotiating the Transition to Modernity*, ed. Ayelet Zohar and Alison J. Miller (New York: Routledge, 2021).
79 For more information on the *goshinei* of Emperor Taishō in the context of three specific prefectures, see: Ono Masaaki, "Taishō tennō no goshinei kafu to sono 'bōgo' keitai no mosaku: Miyazakiken ni yoru Kyūshū, Okinawa chihō kakuken no goshinei 'bōgo' jittaichōsa no imi," *Kyōiku shigakkai kiyō* 48 (2005). See also, Ono Masaaki, "Tennō no shōzō shashin (goshinei) to gakkō to no kankeishi kenkyū" (PhD diss., Nihon Daigaku, 2011).
80 Migita Hiroki, "Masu media no nakano teishitsu: Senzenki 'taishū tennōsei no keiseiteki ni kansuru rekishishakaigaku teki kōsatsu" (PhD diss., Kyoto University, 2006), 144–145.
81 This is in contrast with the Taishō era, wherein the structures were used primarily for the security of the images.
82 Hori, *Promiscuous Media*, 62.

5

FASHION, NATIONAL IDENTITY, AND THE COMMUNITY OF ROYALS

Global Monarchical Visual Culture Between the Meiji and Taishō Periods

In March 2023, NHK broadcast the documentary "Royal Mysteries: Secrets of the Empress' Dress."[1] Reviewing the methods and techniques utilized in the five-year restoration of the 130-year-old *daireifuku* (大礼服), a ceremonial European-style dress with a long train and luxurious embroidery once worn by Empress Shōken, the documentary compares the dress to those found in France and Britain and raises the possibility that the fabric and construction were Japanese, rather than European, as previously thought. Just as the documentary made a splash in the media when it was released, museum exhibitions of Japanese imperial women's dresses are popular events held at regular intervals. Imperial fashion in Japan remains today a means of connecting the current and historic visual monarchy with the populace, in the same way as royal sartorial stories, exhibitions, and social media accounts connect celebrity monarchs to commoners the world over.

As an integral part of royal image making, fashion sent, and sends, many messages to the viewing public. Be it historic costume or the latest trends, the clothing worn by the Japanese imperial family, and also by the crowned heads of other nations as represented in Japanese media, communicated concepts of nationalism, cosmopolitanism, closeness, distance, wealth, and legitimacy. As established in Chapter 4, the clothing worn in formal and official portraiture was a central means of expression, and the Imperial

DOI: 10.4324/9781003376101-8

Household Ministry, along with the imperial family themselves, realized the power held by sartorial selections and image early on in the modern period, harnessing it to project the royal image in a myriad of ways.

This chapter begins by examining the empress' fashions in woodblock prints in the context of the newly globalized sphere of monarchy, considering clothing and national identity. It then contrasts this with images of global monarchy found in photography and amidst imperial expansion, positioning the empresses at a pivot point of Europe and East Asia. The subsequent section takes a comparative and temporal approach to the images of the two modern empresses in the women's magazine *Fujin gahō*, looking at how each empress fit differing versions of the *ryōsai kenbo*, or "good wife, wise mother" ideology in the early twentieth century. The final section analyzes changes in the ideology and how these were modeled by the imperial women.

Clothing and the Global Sphere of Meiji Monarchy

In 1870s prints, and into the early 1880s, Empress Shōken was dressed exclusively in Japanese-style clothing, as she is in *Bankoku ishō kagami* (Mirror of National Costumes of All Nations) (Figure 5.1) by Kobayashi Kiyochika. In this print she wears many layers of fabric indicative of historic court costumes. The form of her body is hidden, and her hair is done in the styles of the Edo and Bakumatsu periods beneath her crown. In 1887, Shōken issued an edict on European-style clothing.

> Now we can no longer restrict ourselves to bowing from a kneeling position, but will have to observe the new (Naniwa) style of bowing while standing. Moreover, if we look at contemporary Western women's wear, we find that it combines a top or jacket and a skirt in the manner of our ancient Japanese system of dress. This is not only suitable for the formal standing bow but also convenient for action and movement and makes it only natural to adopt the Western method of sewing.[2]

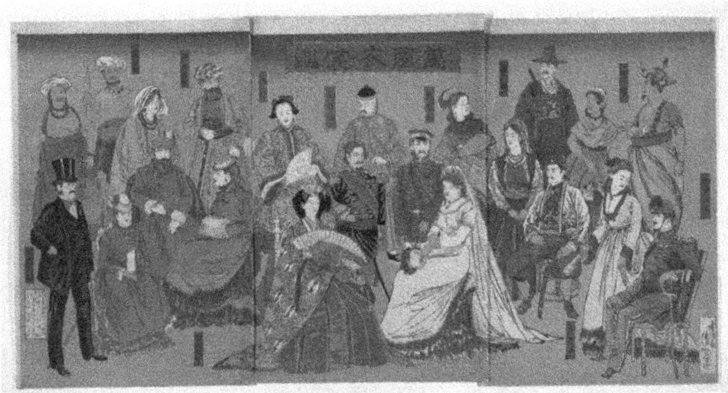

FIGURE 5.1 *Bankoku ishō kagami* (Mirror of National Costumes of All Nations) Kobayashi Kiyochika, 1882, multicolor woodblock print, Metropolitan Museum of Art

The emperor issued an edict on court dress 16 years earlier, in 1871, which states:

> The national polity is indomitable, but manners and customs should be adaptable. We greatly regret that the uniform of our court has been established following the Chinese custom, and it has become exceedingly effeminate in style and character. We should no longer appear before the people in these effeminate styles, and we have therefore decided to reform dress regulations entirely.[3]

It is notable that his edict focuses on Chinese influence and gendered interpretations, while hers is on clothing function and centering modern styles of dress in Japanese history. His edict is concerned with the political implications of global monarchical image and separating Japan from the Sinosphere, while hers concentrates on practicality of movement. Some of the difference lies in current politics; in 1871 Japan was in the early stages of entering the global political and industrial sphere, whereas in 1887 Japan was nearing dominance in East Asia and held a more central role on the world stage. In many of the early Meiji prints of Shōken where she wears historic dress, she is seated, while in later images where she wears European-style attire, she is in an active pose, bringing the utility of newly adopted styles of dress to life in visual culture, with words and images reflecting each other.

Mirror of National Costumes of All Nations was released in 1882, between the imperial dress edicts. Shōken is seated in the foreground, dressed in layers of fabric, with an elaborate crown and large fan that partially obscures both her body and that of Emperor Meiji, standing immediately behind her. The immensity of the pine-decorated fan and its role in hiding the corporeal presence of the Japanese emperor and empress can be read as a nod to historic court practices of keeping the sovereign hidden behind a curtain. In a similar fashion, the tiny trail of the empress' robe that pools on the ground, subtly peeking into the left panel, is reminiscent of the small hints of fabric that represented hidden figures in Heian paintings of court life.[4] These visual references to historic court culture are contradicted by the feminine presence of the Meiji empress as the central focal point of the print, her very existence a sign of the modern monarchy, but also provide an imagined link to the long imperial lineage.

Although Shōken and Meiji are recognizable, the representatives of the other nations are anonymous or imagined: this is not an accurate group portrait of royalty. The British couple that sits immediately to the right of the Japanese imperial pair have some visual similarities to Queen Victoria and Prince Albert in their youth, but Albert died in 1861 and Victoria was in her early sixties at the time of this print. Other represented nations such as France had abolished monarchy, while India was a British colony at the time. The United States was founded on anti-monarchical ideals, or in the case of the vaguely represented Arabia or Africa, the depicted couple were imagined as cultural conglomerations.

While the pairs that the Japanese emperor and empress are surrounded by ambiguously represent the appearance of royals from each region, both the gender balance among represented leaders and the message of the print, that the Japanese royals were at the forefront of global court culture, is clear. Shōken and Meiji are aligned with France, England, and the United States, as read from right to left in the front row. Positioned in the middle ground are Turkey and Russia, again right and left, and in the back are India, Korea, China, Arabia, and Africa, forming a global hierarchy of nations. Shōken's body language and costuming also show her significance in this scene. Most of the other women gaze either at their partners, at each other, or at Shōken, with America and Africa being exceptions. She represents what can be interpreted as the distinctive position of Japan: Shōken and Meiji are the only couple who are wearing different clothing, he in European-inspired military costume and she in historically inspired dress. France, Britain, Russia, and the United States are outfitted in up-to-date 1880s fashions, but Turkey, India, Korea, China, Arabia, and Africa, the non-Euro-American countries, wear historically inspired costumes. Shōken here occupies a space among the world powers of the foreground but dressed in clothing that works to maintain Japan's distinct cultural identity. Although the invented nature of this print means it is not a literal image of court life, it positions Shōken and Meiji at the center of a fantasy of global royalty and leadership, and, like the imagined court scenes from the imperial palace in Tokyo (see Chapter 2), this illusory print allowed Japanese citizens to feel a sense of pride, knowledge, and intimacy with their sovereigns.

Shōken continued to appear in historic costume in a variety of settings, including at the horse racing track at Shinobazu Pond in Ueno Park in a Chikanobu print from 1885.[5] As the imperial image transitioned from woodblock prints to lithographs and on to photographs, historic dress became increasingly rare. Although *Mirror of National Costumes of All Nations* embeds the imperial family in a fantasy of global monarchy, in the context of the Meiji period most buyers would not have viewed the Japanese imperial family alongside their global counterparts. That would change after the turn of the twentieth-century.

The Milieu of Global Monarchy: Positioning the Imperial Family in Europe and Asia

While the public feminine face of the Japanese imperial family was new in the modern period, in other monarchical nations, woman sovereigns were commonplace in the early twentieth century. Early imperial imagery in the women's magazine *Fujin gahō,* introduced in Chapter 3, includes significant coverage of global royalty, particularly that of Europe and East Asia. Images such as a reprinted engraving of the June 3 Berlin wedding of the Crown Prince Wilhelm and Duchess Cecilie in Berlin published in the frontmatter of *Fujin gahō* in July 1905 are similar in style to the Taishō wedding prints from just five years earlier. The scene is composed of a fixed perspective, but the figures are seen from a variety of angles to allow the viewer to see the most action possible. The faces of the matrimonial couple are hardly discernible, with the focus on the officiant and the witnesses, as well as the fashions of the bride and her attendants, a large crowd visible in the background. Other European royals were also featured in the early pages of the magazine, such as the British Queen Alexandra and the wedding of Princess Margaret of Connaught and Prince Gustavus Adolphus of Sweden in 1905, the latter in an engraving that was also featured on the cover of the Illustrated London News. The styles all bear similarity to images of the Japanese imperial family and nobility that shared the same pages, evidence of a global visual language of monarchy.

Members of the Korean and Chinese courts also appeared in *Fujin gahō's* image-heavy front matter. In sharp contrast to the modernity and cosmopolitan glamour of the European images, the East Asian royals were dressed in historic costumes with few signs of contemporaneity, such as the Chinese princess (listed as Princesses Ching and Shun of China), who appeared in September 1909 dressed in traditional costumes and published opposite Japanese nobility in the latest European fashions, riding in fanciful horse-drawn carriages. Just two months after Japan's annexation of Korea, *Fujin gahō* published the formal wedding portraits of Sunjong, Emperor Yunghui, and Empress Sunjeong, listed as "Prince and Princess Lio Shōtokukyū, ex-emperor of Korea," in October 1910 (Figure 5.2). At the time of annexation, the Korean royals were stripped of their titles and brought into the structure of the Japanese nobility, one of many cultural usurpations of the Japanese colonial era.

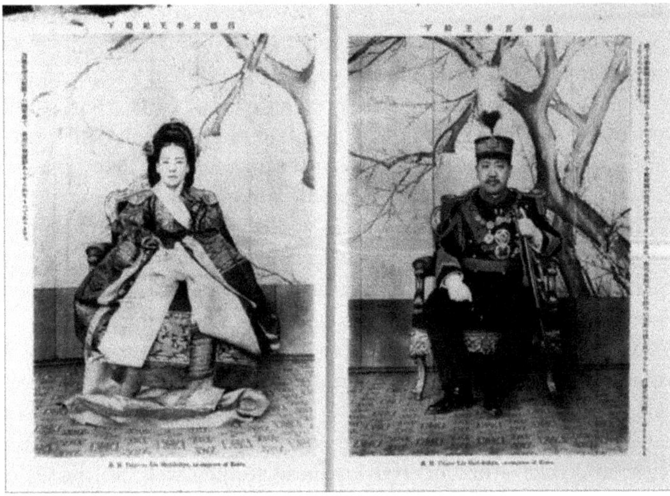

FIGURE 5.2 *Shōtokukyū riō denka and Shōtokukyū riō denka* (Prince and Princess Lio Shōtokukyū, ex-emperor of Korea), *Fujin gahō,* October 1910, n/p (frontmatter)

In their photographs, Emperor Sunjong is pictured seated in an elaborate European-style chair with patterned carpet and a painting of a tree on the backdrop, wearing his military uniform. He sits casually, with a slightly slouched posture, relaxed legs, and blank facial expression, leading him to appear weak when viewed alongside the boastful and confident postures that were common for European and Japanese noblemen in military uniform. Both photographs were shot in front of the same studio background; in his, more of the tree appears at the right side of the photograph, distracting from his clothing, the dark colors of his uniform and the tree blending together, while in Empress Sunjeong's, less of the painted tree is seen, lending an austere effect to the image. She is dressed in a luxurious and elaborate historic costume, the layers of opulent textiles hiding her body and the chair. In both photographs the harsh lighting and high contrast would have felt anachronistic for studio portraiture of royalty in 1910. Although not uncommon for photographs taken outdoors, the flat appearance arising from the dark shadows of Emperor Sunjong's image and the bright highlights of Empress Sunjeong's, together with the combination of him in a military uniform and her in historic costuming, were reminiscent of early Meiji studio portraits and were a subtle way of reinforcing colonial hierarchies. Published more than thirty years after the first Japanese imperial photographs were released, amidst a photo-heavy publication, and at a time when the power of photography and image making were well understood, this pair of images depicts Korean leadership as traditional and weak and enforces the political message of the expanding Japanese empire as a civilizing force.

Common to both European and Asian royal photographs was the central visual role of women. By showing how European royals utilized female sovereigns, the Japanese empresses, princesses, and women of the nobility appeared more moderate to a Japanese audience—the imperial Japanese women were not heads of state, and even when acting as proxies, as in the regency period, they maintained a greater degree of subtlety in their rulership and cultural positioning. The East Asian photographs, by contrast, show a vision of leadership that would have appeared as feminized in the context of early twentieth century Japan. The inclusion of global monarchs in *Fujin gahō* thus served many purposes: it provided legitimacy by demonstrating a distant association with European royalty by means of optical parallels but simultaneously made Japanese women royals appear conservative and less threatening. Concurrently, it worked to include East Asian monarchs in the larger milieu of the Japanese nobility, cementing ideas of empire by utilizing traditional attire and unrefined imaging, which by contrast elevated the cosmopolitan nature of the Japanese imperial family.[6] Furthermore, the didactic function of all imperial and royal images established a conventional form that was normalized by placing it within the sphere of global monarchy.

Royal fashion and the community of global monarchy was an important part of validating, justifying, and securing the role and future of the Japanese imperial family. Utilizing woodblock prints, mass media photography, and fashion was a logical means of promoting the messages of imperialism and legitimacy expressed by the corporate monarchy. In the Shōwa and Heisei years, as well as today, state visits and royal callings remain common means of connecting monarchs around the world, and royal fashions are still analyzed in the mass media, showing the lasting power of fashion and community in maintaining the imperial presence. These globally embedded messages were the outward facing aspect of fashion and national identity for the imperial women, contrasted with domestic values and ideas of the virtues of women as modeled by their empress.

Fashion, Femininity, and *Ryōsai kenbo*

Located at the pivot point of European and East Asian monarchies, the Japanese empresses consistently maintained a conventionally feminine look, positioned with demure gestures and postures, regardless of their sartorial selections being historic or contemporary. While their roles were somewhat flexible, and their identities never protean, the gendered appearance of Shōken and Teimei did not court controversy or push the boundaries of acceptability too far. Elements of empress images from *Fujin gahō* that were intended for a domestic audience, including monarchical dress, staging, and the selection of events covered, indicate how the imperial household utilized soft power strategies to craft the public visual monarchy in a feminine space and show how these images were used to promote the values of *ryōsai kenbo*, or "good wife, wise mother." These virtues were in line with universal traits of queenship such as maternity, piousness, thrift, and, in the modern era, nationalism.

Ryōsai kenbo was a theory of womanhood which had its roots in the late nineteenth century, and as a state ideology it continued through the mid-twentieth century, with subtle changes through time.[7] First coined by school principal Nakamura Masanao in the early 1870s, the concept was made manifest in school textbooks and government policies and trickled down to influence everyday familial gender dynamics.[8] Similar to moral campaigns undertaken around the world in the late nineteenth and early twentieth century, the principles of *ryōsai kenbo* promoted the idea that women should be broadly educated so as to be supporters to their children and husbands and to provide a strong societal foundation vis-à-vis their role as homemakers and home economists, thus positioning women as supporters of national aims within the framework of the home and community.[9] Government officials were concerned about contradictory notions of women: on the one hand there was worry over the "woman problem" (women growing too liberal and free-thinking in their mores), yet on the other hand military officials fretted about housewives being too insular and not having the skills and preparedness as individuals and family leaders to ready their sons and the home front for military activity. These contradictory impulses resulted in the promotion of specific versions of the *ryōsai kenbo* ideology, which differed through the decades, and were modeled in the images of the empresses, princesses, and nobility as published in women's magazines such as *Fujin gahō*.

Conventional gender roles, as they stood in the Taishō period, were constructed during the reign of Emperor Meiji. With the codification of the Civil Code 民法, (*minpō*) of 1898, patriarchy, patriliny, primogeniture, and the monogamous family became legal standards. The *ryōsai kenbo* ideology reinforced these bureaucratic principles with cultural norms, making the government construction of the feminine ideal a comprehensive model in which women were to maintain tradition and care for the family and domestic affairs, and men were to undertake wage labor outside the home, tending to government, business, and industry. Yet these values were ideals and were not reflective of reality; in the mid-Meiji period, for example, women constituted a majority of industrial workers through their participation in silk manufacturing. Social and political tensions regarding the role of women were present throughout the late nineteenth and early twentieth century, but images of the imperial women in the late Meiji period exhibit the conventional form alone.

The first woman of the Japanese royal family to appear in the pages of *Fujin gahō* was Teimei during her tenure as crown princess; the empress herself would appear in the second year of publication, in a July 1906 image depicting Shōken as she read a message to the attendees of a June Red Cross meeting. Shōken is dressed in light colors; the caption tells us her dress was light pink, and she is framed by the banners and poles of the stage. Her subjects, dressed in dark colors, gaze up at the empress from below with heads angled down in a respectful bow, the viewer's perspective also gazing up at the empress as the audience does, from below. This establishes the style of empress images in the pages of *Fujin gahō*: Shōken appears as demure and feminine, her head elevated above her surrounding attendants, and her body above her subjects. The queenly virtues exhibited in the pages of the magazine are the same as those outlined in Chapter 2: maternity, piety, charity, and work, and diplomacy. The banner behind her, constructed of thick stripes, is gathered at the left, making it visually reminiscent of the rising sun flag. Combined with the source of light for the image coming from the left, the empress stands illuminated and reflects this radiance onto her citizens as they appear in front of her, an apt metaphor for her role vis-à-vis the emperor and the women of the realm.

Just a month later, in August of 1906, an image of Empress Shōken was published on the sixth page of *Fujin gahō* (Figure 5.3).

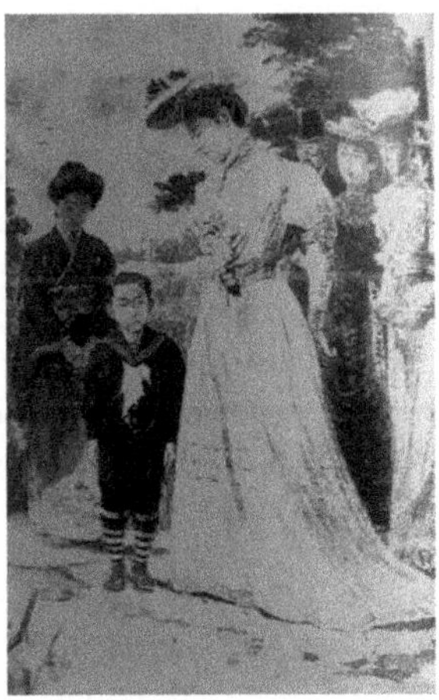

FIGURE 5.3 *Kōgō heika to Kaneko danshaku bessō* (Her Majesty the Empress Visiting Baron Kaneko's Villa), *Fujin gahō*, August 1906, page 6

Captioned *Kōgō heika to Kaneko danshaku bessō* (Her Majesty the Empress Visiting Baron Kaneko's Villa), Shōken is shown in a matronly role, exhibiting a highly conventional feminine appearance and serving as a model for both the concept of the imperial mother (*kokubo*), as well as standards of imperial feminine beauty and propriety in the late Meiji period. Empress Shōken is depicted at the center of the frame; she is taller than the other people in the composition, and the placement of her in the foreground, combined with her central location, provides her with a more striking presence than the attendants standing off to the right of the picture plane, as she rests her hand atop the head of the young Kaneko boy.[10] Her posture is regal and confident, and her facial expression is calm as well as neutral. The way in which she gently pats the young child's head, as well as her soft expression and carriage, provide a maternal feel to the piece, her hat sheltering the boy. In regard to her fashions, the lines in the drapery folds of her skirt, combined with the large adornment on her bodice, give an element of stability and strength to her form. Although in life Empress Shōken was petite in stature, in this image, partially through the use of perspective, and also through artistic liberties, she possesses a grace and elegance in her exaggerated figure, dominating the picture plane. The dress that she wears is significantly corseted, with a fabric belt emphasizing the small size of her waist. Additionally, the light color of her garb stands out against the dark hues of the surrounding figures and the tree in the background; this brightness emphasizes her monarchical stature and, combined with the sweeping lines of her skirt and bodice, leads the eye to the outline of her facial profile.

Other images of Empress Shōken featured in *Fujin gahō* include photographs, etchings, and reproductions of paintings and show the empress sporting a similar sartorial style. In each, Shōken wears a floor length, corseted, S-shaped dress and a large wide-brimmed hat, as was the fashion of the first decade of the twentieth century.[11] Her dress includes the slight flare at the ankles and the snug hips that were popular in the years leading up to 1909, as well as the flounced blouse with buoyant fabric comprising the shoulders and upper arms that was so common in the silhouettes of the day. Furthermore, in all of the reproduced images, Empress Shōken wears the lavish, opulent millinery style that marked fashion in the 1900s; her hats, topped with large floral décor and full ribbons, include a small veil, which was often used when in transit, as it would assist in keeping the hat balanced upon the head. The fashion serves two purposes: first off, through composition choices and details, Empress Shōken's clothing works to distinguish her figure from the others in the image; second, the styles are an example of in vogue trends that were acceptable for women of upper and upper-middle class to wear, such as tight, corseted bodices; layers of gathered fabric on the front of the torso; a wide-shouldered silhouette with fitted sleeves in the forearm; and a flowing, long skirt with a slight bustle.[12]

Numerous scholars have addressed the importance of clothing for the monarchy throughout time and across cultures. Specifically, historian Kate Strasdin's work on Queen Alexandra (1844–1925, r. 1901–1910) is relevant for her theorizing of the monarchical wardrobe as both a material and conceptual notion that provided a space to create powerful messages for multiple audiences.[13] Considering the role of the corporate monarchy—in this instance comprising tailors, attendants, and dressers—Strasdin's argument that clothing is a means of understanding the larger workforce that constitutes the royal apparatus is relevant for the later *Fujin gahō* photographs and also for reading the clothing archive itself. In the pre-photography images though, the empress' clothing can be best understood in a context of artistic interpretation: the fashions of Empress Shōken are not a reflection of reality but an expression of her values. Regardless of their tie to reality, the fashions of the Japanese modern empresses, together with the settings, postures, subject matter, and media outlet, communicate the values of queenship of relevance to the specific situation.

Each of these images also presents Empress Shōken with an averted gaze. In every instance, the monarch is either looking down at an object or upon her subjects or, in the case of a carriage image, off into the distance. This stands in sharp contrast to later empresses, who on multiple occasions gazed directly into the camera. Shōken's attendants and subjects also avert their gaze, thus lending a tense feeling of reverence to the scenes. The downcast eyes of those represented in the compositions work to lead the viewer to the central empress figure, who is located at either the top of or the center of the image.[14]

In the Meiji period, the *ryōsai kenbo* ideology was relatively conservative, as the conception of "good wife, wise mother" was still emerging from earlier philosophies of women's positions, which included Confucian-influenced ideas of women as belonging strictly within the domestic realm. The images of Empress Shōken featured in the early days of *Fujin gahō* were created before upper-class women held jobs in the public sphere and at a time when feminist movements were harshly controlled. These factors led to monotonous public images of Shōken interacting primarily with the young and ill, resulting in a conservative account of maternal and feminine roles.

In addition to these concerns, Empress Shōken was seen visiting the Tokyo Industrial Exhibition in the August 1, 1907, edition of *Fujin gahō*. The Meiji government recognized women as an integral part of the modern Japanese nation, not just for their contributions to homemaking, child rearing, and caretaking but also for their heavy involvement in factory work. The majority of textile factory workers in the late nineteenth century were women, and as such they were responsible for one of the largest sources of economic power and foreign income in mid-Meiji Japan. Maintaining the productivity of the female workforce was of the utmost importance to the national project; one way to encourage morale among the youthful workforce was for the empress to acknowledge their contributions. The realities of women's participation in industrial production were generally hidden from public view, and when they were widely visible in woodblock prints, imperial visits, or at model factory displays at the fairs, the conditions were presented as far safer and more sanitary than they were in reality. As a symbol of female leadership who visited factories and the industrial exhibitions which featured manufactured textiles, and who shared physical space with women workers, Shōken showed women of the working classes how important their work was to the nation. This also fulfilled her role as mother of the nation and continued her association with sericulture, which was addressed in Chapter 2.

Katano Masako identifies the *kokubo* (国母, mother of the nation) as a crucial component of the modern court revolution that created a permanent, compulsory imperial household. She details Shōken's development as a public figure and the shift in activities of the imperial women which emerged over the late nineteenth century, determining that this change was key to the court revolution.[15] Reinforcing the repetition of the visual monarchy in vernacular media such as *Fujin gahō* was central to this crafting of imperial identity. As Shōken never had biological children of her own, picturing her as a caretaker was a way to link her to maternal roles, which was of particular interest in the context of women's magazines. The strategy of adoption to ensure succession and to maintain a queen's place in the royal family was utilized in a variety of times and places, including Joseon Korea and seventeenth-century Nayaka South India, and the promotion of the ideal of mother of the nation was used by other childless queens, including Mary and Elizabeth Tudor and Anne Stuart, all evidence of the centrality of maternity to global queenship.[16] Furthermore, the formal elements of the images also show a soft, caring femininity that connected Shōken to sentiments of family and motherly qualities, both of which were important in cementing the feminine roles of the newly public imperial family.

Evolving Values and Changes in Media: *Ryōsai kenbo* and the Rise of Imperialism

With the conventional media form of the empress established in the first few years of publication, imperial images in *Fujin gahō* remained stable over the 1910s. Reproduced engravings and paintings were slowly eliminated, replaced by photography, and layouts changed to include a handful of images set against decorative backgrounds and frames, as opposed to a single image on a page. At the start of the Taishō era, not much differentiated the representations of the empresses in the pages of the magazines; the newly crowned Empress Teimei was envisioned in a similar fashion to her predecessor, as a fashion icon and representative of conventional *ryōsai kenbo* values. It is within the details and nuances of the images over time that the differences in women's social roles are evident: over the course of the 1920s, *ryōsai kenbo* ideologies changed, in concert with the imaging of the empresses. Empress fashions were an important component of their images as arbiters of *ryōsai kenbo* values—to successfully promote the role of the good wife, wise mother, empress images necessitated a stylish demeanor, so as to be a desirable role model.

By the 1920s, Japan held a secure position in international political spheres and had thoroughly modernized, yet there were still domestic concerns regarding the balance between modernity and identity.[17] As women were seen as symbols of the new commercial culture, and as their roles had changed in a more drastic way than their male counterparts, much of the anxiety regarding the loss of identity and traditions was directed toward women, whose roles and choices were scrutinized and judged to a higher degree than those of their male counterparts.

With the competing needs for an appropriate role for women to play in the development of the Japanese empire, and the desire to steer women away from morals which were deemed inappropriate or unacceptable in Taishō Japan, came the development of a Taishō-specific *ryōsai kenbo* ideology. The philosophy was expressed to the general citizenry in a variety of modes, most conspicuously via state-issued textbooks. For example, in the 1930 version of the upper-level ethics reader, *The Revised Morals Teachings for Young Girls*, young women were instructed on the role of the married couple within the family unit and that in Japan the family should model itself after that of the imperial household, ensuring the continuity of the nation into the future.[18]

The "good wife, wise mother" of the 1920s was decidedly different from her Meiji predecessor in a few key ways and in response to three key social changes: the rise of so-called "woman problem" (婦人問題, *fujin mondai*), the participation of European and American women in home front activities during the First World War, and a concern over deteriorating living conditions in the post–First World War era.[19] In response to these changes, the "good wife, wise mother" was expected to contribute to society not just through childrearing and domestic work but also through part-time or occasional work outside the home. As Koyama Shizuko states, "again, there came to be an expectation that women, rather than pursuing a masculine role by seeking employment, should display suitably feminine moral characteristics, such as kindness, in their engagement in social work for the betterment of society."[20] Taishō women were not expected to mimic the roles of men, nor were they confined to family life as in the Meiji period, but rather they were to take on a distinctly feminine role in supporting the nation and empire. The expanded concept of the *ryōsai kenbo* is further explained by Barbara Sato:

> For a woman, it was no longer enough to simply look after her husband in order to be considered a good wife. Rather, the understanding of a "good wife" had altered to include the management of family consumption and an awareness of her contribution to the national economy.[21]

As the roles of women were changing in response to consumer culture, military concerns, and fretting over morality, it follows that the visual roles of the empresses were also to undergo changes throughout the early twentieth century, with less attention to conventional femininity and an increase in public appearances related to political concerns.

While feminist movements such as Seitōsha attempted to counter the limitations of *ryōsai kenbo* and campaigned for expanded roles and rights for women outside of the ideological constraints of the doctrine, the changes in the official ideology in the 1920s made *ryōsai kenbo* ideas more palatable to average citizens. There was an understanding among government officials that the doctrine was seen as old-fashioned, and as these officials worked to continually promote it, they also saw the necessity of keeping it relevant to women.[22] As women, and men, became accustomed to and accepting of consuming images of women in the media, it became increasingly important to provide acceptable female images which supported government ideologies. Simultaneously, as women gained greater voices in society, it became necessary for *ryōsai kenbo* ideologies to appear adaptable to women's concerns and to seem as if the ideology were produced for consumption by women.

Creating the illusion that *ryōsai kenbo* values were innate, internalized, and instinctual to women, rather than a top-down doctrine, was important to promoting the concept to the public. If the *ryōsai kenbo* ideology was seen as something which appeared to be a natural, self-motivating impulse rather than a state-constructed ideology, it would be much more successful. To achieve this normalization of the value system made women feel as if the ideology were an internal instinct, and one with great importance; this was accomplished by appealing to the maternal component of *ryōsai kenbo*. In what cultural historian Michiko Mae claims was an "example of a modern doctrine concealed as a Japanese cultural tradition," women had three main roles in the *ryōsai kenbo* system: as birth mothers to citizens and soldiers, as the transmitters of national culture and identity, and as a symbol of what men needed to protect.[23] For the most part, these core concepts remained the same even as the nuance of the ideology evolved with society. Constructing the good wife, wise mother as an important figure who was central to the success of Japanese society was in part accomplished by using the empress as a fashionable role model; if *ryōsai kenbo* was important enough for the imperial household to perform, surely it should be emulated by the masses. Requisite for this model was an empress that was desirable for emulation: an aspirational and compelling celebrity royal.

As was the common style in the 1920s as well as previous decades, Empress Teimei's clothing in the *Fujin gahō* image set exhibits a straight silhouette with little emphasis on the curved and constricted form of the female anatomy. Her clothing mirrored the international trends for women to wear smaller hats and tailored suits which drew their inspiration from menswear. By the late Meiji period, most urban men had adopted suits as their common dress.[24] Although women had fully adopted Euro-American hairstyles by the 1890s, and had incorporated other accessories such as handbags and umbrellas, it was not until the 1930s that women fully adopted Euro-American-style dress, and even then it was not as common as Japanese styles.[25] Within the realm of Japanese-style clothing, the kimono styles that were worn by Japanese women in the 1920s had changed dramatically from those of their grandmothers.[26] Elements of Euro-American fashion, such as hats, leather shoes, and overcoats were mixed in, creating a hybrid of styles. The construction of the kimono itself had also changed, with the *obi* (kimono belt) worn higher on the waist, mimicking the straight-silhouetted menswear-inspired fashions that were so popular in Europe and the United States. Furthermore, the fabrics of the early twentieth-century kimono incorporated modern patterns, weaves, and materials.[27] Thus, by the Taishō period, the categories of Japanese-style and European-style clothing were not as clear cut as they once were. When fashions did change, concepts of thrift, ease of wear, and freedom of movement all contributed to the move from Japanese clothing to European styles. That the silhouette of Japanese and European dress styles was similar in the 1920s also was a probable contributor towards the shift in fashion; the slim, straight look of European-style dresses was markedly similar to kimono lines, making the transition easier.[28]

Since the Meiji period, the women of the imperial household were frequent visitors to the many cultural exhibitions held in Tokyo, an activity reflected in woodblock prints and subsequently in photography. In July 1922, the women's magazine *Fujin gahō* published a photograph of Empress Teimei as she left the Peace Exhibition in Ueno Park (Figure 3.1). In the photograph, she looks directly at the camera as she walks away from the exhibition building, with the light color of her parasol and dress framing her face. Her expression is serious and flat; this is not the soft, gentle face which was common with her processor Empress Shōken, but rather Teimei bears the visage of a monarch with additional clout and a more prominent role in the court structure and larger society.

In addition to the sartorial style of Empress Teimei, the gaze of the female monarch was a feature that distinguished her from her predecessor and marked the newness of her comportment; the men in the photograph look at her, but she looks at the photographer and, by proxy, the viewer. In the imperial woodblock prints of the Meiji period, Shōken was typically the central subject, but the compositions, colors, patterns, and her invented, stylized facial expressions lent a visual uniformity to the woodblock prints. The photographs of the Taishō period, by contrast, show the empress outside of the palace walls and, by the nature of the medium, lend her a sense of agency.

The text accompanying the photograph states that Teimei stayed at the park until evening to enjoy the night scenery. This phrasing contributes to a reading of her as independent and modern; like so many women interested in exploring their city, she was out in the evening hours, and while accompanied by her court handlers, she was without her husband, a fact that is accentuated by the space around her.[29] The composition of the image, combined with the comportment of the empress, shows that the parties involved in creating this photograph were savvy to the powerful role of vernacular media in constructing the visual monarchy and actively deployed photographers, handlers, and the empress herself to make the images successful. Numerous examples show the same phenomenon, Teimei strolling through gardens, the sole figure in the frame; Teimei as she departs museum exhibitions, views citizens performing traditional dances, or visits notable schools. In nearly every example, she is distant but close enough to view her clothing, and in most images her figure is framed by the architecture of the location.

Just one month earlier, *Fujin gahō* published a photograph of Teimei together with the Prince of Wales and Crown Prince Hirohito viewing cherry blossoms at the famed Shinjuku gyoen (Figure 5.4). As they process through an unremarkable section of the park, which was originally a private residence but transitioned into an imperial garden by the early twentieth century, Hirohito looks at the camera, dressed in military uniform. Teimei walks in the middle of the path, her bright white dress and hat attracting the eye at the center of the photograph. The only other woman in the image is one of the princesses of the blood, dressed in a more subdued tone with a large black boa and hat, her position near a large tree visually pulling her figure into the background. At the right is the Prince of Wales, standing separate from the rest of the group as he walks forward and gazes to the side. This image is remarkable in that it shows Teimei in the same frame as her son, a rare instance of this familial closeness that was published during the Taishō period, and it also shows Teimei hosting a foreign royal, and a male prince, at that, once again positioning the Japanese imperial family in the milieu of global monarchy. Photographs of the cherry blossom viewing were

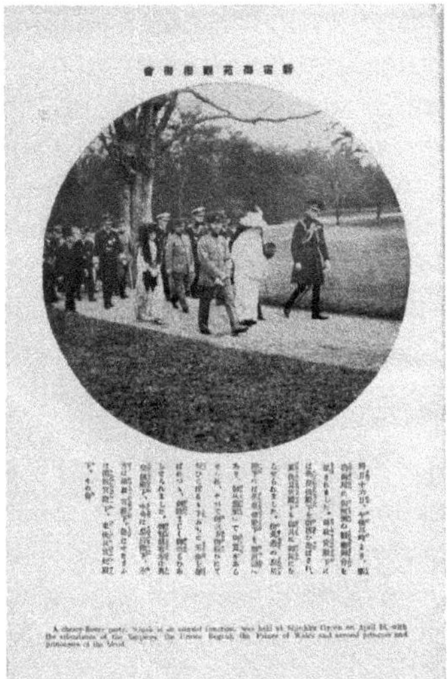

FIGURE 5.4 *Shinjuku gyoen kan-ō gokai* (Gathering to View Cherry Blossoms at Shinjuku Gyoen), *Fujin gahō*, June, 1922, n/p (front matter)

published across newspapers and magazines. In other available versions the image is cropped closer, and Teimei can be seen with a smile on her face, also a distinct and remarkable difference from the vast majority of her photographic record. While the Shinjuku gyoen photograph is an anomaly, it was not completely out of form and represents one end of the spectrum of empress images in the late Taishō period, one that lent the empress a relatable and engaging public persona.

The alluring celebrity persona that was constructed through Teimei's sartorial selections and common activities imbued the popular empress with an aura of trust among her people, one that her handlers at the Imperial Household Ministry could utilize in order to promote specific *ryōsai kenbo* values to the general populace, allowing the visual monarchy to act in a "soft power" fashion.

This chapter examined the fashions of Empress Shōken and Empres Teimei in the context of the global monarchy as well as in their roles as exemplars of *ryōsai kenbo* values in the pages of *Fujin gahō*. Acting as the exemplary woman of the realm, the empress figure was a slate on which to inscribe the values and virtues of the day, just as queenship has always acted as both a mirror of and an influencer on social values. In the Meiji and Taishō periods, these values were rapidly changing along with the empress image and empress role, transformations that were occurring in the public sphere. Flexible through time, the image does not reflect the empress as individual—her agency is difficult to discern in any specific image—but shows the sum influence of the corporate monarchy, including artists, the Imperial Household Ministry, the press, the citizenry, and the empress herself. Woodblock prints and magazines are both commercial goods sold on the open market, and the success of the celebrity royal image is dependent on its relatability as well as its glamor and splendor, all traits that were exhibited in the fashionable, global empresses of modern Japan.

Notes

1 *Kōgō no doresu no nazu*, NHK, aired March 18, 2023, www.nhk.jp/p/ts/98L4Y9JJ62/episode/te/6678RN8VNV/.
2 This translation can be found in: Keiichiro Nakagawa and Henry Rosovsky, "The Case of the Dying Kimono: The Influence of Changing Fashions on the Development of the Japanese Woolen Industry," *Business History Review* 37, no. 1&2 (1963).
3 This translation can be found in: Nakagawa and Rosovsky, "The Case of the Dying Kimono."
4 Melissa McCormick, *The Tale of Genji: A Visual Companion* (Princeton: Princeton University Press, 2018).
5 This print can be found in the Scripps College Collection, https://ccdl.claremont.edu/digital/collection/cyw/id/135/.
6 Chinese dress was also fashionable in the 1910s and 1920s, and oftentimes hybrid styles of clothing were featured in paintings, as well as magazines. Tsuyoshi Kaizuka, ed., *Egakareta Chaina doresu: Fujishima Takeji kara Umehara Ryūzaburō made: tēma tenji* (Tokyo: Bridgestone Museum of Art, 2014). This type of dress was wrapped up in colonial issues of femininity and power; for further discussion of these complexities:

Ikeda Shinobu, "The Allure of a 'Woman in Chinese Dress': Representation of the Other in Imperial Japan," in *Performing "Nation": Gender Politics in Literature, Theater, and the Visual Arts of China and Japan, 1880–1940*, ed. Doris Croissant, Catherine Vance Yeh and Joshua S. Mostow (Leiden: Brill, 2008).

7 Kurazumi Yuko, "Kindai joshi dōtoku kyōiku no rekishi: Ryōsai kenbo to joshi tokuseiron to iu futatsu no isō," *Tokyo daigaku dagakuin kyōikugaku kenkyūka kyōikugaku kenkyūshitsu* 34 (2008). Kawamoto Aya argues for the *ryōsai kenbo* as a reforming device in both Japan and Korea that functioned to bring women into the modern nation. Kawamoto Aya, "Chōsen to Nihon ni okeru ryōsai kenbo shisō ni kansuru hikaku kenkyū: Kaikokuki kara 1940 nendai zenhan o chūshin ni," *Osaka shiritsu daigaku shakaigaku kenkyūkai* 11 (2010).

8 He first mentions the phrase in 1875 in the *Meiji Six Journal.* Sharon Sievers, *Flowers in Salt: The Beginnings of Feminist Consciousness in Modern Japan* (Stanford: Stanford University Press, 1983), 22. Nakamura was the principal of Tokyo joshi shihan gakkō, the first normal school for girls opened by the Meiji government. Mara Patessio, *Women and Public Life in Early Meiji Japan: The Development of the Feminist Movement* (Ann Arbor: Michigan Monograph Series in Japanese Studies, 2011), 27.

9 The concept of *ryōsai kenbo* was created in opposition to earlier Tokugawa models of women in society that claimed women should be subservient to their husbands and wherein education for women was not considered necessary. See Kumiko Fujimura-Fanselow, "The Japanese Ideology of 'Good Wives and Wise Mothers': Trends in Contemporary Research," *Gender and History* 3 (1991).

10 This is the only image in which an artist is attributed in the caption. 『内田千秋君筆』 *Uchida Chiaki kun fude*, or the brush of Uchida Chiaki, is included parenthetically at the end of the image caption. *Fujin gahō*, August 1, 1906, page 6. The elder Kaneko was a well-known diplomat who was influential in Japanese international diplomacy.

11 For further detail on the fashion trends of the 1900s and 1910s, see: Elizabeth Ewing and Alice Mackrell, *History of 20th Century Fashion* (London: B.T. Batsford, 1997).

12 Aoki Junko argues for Shōken's clothing, as well as that of other noblewomen, as an example of the imperial family

promoting acceptable fashion. Aoki Junko, "Zasshi 'Kōzoku gahō' ni miru kindai kōzoku fuasshon no imeji," *Contentsu Bunkashi Kenkyū* 8 (2013).

13 Kate Strasdin, *Inside the Royal Wardrobe: A Dress History of Queen Alexandra* (London: Bloomsbury Academic, 2017).

14 In the carriage image from May 15, 1908, she is centered on the top to bottom axis, but not the right-left axis; however, she is framed by the large, dark carriage in which she rides.

15 Katano Masako, "Kindai kōgōron," in *Jendā to sabetsu*, ed. Amino Yoshihiko, vol. 7 of *Tennō to ōken o kangaeru* (Tokyo: Iwanami shoten, 2002), 81.

16 Elena Woodacre, *Queens and Queenship* (Leeds: Arc Humanities Press, 2021), 44.

17 Stefan Tanaka, *Japan's Orient: Rendering Pasts into History* (Berkeley: University of California Press, 1993; rpt., 1995), 3.

18 Miriam Silverberg, *Erotic Grotesque Nonsense: The Mass Culture of Japanese Modern Times* (Berkeley: University of California Press, 2006), 148. For an analysis of late Meiji *ryōsai kenbo* education, see: Jiang Hua, "Kōtō jogakkō ni okeru ryōsai kenbo kyōiku no jissai ni kansuru kōsatsu—kōchō nado no kunwa, kōkun, seitokokoroe, ryō seikatsu nado no bunseki o chūshin ni shite," *Waseda daigaku daigakuin kyōikugaku kenkyūka* 19 (2011).

19 Koyama Shizuko, "Domestic Roles and the Incorporation of Women into the Nation State: The Emergence and Development of the 'Good Wife, Wise Mother' Ideology," trans. Vera Mackie, in *Gender, Nation and State in Modern Japan*, ed. Andrea Germer, Vera Mackie and Ulrike Wöhr (New York: Routledge, 2014), 92–93.

20 Koyama, "Domestic Roles and the Incorporation of Women into the Nation State," 94.

21 Barbara Sato, *The New Japanese Woman: Modernity, Media, and Women in Interwar Japan* (Durham: Duke University Press, 2003), 96.

22 Kathleen Uno, "Womanhood, War, and Empire: Transmutations of 'Good Wife, Wise Mother' before 1931," in *Gendering Modern Japanese History*, ed. Barbara Molony and Kathleen Uno (Cambridge, MA: Harvard University Asia Center, 2005), 510. She quotes from a 1929 publication which attempted to argue that the ideology was unfairly labeled as old-fashioned and moved to once again make it popular among young women by emphasizing its necessity for success in the imperial project.

23 Michiko Mae, "The Nexus of Nation, Culture and Gender in Modern Japan: The Resistance of Kanno Sugako and Kaneko Fumiko," trans. Leonie Stickland in *Gender, Nation and State in Modern Japan*, ed. Andrea Germer, Vera Mackie and Ulrike Wöhr (London: Routledge, 2014), 74–75.

24 Throughout the early twentieth century, close to half of the Japanese population remained in rural, agricultural areas. These citizens kept Japanese dress as their standard clothing style. The change from Japanese to Western style suits for men is sometimes attributed to the change in the Japanese political world from colonized to colonizer. See: Mina Roces and Louise Edwards, "Transnational Flows and the Politics of Dress in Asia and the Americas," in *The Politics of Dress in Asia and the Americas*, ed. Mina Roces and Louise Edwards (Eastbourne: Sussex Academic Press, 2007), 10.

25 Historian Toby Slade attributes this shift to increasing numbers of Japanese citizens growing comfortable with European dress after wearing Western-style school and military uniforms and to the change in popular styles towards those which would accommodate active lifestyles. Toby Slade, *Japanese Fashion: A Cultural History* (Oxford: Berg Publishing, 2009), 58.

26 Tanida Etsuji, *Nihon fukushokushi* (Tokyo: Koseikan, 1989).

27 Annie Van Asche, "Japanese Kimono Fashion of the Early Twentieth Century," *Textile Society of America Symposium Proceedings*, Paper 799 (2000), http://digitalcommons.unl.edu/cgi/viewcontent.cgi?article=1800&context=tsaconf

28 Liza Dalby, *Kimono: Fashioning Culture* (New Haven: Yale University Press, 1993), 126–128.

29 Yokohama bijutsukan, *Fuasshon to āto uruwashi tōzai kōryū* (Yokohama: Yokohama bijutsukan and Kyoto fukushoku bunka kenkyū zaidan, 2017). Bunka gakuen fukushoku hakubutsukan, *Meiji, Taishō, Shōwa senzenki no kyūteifuku—yōsō to shōzoku* (Tokyo: Bunka Gakuen Fukushoku hakubutsukan, 2013).

6

MOURNING AND MEMORY

The Visual Politics of Imperial Funerals and Memorial Sites

On May 17, 1951, Empress Teimei died of a heart attack at age 66. At the moment of her death, postwar Japan was on the verge of immense changes, as only four months later the Treaty of San Francisco was signed, leading to the official end of the U.S. occupation of Japan in April 1952. In the early 1950s, the Japanese national economy was starting to recover from the devastating effects of the war, and Teimei's passing, the first major imperial event in the postwar period, was an important marker of the change in the family's status from political and military figures to cultural icons. Likewise, the first public imperial funeral of the modern age was for a woman, held fifty-five years earlier when Empress Dowager Eishō passed away in 1897.

Imperial funerals in the early twentieth century were commemorated as national holidays and marked with grand processions, all of which were dictated by a series of imperial edicts and Imperial Household Law. In the years just after Japan conceded defeat in 1945, however, much of the bureaucracy of the Imperial Household Agency was dismantled or downsized, and the role of the imperial family in Japanese public life was significantly diminished as compared to the decades between the 1870s and 1940s. As a result, there was uncertainty as to what form Teimei's funeral should take, yet in the end a large state funeral was held. The event was only one of two funerals for a Japanese empress in the twentieth century, the other being Shōken's funeral in 1914.[1] For Teimei, as for Shōken, Japanese citizens lined the streets of Tokyo to pay their respects and to view the funeral procession. But in

DOI: 10.4324/9781003376101-9

the postwar context of Teimei's mourning, U.S. servicemen joined the event, and photographs and film footage of the funeral were seen around the world, making it a truly international occasion.

As shown throughout this book, imperial institutions and conventions that are presented as timeless, ancient, and unique to Japan are in fact often recent innovations with parallels in other modern monarchies, and the frequent characterization of the modern Japanese imperial family as purely patriarchal and patrilineal overlooks the fact that they often drew upon royal women for public legitimacy and clout. These principles hold true for imperial funerals and burial practices in the modern era. While Shōken's 1914 funeral drew upon the pageantry of her husband's memorial only two years earlier, it was Empress Dowager Eishō's funeral in 1897 which future funerals were based upon.

The first two sections of this chapter look at the early twentieth century funerals of Eishō and Shōken, following a trajectory of media immediacy: first examining quickly published mass media images from the days and weeks after death, then commemorative funerary photo albums which took a broader view and were published for years after the event. Arguing that the visual culture of funerary events was critical to cementing the empress as a focal point in the modern imperial family and to providing the modern royal women a place in the traditional side of the visual monarchy, this chapter concludes with Teimei's funeral in 1951 as the first postwar imperial event, one which was covered in the domestic and international media, showing the transition to the era of the Japanese symbol monarchy.

Modern imperial funerals took on the form of imagined ancient rites as they were recorded in historical accounts.[2] These "traditional" rituals provided the state, and the imperial family, with legitimacy and authority.[3] Atsuko Hirai shows that the Tokugawa shoguns formalized state mourning, practices that were modernized in the Meiji period, specifically in the context of Eishō's funeral.[4] Adrian C. Mayer states:

> Meiji's funeral, therefore, achieved a double purpose for its organizers. By changing the content, they symbolized the new age that had dawned with the Restoration. Yet, by making

> their innovations in a traditional Japanese idiom, by reverting to the customs followed by Emperors in a previous millennium, they expressed the stability, centrality, and continuity of the monarchy.[5]

That the men of the imperial household were viewed in this dual fashion is in keeping with the emperor's public positions. However, while acting as the holders of tradition, the empresses were often envisioned in print and photographic form as more modern than their male partners as they participated in charity, visitation, and diplomatic activities, standard practices for queens the world over. Funerals were a visual means to balance the empress' modernity and to position them within the imagined history of the imperial family.

The images analyzed in this chapter were created or selected by a broad group of bureaucrats, journalists, graphic designers, and everyday citizens for posthumous distribution, consumption, or collection, with the benefit of hindsight and with the intention of memorializing. In this sense, the narratives and aesthetics are of a different scope and strategy than other images examined in this book, which were generally created during the lifetime of the sovereigns. The very act of memorializing, historicizing, and creating cultural memories of a public figure in this way worked to unify imperial historical memory across society and to place women as celebrity figures central to the Japanese imperial institution and the visual monarchy.

Eishō and Shōken: Women and the Innovation of Public Imperial Mourning

The first imperial funeral of the modern age was that of Empress Dowager Eishō. Born in 1835 as Kujō Asako (九条夙子), Eishō was a child of the nobility, or *kuge*, matched at age 13 to then–future Emperor Kōmei. After bearing two daughters who died in infancy, she gave birth to then–future Emperor Meiji in 1852. As Kōmei passed away when Meiji was just fifteen, it is often reported that Emperor Meiji was close to his mother. During her lifetime, Eishō was represented in a limited number of photographs and paintings, none of which were widely distributed. Eishō was, by all accounts, the last empress consort to live outside of the public eye. In death, though, she would provide a model for future ritual functions.

The 1897 funeral of the former empress consort was a shift from earlier rites, particularly in comparison to those of Emperor Kōmei in 1867.[6] Kōmei's funeral took place prior to the revolution in imperial representation and before the advent of mass media, visual monarchy, and the modernization of the Japanese imperial family. Eishō's funeral, which Emperor Meiji called for "as a standard for the future," was funded by the state, and her death was widely reported in the newspapers.[7] Yet, as a matter of law and per the wishes of Eishō herself, the ceremonies were a private, family affair.[8] Eishō's funeral also took place before the widespread distribution of photographs in the mass media. Although this meant that Eishō's funeral acted as a test run for modern imperial mortuary practices, it was conducted without an audience, something that would change dramatically with the Meiji imperial couple.

The private funeral was, however, represented in visual culture. The triptych woodblock print, *Kyoto Ōmiya gosho yori ryōtsunonawa shingoryō e go sonkan no zu* (Empress Dowager Eishō's Funeral) (Figure 6.1) by Harada Kōkyo (原田耕挙,

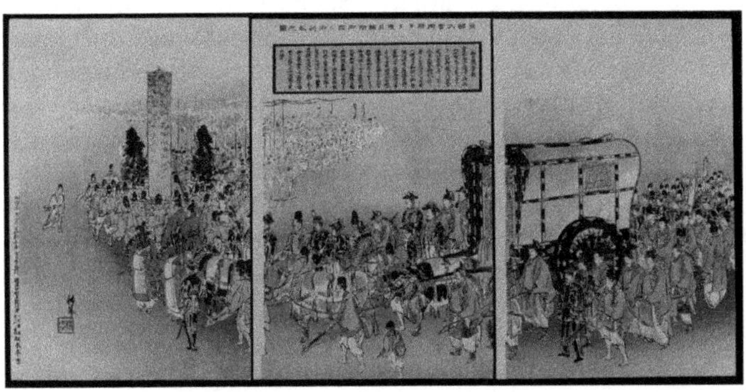

FIGURE 6.1 *Kyoto Ōmiya gosho yori ryōtsunonawa shingoryō e go sonkan no zu* (Empress Dowager Eishō's Funeral), February 5, 1897, Harada Kōkyo, Jordan Schnitzer Museum of Art, University of Oregon, Eugene, Oregon, 2021:36.13a-c

1863–1925), dates from February 5, 1897, two days prior to the memorial service. The print acted as both an announcement of Eishō's funeral but also a model for later rites of internment. The large oxcart and lengthy procession were represented in a contemporary style with few details from the surrounding landscape. The procession, which took place in Kyoto, seemingly moves through empty space, a common means of perspective in two-dimensional media. The Japanese public was well aware of Eishō's passing: in addition to the period of mourning declared at court, citizens were to abstain from song, dance, and music for thirty days; black streamers were flown in public in lieu of flags; and criminal executions were paused for fifteen days after her death and again on the days of the coffin's departure and her burial.[9]

Donald Keene argues that the absence of Buddhist elements in the funeral was surprising, as these were replaced by Shinto rites, a new development in the Meiji period.[10] But there were Buddhist elements of the empress dowager's funeral that were conducted in private, even if they were not documented in visual culture.[11] The print, as with other public-facing funerary visual culture for Eishō, has a typically Meiji hybrid feel. The lines of attendants that flank the oxcart are dressed in either European-style military costume or historically inspired Shinto robes. The dynamically weighted lines used to outline the human figures and the increasing abstraction given to the procession as it advances into space lend a sense of movement to the image. Amidst the human chaos of the scene, the oxcart looms large and seemingly static, its design precisely rendered in fine lines and meticulous detail. Considering this event was a funeral for a woman, it is interesting that every person represented is male, as the majority would have been, showing that while the Imperial Household Ministry allowed for a feminine presence by way of the empress' public personae, it was still a highly masculine and patriarchal organization.

Similar prints were produced in 1912 upon the death and funeral of Emperor Meiji, whose passing also included vast amounts of photography, a first for an imperial funeral. Yasuda Hanpo's (安田半圃, 1889–1947) hexapytch woodblock print *Nijūbashi-gai gotaisō no zu* (His Imperial Majesty's Funeral Outside Nijūbashi) (Figure 6.2), September 1912, borrows from

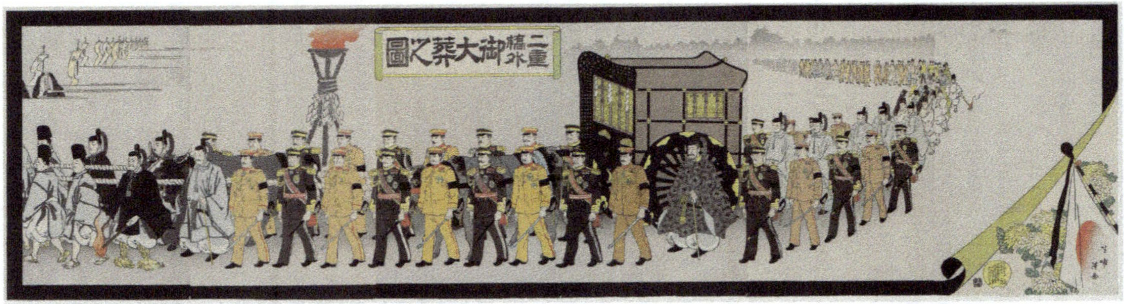

FIGURE 6.2 *Nijūbashi-gai gotaisō no zu* (His Imperial Majesty's Funeral Outside Nijūbashi), September 1912, Yasuda Hanpo, multicolor woodblock print, Collection of the Museum of Fine Arts, Boston

the style of the 1897 Eishō funeral procession triptych by including very little background setting, abstracting the procession as it recedes into space, and featuring the oxcart as the dominant subject, offset at the right of the image. Meiji's print, however, is in the unusual hexapytch format and has a far more regimented style with additional military attendants. Whereas the Eishō funerary print is dynamic, calligraphic, and gestural in style, the Meiji funerary print is disciplined, structured, and cadenced. Furthermore, the Meiji print is a skeuomorph of a handscroll: at the bottom right is the representation of rolled paper, exposing chrysanthemums and a Japanese flag.[12] While it is tempting to attribute these subtle differences to gender, personality, or funerary developments, it is more likely that the variances are a result of artistic liberties taken by the individual producers, for in death empresses received similar treatment to emperors. This equality in death is seen in other monarchies; John Carmi Parsons writes on the surprising equal treatment of medieval English queens and kings in death, arguing that it was important to include the maternal queen in the royal lineage and that it was easier to do so after her passing than during her lifetime, when she still had influence at court.[13]

Emperor Meiji's funeral was also widely represented in photographic material, including newspaper spreads, postcards, and photo books. His funeral marks the first time that photographic reproductions of imperial mourning were created and distributed on a large scale, and imperial funeral iconography as developed in 1912 would impact Empress Shōken's funeral in 1914, Emperor Taishō's funeral in 1926, and to a lesser degree Empress Teimei's funeral in 1951. Meiji died on July 30, but his funeral took place on September 12 to allow for the proper timing of rites and rituals. Numerous photographs of the funeral procession flooded the media and were subsequently utilized in other forms of visual culture, such as the postcard, *Meiji Jingū minami seimon* (Meiji Shrine South Gate).[14] The postcard contrasts a photograph of a procession of Shinto practitioners from Meiji's funeral with a static image of the Meiji Shrine and a portrait of the emperor late in life. The warm orange and peach tones of the autumn maple leaves match the color of the *torii* and inform us of the fall season, while the blue shadows of the pine tree silhouettes and the green background are reminiscent of the natural environment of the Meiji Shrine. The gold of the *shimenawa* and *kami* provide a further hint of the autumn season of the funeral and are a nod to imperial luxury. The postcard taken as a whole exhibits the new public concept of mourning: the portrait to remember the emperor in his human form, the funeral procession to commemorate the ritual act of his final rites, and the shrine architecture to place him in the lineage of emperors as sacred presence. As with woodblock prints, postcards were commercial objects; therefore the use of Meiji's funeral as the subject of this card, and many others, shows the popularity of the theme to average citizens, who probably would have also viewed images of the 1901 funeral of Queen Victoria or the 1908 funeral of Empress Dowager Cixi.

As evidenced by the signs in this postcard, modern state funerals had a decidedly Shinto flair, but owing to the official separation of state and religion in the 1889 constitution, the term *kōsōshiki* (公葬式, public funeral ceremony) was the preferred phrasing.[15] Historically, funerals were customarily in the realm of Buddhism, not Shinto. Likewise, the practice of full-body burial of the emperor was not always practiced. In the past, emperors were cremated in the Buddhist tradition but the rise of Confucian sentiments in the Edo period led to Emperor Gokōmyō's secret burial in 1654, with the addition of rituals to make it seem as if he was cremated. The practice of differing public and private burial acts continued until Emperor Kōmei's death in 1867, the first to be a publicly acknowledged burial of the imperial body, evidencing the diversity of imperial funerary practices.[16]

Seventeen years after Eishō's passing, and two years after Emperor Meiji's, Empress Shōken's 1914 funeral was the first public memorial event for a modern empress. Emperor Meiji had died only two years earlier, leaving the imperial bureaucracy, media apparatus, and Japanese citizenry prepared for a large-scale funeral. Upon Shōken's death on April 9, 1914, funerary rites, rituals, and events commenced.[17] Newspapers immediately began to run full-page articles recounting her life and detailing the plans for the funeral, often accompanied by her reproduced *goshinei* or similar portraiture from her youth, both in Heian-style robes and European-style dresses. In the days immediately prior to the funeral on May 26, the *Asahi shinbun* (Asahi newspaper) included portraits identifying the nobility and dignitaries who would participate in the funeral, descriptions and photographs of the hearse, and maps of the planned procession route. Special editions of the newspaper on the eve of the funeral day were laden with photographs showing lines of military participants, Shinto priests, the funerary train, crowds of mourners in a deep bow as the remains passed by, and the mausoleum site at Fushimi, Momoyama, as well as reproductions of Shōken's poetry and calligraphy. Absent in this media mix were photographs of the death bed or the dead body, owing to cultural norms. This provides a stark contrast with media coverage of concurrent European monarchical passings, where the ill king or queen and later their death portraits were often published in mainstream media.[18]

In one example of Japanese media coverage, on April 13, 1914, the *Osaka Asahi shinbun* printed a group of photographs at the top of page four. Three of the photographs show the carriages of nobility as they enter or leave the Aoyama site where Shōken's remains lay while awaiting the state funeral, the fourth image a photomontage of two officials bent at the waist in a deep bow with their shadows rendered on the blank page with drawn hatch marks. These kinds of images—groups of public mourners, citizens bowing in respect, horse-drawn carriages, and architectural facades hiding the intimate act familial bereavement—were repeated in newspapers and magazines throughout the months of April and May as the performed act of national remembrance became part of the public consciousness. In addition to the platitudes that fill the page just below the photographs with headlines such as "Omegumi shison ni oyobu" (Grace unto her descendants), the bottom section of the page includes translated obituaries from the foreign press, including segments of text from the *England Telegraph* and the *New York Post*, primarily selected from powerful nations in the Euro-American sphere.

These images, and many others like them, combined in the mass media to inform the citizenry how to properly mourn the imperial family, and notably the gendered differences between the visual memorialization of empress and emperor were minor. The articulation of an imagined past was packaged for consumption and functioned in a didactic fashion, envisioned as atemporal yet combined with new precedents such as the very presence of empresses themselves. The formula of mourning images across early twentieth century media was less about the individual person or personae of Eishō, Meiji, or Shōken and more about the pageantry that justified and authenticated the imperial family as an institution.

The Empresses in Funerary Photo Books

In addition to the flurry of mass media photography published at the time of the imperial funerals, memorial photograph books were also published by a variety of groups, including the Imperial Household Ministry, military-affiliated associations, and periodical publication houses. Determining the distribution channels or audience reception of these books is beyond the scope of this chapter; however, the relatively widespread availability of the publications in archives and libraries, as well as the materials used for the various volumes indicates that they were fairly common objects.[19]

Produced in the weeks after the ceremonies and therefore one step less immediate than the instantaneous newspaper coverage, memorial books present the funerals in a documentary fashion. Some include lengthy didactic texts covering the life of the deceased or a description of the event; others just have brief descriptions of the photographs in Japanese and English. The monochrome photographs are high in contrast, brightly lit, and crisp in their printing. As objects of consumption, the photo books are luxurious, with gold embossed details, thick paper, and attention to detail as seen in the interleaving, but simultaneously the volumes are mass produced, unemotional, and formulaic, representing the funerals as timeless impersonal events. The standardized nature of these books shows that they were intended as documents of funeral pageantry, not records of the person or even personae of the empresses and emperors, and their mass consumption is a nod to the celebrity status of the monarchs.

The leather-bound volume *Shōken kōtaigō taisōgi shashinchō* (Empress Dowager Shōken Funeral Photo Book), published in 1914, includes detailed documentation of over eighty photographs of Shōken's funeral procession, mausoleum, and funerary implements. The book presents the event in full but does not include portraiture of Shōken or text documenting her life, only documentary-style photography with brief captions in Japanese and English that label the items or events in terse, brief language. Read in its entirety, the book presents primarily men in the procession and empty scenes with the empress' presence suggested by her tomb, her funeral train, or the oxcart that transported her remains. In comparing the memorial photo books of Shōken and Teimei, Teimei's have a more clinical feel, but this is a subtle difference. The procession in Shōken's book is often blurry with movement, includes more "ritualists" in the photographs, and is less staged than that of her successor. Among the photographs in Shōken's book that are more dispassionate in appearance, such as those of the funeral train or the mausoleum, the angles, composition, movement, and show a more human presence and scale, particularly as contrasted with Teimei's funeral book, which will be addressed at the end of this chapter. Like many photographs in Shōken's book, *General View of the Mausoleum* (Figure 6.3) is shot from a top-down angle and includes a small, anonymous official figure, providing a sense of scale. The structures are distant, and therefore small, but not imposing. The fence in the foreground and the single structure at the left are partially outside of the picture frame, giving the viewer a sense of a complete picture, and the soft lighting lends a sense of calm. These photographic strategies unify the book, making it appear as a complete record of the event.

Other types of funerary documentation can be found among the records of Meiji Jingū, where Shōken and Meiji's *kami* are enshrined. Published by the Teikoku gunjin kyōikukai (Imperial Soldiers Education Association) just after the opening of Meiji Jingū in 1920, *Meiji Jingū oshashinchō: fu gozōeikiroku* (Meiji Shrine Photo Book: Appendix Record of Construction) provides detailed documentation of the inner and outer precincts of the shrine upon its opening to the public.[20] The bound volume includes maps, textual documentation of the structures and brief written

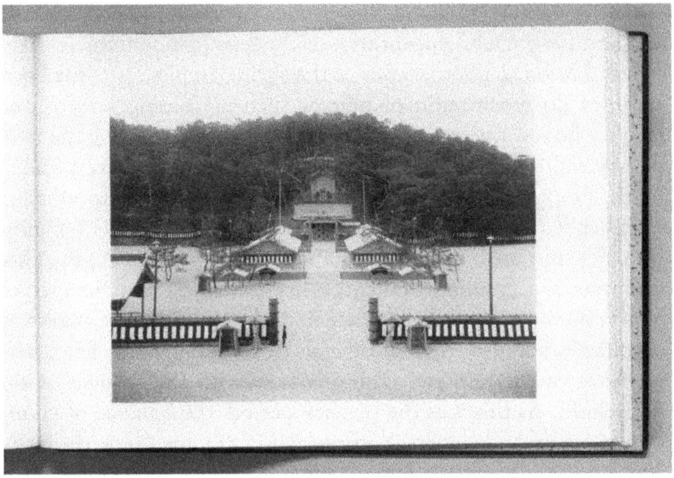

FIGURE 6.3 "General View of the Mausoleum," *Shōken kōtaigō taisōgi shashinchō* (Empress Dowager Shōken Funeral Photo Book), August 1914, Taisōshi, p. 268. National Diet Library Digital Collections

recollections of Meiji and Shōken, and dozens of photographs of the shrine structures, both as architectural documentation and with a human presence. The first pages of photographs include a profile image of Emperor Meiji in his elder years, contrasted with Empress Shōken's photograph from the 1880s; while the emperor visibly aged in the public forum, the empress remained youthful in her reproduced image. Potential reasons for this eternal youth could come from cultural preferences for female beauty but also from the lack of precedent for an aging empress in visual culture; the invisibility of the *gon no tenji* and *kōgō* of the past and the emphasis on maternity in the court women meant that there was no model for an elder empress. Furthermore, caricatures of older women monarchs in global media, including Victoria and Cixi, could have led the Imperial Household Ministry to be concerned with the reception of images of an older woman. While not as extreme as the legislated "mask of youth" seen for Elizabeth I in sixteenth-century England, the images of Shōken demonstrate a concern for the vital appearance of the female monarchs.

In addition to photographs of the shrine architecture, the book includes documentation of objects such as folding screens and lacquer boxes, the construction of the shrine, including the temporary railroad built into the site and the laborers at rest and at work. Empress Teimei is also shown visiting the site to worship together with a group of princesses, bringing an active feminine presence into the book. Read as a whole, the majority of the photographs are either documentary-style architectural images or have a dominating male presence in the form of groups of visiting dignitaries and government officials or Shinto priests. The active presence of the imperial family is seen with the women of the household. As this was the regency period, the balance of young crown prince and empress consort acting as imperial proxy was a standard representation (see Chapter 4). Yet in the context of the album as a whole, the feminine imperial presence is manifested as youthful in the case of Shōken's portrait and influential in the case of Teimei as imperial proxy; in other words, the women are a central part of the monarchy, both in life and in death.

With the death of Emperor Taishō in 1926, the primary method of funeral coverage in the media came in the form of periodicals such as newspapers and magazines; however, memorial publications were also produced after his passing. One of Emperor Taishō's memorial publications, *Taishō tennō goshashinchō* (Emperor Taishō Photo Book), published two years after his death, is a photographic record of his life, with an emphasis on family.[21] With a lush gold illustrated cover, a calligraphy-style title block, and graphics of a paulownia tree and two phoenixes, this book includes Taishō's *goshinei* as the first page, moving on to Teimei's *goshinei*, both framed by a graphic chrysanthemum border. The *goshinei* of Hirohito and Kōjun is surrounded by a graphic phoenix border, as is a photograph of Princess Teru (Shigeko) as a baby, with a paulownia border. Each of these studio portraits of the imperial family include the official chrysanthemum seal of the imperial household at the top of the page in embossed gold. The publication details Taishō throughout his upbringing, with a few highlights of his reign, and extensive photographs of his funeral, including an inset newspaper clipping of the funeral procession. His children, as well as his sisters and their families, are also documented in the many pages of photographs, indicative of the transition in the imaging of the imperial household to a focus on the nuclear family. Interestingly, this publication includes a significant number of photographs of Teimei, including a full-color image at the front that shows her as she attends an exhibition of European-style oil painting in 1925.

Near the end of the *Taishō tennō goshashinchō* is a full-page spread on Empress Teimei that includes six photographs of the then empress dowager. The images are familiar and include her visiting the Peace Exhibition in 1922, speaking before the Red Cross, and visiting victims in the wake of the 1923 earthquake, actions which are labeled with the term "*kokubō*" (国母), or mother of the nation, a designation that was used on previous occasions. In contrast, the book also includes a single-page spread on Emperor Taishō as a "*jifu*" (慈父), or loving father, consisting of a photograph of Taishō with his two elder sons as toddlers, Hirohito and Yasuhito (Prince Chichibu), and a second photograph of the emperor visiting Korea while he was crown prince. This representation of the emperor as a father of his own progeny and the empire but the empress as only mother of the nation is remarkable, as it removes both the biological and emotional maternal agency of the empress figures. The 1907 Korea photograph includes important Japanese military and political leaders such as Arisugawa Takehito and Itō Hirobumi, then the resident-general of Korea while it was a Japanese protectorate, as well as Crown Prince Yi Un of the Korean Imperial House, then only ten years old. Taishō was the first member of the Japanese royal family to travel overseas, and at the time of its creation, this photograph was an important means of exhibiting the relationships between the Japanese and Korean imperial households, as well as showing the Japanese colonial government presence in Korea.

Beyond the pages of this specific photo book, funerals were deeply involved with colonial and global monarchical relationships. Starting with Eishō's funeral in 1897, the Japanese government required colonial territories to adopt mourning protocol such as multi-day prohibitions on music or prisoner executions, and around the same time the Meiji imperial family adopted the practice of recognizing the passing of global monarchs with the same court memorial etiquette they practiced for domestic imperial deaths.[22] These two sides of memorial practice, colonial and global, show how the imperial institution was activated for a variety of political purposes both at home and abroad, in a manner similar to other monarchies of the era.

A second Taishō funeral book, *Taishō tennō gotaisō shashinchchō* (Funeral Photo Book for Emperor Taishō), contains similar photographic content, but with far less emphasis on Teimei.[23] Bound in a traditional Japanese style, the publication includes images of Taishō's life and reign but is focused on the funeral itself. The book starts with photographs of the funerary procession, with the *goshinei* placed after the table of contents. The emphasis on family and lineage is visually evident with the inclusion of Hirohito and Kōjun's *goshinei* and an overlaid portrait round of the infant Princess Teru, but there is no single section devoted to Teimei, and the vast majority of the photographs document the funeral, funerary rites, funeral attendees, and the mortuary monument.

The difference between the two publications—with the first book including a family-oriented memorial of Taishō and the second focused on the funeral itself—shows that the evolution of the imperial image was not always linear and that the general stylistic changes discussed throughout this book and in this chapter show a corporate approach to visual monarchy rather than a purely propaganda-based approach, meaning while images were subject to censorship, they were not exclusively state issued. A balance in publicly driven interest, media selection, artistic choice (even when anonymous), and the agency of the imperial family themselves, as detected in their body language, combined to form the media milieu of the modern imperial family.

An examination of the funeral books leaves many questions unanswered. The varied organizations that published the books, such as the Imperial Soldiers Education Association or the Citizens Education Association, hint at the audience for these documentary publications, but we are left wondering how they were utilized by those who possessed them. The messages in the books, be they for emperors or empresses, is one of pageantry and atemporality. These didactic, image-heavy documents worked to articulate the new practice of a large, public state funeral for the members of the imperial family while justifying the precedent through images that represent seemingly timeless and authentic death rituals.

The publication of these books, often two years after the death of the empress or emperor commemorated within, worked to cement the social memory of the monarchs after their passing. Buddhist periodicals would often publish short textual commemorations for the members of the imperial family on regular occasions after their death, but there are few visual or public means of commemorating the historic members of the imperial family.[24] In Japan public sculpture of historic figures is fairly rare, and members of the modern monarchy do not appear on stamps or currency. Sociologists have used the term "social memory" to examine "particular sets of practices like commemoration and monument building and general forms like tradition, myth, or identity."[25] Widely distributed photo books, as well as participation in or viewing of the funeral rites functioned to cement the centrality and importance of the imperial family in the social memory of the Japanese populace, as would holidays such as Meiji setsu, now called Culture Day (November 3).[26] The Meiji Memorial Picture Gallery (聖徳記念絵画館), a Tokyo museum housing eighty paintings commemorating Emperor Meiji and built over the course of twenty years, also served to cement the imperial couple in the public space of the capital.[27] Both of the forms of public, visual funerary commemoration examined thus far—mass media coverage and photo books—worked to establish imperial funerary rituals in public memory, creating a baseline of "tradition" that would be utilized in the postwar years.

Teimei's Funeral: Postwar Transitions and Nostalgia

With the end of the Pacific War in 1945, substantial changes occurred in the emperor system, as well as with the imperial family's place in Japanese society.[28] While many of the imperial practices set out in the 1889 Constitution remained, such as excluding women from the throne and the system of primogeniture, other practices, such as state-managed Shinto and the system of nobility, were removed from the law.

Teimei's passing was marked in Japanese newspapers with textual proclamations on May 17, followed by more in-depth coverage on the front pages of daily periodicals on the following day. The photograph published in the *Asahi shinbun* on May 18, 1951 (Figure 6.4), shows Teimei in her years as the empress dowager in a closely cropped image. The accompanying articles recount her life and the era of her rule. The image shows her not as a

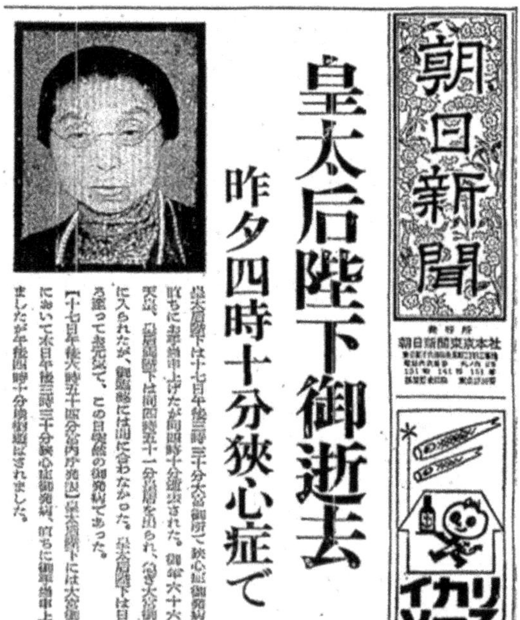

朝日新聞

皇太后陛下御逝去

昨夕四時十分狭心症で

皇太后陛下は十七日午後三時三十分大宮御所で狭心症御発病、直ちに御手当申上げたが同四時十分崩御された。御年六十六。天皇、皇后両陛下は同四時五十一分御所を出られ、大宮御所に入られたが、御臨終には間に合わなかった。皇太后陛下は日ごろ至って御元気で、この日突然の御発病であった。

【十七日午後六時五十分宮内庁発表】皇太后陛下には大宮御所において本日午後三時三十分狭心症御発病、直ちに御手当申上げましたが午後四時十分崩御遊ばされました。

イカリソース

FIGURE 6.4 *Kōtaigōheika goseihō* (The passing of her majesty the Empress Dowager), *Asahi shinbun*, May 18, 1951, page 1, Tokyo morning edition

youthful empress but rather as a grandmotherly dowager along the visual lines of other widowed modern queens such as Queen Victoria; Teimei's hair is tightly pulled back, and she wears a high collar, strands of jewelry, and small framed spectacles, a far cry from the on-trend fashions of her youth. It is likely that this photograph was selected in an attempt to neutralize the politics of the imperial family at a time when their position was precarious and to make her an easily identifiable and comforting figure. While Teimei's death sparked memories of the 1910s and 1920s, to reminisce about the era of her husband's rule was also to recall Japan at a time when it was on the road to empire and in the build-up to the war years. Remembering Teimei at the height of her reign was fraught with challenging historical memories. The selection of a photograph of the empress in her elder years carried many fewer recollections and was a safer choice. Furthermore, the photographs selected for the funeral remembrances did not show Teimei as a powerful figure or as the outgoing public figure that she was in the 1920s when she acted as an imperial proxy or military mother, but rather they represent her as a subdued older woman. This re-remembering was likely part of a larger continuing strategy of promoting conventional gender roles for the imperial household; throughout the modern period this was the standard empress representation, with the exception of Teimei during the regency years. In the funeral imagery, the anomaly of her final years as empress were concealed.

Occurring at the end of the occupation, and at a time when both the symbol monarchy and the U.S.–Japan narrative were established, Empress Teimei's funeral was an event that cemented the postwar position of the imperial family as cultural symbols. Stephen Large argues that the funeral of Empress Teimei, as well as the investiture and wedding of the Crown Prince in 1952 and 1959, respectively, were, "ceremonial occasions [that] catered to a sense of popular nostalgia for the idealized cultural traditions of the court."[29] The domestic press coverage of Teimei's funeral included images of horse-drawn carriages, a symbol of the monarchy since the days of Emperor Meiji's processions, and the length of coverage was relatively brief: she was memorialized immediately after her death, and her funeral made the front pages of the daily newspapers when it occurred the following month. This was not an event which was dwelled upon in the media.

Teimei's death was marked with an imperial funeral procession in the style established by Emperor Meiji and Empress Shōken only forty years earlier. Her state funeral, which included the *Rensō-no-gi* (斂葬の儀, Ceremony of the Funeral and Entombment), took place on June 22, 1951, after which she was buried at the Musashi Imperial Mausoleum (武蔵陵墓地, *Musashi ryōbochi*) in Hachiōji, just west of Tokyo. The funeral was conducted in accordance with the various imperial edicts and imperial mortuary laws, which were put into place between 1909, just before the passing of Emperor Meiji, and 1926, immediately before the funeral of Emperor Taishō.

Press coverage was not the only means of representation that the Imperial Household Agency used to record Teimei's funeral. A variety of memorial books were released in 1951 to commemorate the life of the empress, including one recording Teimei's poetry, published by Dainishobō, and one remembering her life, published by the Dainippon Silk Foundation. Both of these books include a selection of photographs amidst the text and draw on the distanced images of earlier imperial funeral photo books.

More interesting for the purposes of this study is the 1951 all-photograph publication *Teimei kōgō daisōgi shashinchō* (Photo Book of Empress Teimei's Funeral). Produced by the Imperial Household Agency, the book includes documentary style, detailed monochrome photographs of the funeral setup; the carriage along the route; citizens viewing the procession; the imperial family and foreign dignitaries in attendance; ritualists conducting the ceremonies; and images of the funerary carriage, train, and mausoleum, as well as a rubbing of the gravestone. The album presents an unemotional, and at times clinical, visual representation of Teimei's funeral. Most of the mourners are depicted at a distance, and the imperial family are shown lined up in a nearly geometric fashion, framed by the photographer as dispassionate figures. Some of the images are stark and cold, such as that of the funeral carriage, which has no human presence whatsoever (Figure 6.5). This specific photograph of the carriage is shot at a straight angle, with no indication of the surrounding environment

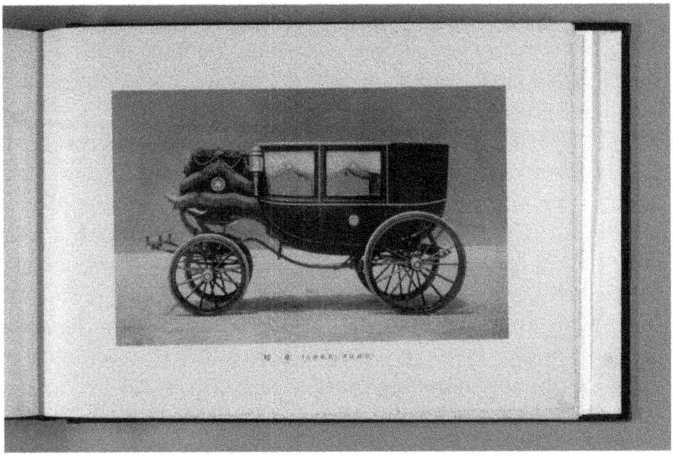

FIGURE 6.5 *Teimei kōgō daisōgi shashinchō* (Photo Book of Empress Teimei's Funeral), 1951, published by the Imperial Household Agency, National Diet Library Digital Collections

aside from the bright, top-down lighting. The carriage shaft and driver's seat are empty, just like the body of the carriage, where the empress' remains rode. The image is simultaneously clinical and harsh but also ghastly and unsettling. This publication, as well as the memorial articles, are a departure from media representations of Empress Dowager Eishō, Emperor Meiji, Empress Shōken, and Emperor Taishō's funerals. In the earlier, prewar instances which occurred in 1897, 1912, 1914, and 1926, respectively, the sovereigns were shown in images from their younger days, and a nostalgic, warm tone can be read from the published photographs.

In seeking cultural context for these differences, it is noteworthy that Teimei's funeral occurred at a distinct political and social moment, situated as the first postwar imperial public event but also the only imperial funeral during the long postwar period; the next major funeral would take place in 1989 with Hirohito's passing, and an empress' funeral would not again take place until 2000, when Kōjun died after a prolonged period of health problems and absence from the public sphere. Furthermore, the political events immediately surrounding the funeral of Empress Teimei had a great impact on how the memorial was represented in visual culture.

Only one month prior to Teimei's death, in April of 1951, United States president Harry Truman dismissed Douglas MacArthur from his position as commander of the occupation. When MacArthur left Japan on April 16, he was sent off with a fond farewell, but only a few weeks later his reputation changed when he testified before the U.S. Senate. In three days of testimony, MacArthur used paternalistic language to describe the Japanese people, going so far as to describe them as "twelve-year-olds."[30] Important to remember here is that MacArthur was key in preserving the imperial family's place in Japanese society after the war, keeping Hirohito from being tried as a war criminal. With MacArthur's removal, the Imperial Household Agency, and the imperial family, were undoubtedly concerned about maintaining the support of the U.S. occupying forces. With Japanese feelings toward MacArthur pivoting rapidly in the weeks just prior to Teimei's death, and uncertainty surrounding the position of the new occupation leadership vis-à-vis the imperial family, caution was crucial in how the imperial funeral was presented to the domestic and international public. The photographs published in both the memorial book and the popular press attempted to generate a neutral impression; they do not indicate a great sense of nostalgia, and in using the horse-drawn hearse as the primary symbol, the images attempt to create a cultural impression rather than an emotional response or loyalty to an individual. This is a series of images which walk the line between maintaining an institution that was under threat of both domestic irrelevance and international intervention while cautiously holding back from being overly celebratory or nostalgic. They are easily defined by what they are not: not enthusiastic, not nostalgic, not nationalist, and not triumphant.

The documentary style is reflected in other media as well. For example, *Jikei* magazine from August of 1951 includes a layout with photographs in a similar style to the *Daisōgi shashinchō* but also exhibits Teimei's grandmotherly portrait and an image of her together with her extended family, giving a more human feel to the memorial but retaining a somber character. Still, the funeral carriage amidst the procession was among the more popularly published photographs, with *Asahi camera* running an image of the carriage in September of 1951, the Christian magazine *Koei* running a photograph in October of the same year, and *Shinbun gekkan* including one in June of 1951. This procession image can also be seen in the international media coverage of the event, including at the right side of a two-page spread in *Life* magazine.

The global political climate had changed dramatically by 1951, and interest in Japan and Japanese culture was once again heightened in Europe and the United States in the postwar years. Magazines such as *Life* carried features which mentioned the funeral and briefly discussed the life of Empress Teimei. A two-page photograph spread published in the magazine emphasized Japanese traditional culture in the images, reinforcing that the citizens of Japan were ruled by democracy in 1951 and that they were the former subjects of Teimei. In doing so, this spread reminds readers of the greatness of Japanese culture but also that Japan's empire was a vestige of the past. The brief article states that after Taishō's death, Teimei, "silently watched the rise and fall of his Empire from the seclusion of the Omiya Palace."[31] It removes her power when referring to her as a "frail little Dowager Empress" and with the imagery reinforces a vision of Japan as an exotic culture stuck in the past. With photographs including peasants farming without machine labor; a steam engine; former subjects seated on straw mats in front of low, wooden structures; and Shinto priests in traditional costumes, the images of these pages do not exhibit Japan as a world power which presented an economic or military threat.

The Potential Future of Imperial Funerals

Empress Teimei was the second empress to receive a large funeral monument, on par with and located next to that of her husband. Her monument at the Musashi Imperial Graveyard is a large earthen structure, similar to the style of a Buddhist stupa. The style of her grave, as with that of her husband's, is in the same form that imperial monuments took since the twelfth century and the same as Shōken's. Taishō and Teimei were the first to be buried near Tokyo, at a site that now includes their successors Hirohito and Kōjun.

In 2012 Emperor Akihito and Empress Michiko released a statement indicating that they desire cremation, the standard interment of most common citizens. The practice of large-scale imperial burials seems to be coming to a close; however, the Musashi Imperial Graveyard is still used for memorial commemorations and visited by members of the imperial family, with the visits frequently covered in the news. The practice of large state funerals for the imperial family is also potentially in question. Hirohito's funeral in 1989 and Kōjun's in 2000 were significant affairs, but the present changes in the imperial family's desires leave many unanswered questions. The 2019 Reiwa transition gives some hint that there will still be significant state events marking imperial transitions. Polling from the time of the transition that shows that there is still a public appetite for the Japanese monarchy, with some 80% responding positively to the imperial family.[32] As of March 2021, a government panel was convened to study the transitions of the imperial family; the resulting policy shifts may also lead to future changes in imperial funerals.[33]

Chapter 4 shows that during the regency years of 1920 to 1926, Teimei's image was a departure from that of her predecessor, Empress Shōken, and her successor, Empress Kōjun. Teimei had a stronger, more independent presence, as depicted in domestic media photographs. She was imaged as far more independent and modern than Shōken and far less conventional and maternal than Kōjun. Teimei was never shown in the same photographic frame as her husband, and only after she became empress dowager was she shown with her children and grandchildren in a single frame. In a similar fashion, Teimei's funerary images were an anomaly: dispassionate and cautious. These removed, distant images were part of the reassessment and reimaging of the imperial family in the postwar years and were a specific response to the political events of the spring of 1951. In the midst of the changing leadership of the occupying forces, it was crucial for the Imperial Household Agency to put forth an image that was not overly nostalgic or nationalist but which simultaneously exhibited the centrality of the imperial family as a Japanese cultural institution.

Imperial funerals were a critical component of social memory, and memorials acted to further entrench the position of the Japanese royal family in society. The atemporality and articulation of tradition evidenced in the visual culture surrounding funerary and memorial events worked to authenticate and justify the position of the modern institution. The pageantry simultaneously envisioned the celebrity culture of a global, modern monarchy but one which was bound to Japanese culture and history. The differing immediacy of media addressed in this chapter show how a single event was memorialized across newspapers, magazines, and photographic memorial books. Furthermore, from Eishō's funeral as the first public imperial memorial occasion of the modern age to Teimei's funeral as the first postwar imperial event, the central importance of women to the public image of the imperial household is evident in memorial affairs. As in life, in death, the modern Japanese empresses operated on the level of their husbands, cementing the visual monarchy in Japanese culture.

Notes

1 Eishō, empress consort of Emperor Kōmei (Meiji's father), died on January 11, 1897, but she did not live a public life in the same fashion as Shōken or Teimei. Kōjun died on June 16, 2000, and had a large, public funeral. Nakayama Yoshiko, Meiji's biological mother, died on October 5, 1907, and Yanagihara Naruko, Taishō's biological mother, died on October 16, 1943. Both Nakayama and Yanagihara's passings were covered in the mass media, but as *gon no tenji*, they did not receive the same commemoration as the empresses.
2 Atsuko Hirai, *Government by Mourning: Death and Political Integration in Japan, 1603–1912* (Cambridge, MA: Harvard University Asia Center, 2014).
3 Takashi Fujitani, *Splendid Monarchy: Power and Pageantry in Modern Japan* (Berkeley: University of California Press, 1996), 148.
4 Hirai, *Government by Mourning*, 366.
5 Adrian C. Mayer, "The Funeral of the Emperor of Japan," *Anthropology Today* 5, no. 3 (June 1989): 5.

6 Edmund Gilday, "Bodies of Evidence: Imperial Funeral Rites and the Meiji Restoration," *Japanese Journal of Religious Studies* 27, no. 3 (Fall 2000).
7 Gilday, "Bodies of Evidence," 289.
8 Gilday, "Bodies of Evidence," 289–290.
9 Donald Keene, *Emperor of Japan: Meiji and His World, 1852–1912* (New York: Columbia University Press, 2002), 530–532.
10 Keene, *Emperor of Japan*, 532.
11 Takagi Hiroshi, "The Buddhist Faith of the Japanese Imperial Family after the Meiji Restoration," *Japan Review* 25 (2013): 29.
12 An additional print of the same subject is *Aoyama Gotaisō shikijō sōmonzen no zu* (Illustration of the Main Gate at Aoyama During the Imperial Funeral Ceremony), Yasuda Hanpo, September 1912, triptych woodblock print, collection of the Boston MFA, https://collections.mfa.org/objects/155303.
13 John Carmi Parsons, "'Never Was a Body Buried in England with Such Solemnity and Honour': The Burials and Posthumous Commemorations of English Queens to 1500," in *Queens and Queenship in Medieval Europe*, ed. Anne J. Duggan (Suffolk: Boydell Press, 1995), 317–337, 333.
14 This image can be found in the Lafayette College collection, https://ldr.lafayette.edu/concern/images/9p290b45j.
15 Andrew Bernstein, *Modern Passings: Death Rites, Politics, and Social Change in Imperial Japan* (Honolulu: University of Hawai'i Press, 2006), 98.
16 Bernstein, *Modern Passings*, 47.
17 Kunaichō, *Shōken kōtaigō jitsuroku*, vol. 2 (Tokyo: Kunaicho, 2014), 742–756.
18 Christopher de Spiegeleer, "'Her Death Is as Saintly as Her Life'. Media Representations of Royal Deathbeds in Belgium, 1850–1910," *Mortality* 24, no. 4 (2019): 450–466.
19 As extremely detailed archival records document every aspect of imperial funerals, it is likely that there are documents showing publication house orders for the photo books from the various groups that published them, but the records are only partially accessible and are not indexed in a way that allows for searching by subject. For example, for Shōken's funeral, over 500 pages of archival materials related to her funeral planning are available as digital scans on the National Diet Library and National Archives databases, listed by date. For Taishō's funeral, a 587-page book provides funeral documentation but without an index. Further research into the details

of the production of the photo books is a potential topic for future research. *Taishō tennō godaisōgi kiroku* (Tokyo: Keishichō, 1928).

20 Teikoku gunjin kyōikukai, *Meiji Jingū oshashinchō: fu gozōeikiroku* (Tokyo: Teikoku gunjin kyōikukai shuppanbu, 1920).

21 *Taishō tennō goshashinchō* (Tokyo: Taishō tennō goshashinchō kankōkai, 1927). The book remains in copyright.

22 Hirai, *Government by Mourning*, 366–367.

23 *Taishō tennō gotaisō shashinchchō* (Tokyo: Dai Nihon kokumin kyōikukai, 1927).

24 For example, Teimei was commemorated in *Rokudai Shinpo* the month after her passing, June 1951, and again in October, 1951 and May 1952.

25 Jeffrey K. Olick and Joyce Robbins, "Social Memory Studies: From 'Collective Memory' to the Historical Sociology of Mnemonic Practices," *Annual Review of Sociology* 24 (1998): 105–106.

26 Originally called Tenchō setsu, the holiday commemorated Emperor Meiji's birthday throughout his reign. It was discontinued between 1912 and 1927, then reinstated as Meiji setsu. After 1948 the holiday was termed Bunka no hi, or Culture Day. Kogakuin University, "Meiji setsu," *Encyclopedia of Shinto*, http://eos.kokugakuin.ac.jp/modules/xwords/entry.php?entryID=894.

27 Yoshiko Imaizumi, "The Making of a Mnemonic Space: Meiji Shrine Memorial Art Gallery 1912–1936," *Japan Review* 23 (2011): 143–176.

28 Kawanishi Hideya, *Kindai tennōsei kara shōchō tennōsei e: "Shōchō" e no dōtei* (Tokyo: Yoshida shoten, 2018), 137–138.

29 Stephen Large, *Emperor Hirohito and Shōwa Japan: A Political Biography* (London: Routledge Japanese Studies, 1996).

30 Michio Kitahara, "Douglas MacArthur as a Father Figure in Occupied Japan After World War II," *International Social Science Review* 64, no. 1 (Winter 1989): 24.

31 "Japanese Bury Their Dowager Empress," *Life Magazine*, July 9, 1951, 33.

32 *The Japan Times*, "Nearly 80% in Japan Support Having Women the Throne and 82% Feel Affection for New Emperor," May 2, 2019. Digital.

33 Nakata Ayako and Narasaki Takashi, "Kōi keishō nennai ni ronten seiri e yūshikisha kaigi ga giron sutāto," *Asahi Shinbun Digital*, March 23, 2021.

CONCLUSION

On April 30, 2019, Emperor Naruhito was enthroned at the Imperial Palace in Tokyo. The images of the first and second enthronement, six months apart, were widely published in the global news media. As the current succession crisis of the imperial family is well known, commenters on social media were quick to point out the gender gap in the photographs: the emperor and empress stand upon a dais as he takes his vows, but off to the side the number of imperial women far outnumbers the men.

In the aftermath of World War II changes in the Imperial Household Law of 1947 dramatically constricted the number of members of the nobility and forced the women of the imperial household to rescind their status upon marriage. This reduced the number of members of the imperial household, resulting in the twenty-first–century succession crisis. Emperor Naruhito (徳仁) and Empress Masako (雅子) have only one daughter, Aiko, Princess Toshi (敬宮愛子内親王, b. 2001). Under Japan's current system of agnatic primogeniture, she is unable to become *tennō*, meaning that Naruhito will have to abdicate the throne to his younger brother Fumihito, Prince Akishino (秋篠宮文仁親王), declared heir to the throne in November 2020. It is assumed that Fumihito's single son Prince Hisahito (悠仁親王, b. 2006) will eventually inherit the title of *tennō*. Having a single heir apparent leaves the monarchy in a precarious position and means that the gender dynamics of family photos will have a higher number of women for the foreseeable future.[1] While the specifics of the succession crisis are distinct to the postwar period, the visually

DOI: 10.4324/9781003376101-10

feminine context for the imperial family is not new: as discussed in Chapter 2, images of the imperial family populated by a majority of women were common in the Meiji period.

As this book has shown, the imperial family was a central component of the modern Japanese state throughout the modern era. In the Meiji and Taishō periods, the biographies and lives of the emperor, empress, and their immediate family members were promoted through mass media sources, and their public image, as constructed by government agencies, had a major impact on conceptions of family and gender relations in the modern era. Many of the behaviors, rituals, and functions performed by the imperial family were established during the Meiji period and codified during the Taishō reign. It was during the Taishō period that most of these activities were performed in public for the first time and during the early Shōwa period that imperial rituals and rites came to be understood as normative, regular state functions.

By examining the key theme of the visual monarchy and investigating how common themes of queenship such as charity, piety, and maternity were promoted and communicated to the public vis-à-vis images, this book has shown how the office of the Japanese empress evolved over the modern era and transformed in tandem with the women occupying the role. This change itself was similar to developments happening in other nations around the world: the switch to the celebrity monarch was a major shift in how monarchy was conceptualized and worked as a means for institutional preservation in an era when religious justifications for hereditary thrones were waning. The simultaneous growth of mass media allowed for global celebrity culture to thrive in the modern visual environment. Against this backdrop the women of the imperial household, as part of a corporate monarchy, reshaped the very ideals of queenship in the modern era as the Japanese monarchy itself went through dramatic moves from hidden to visible, a culture of court consorts to one of monogamy, exclusively religious to holding a political position, and private to public, among others.

Furthermore, the biographical accounts provided within Part I and elaborated upon throughout this book are part of a larger contemporary movement to uncover women's history and bring women's stories further into the fold of mainstream scholarship.

While the empresses themselves were extraordinarily visible during their lifetimes and today maintain an important position in the visual monarchy, their stories are often opaque and obscured, overshadowed by the emperors, making it difficult to ascertain certain details of their lives. Drawing on diverse methodologies from gender studies and art history, as well as conventional archival methods, allows for more breadth in the narrative biographies of these imperial women. Decidedly there is more work to be done; this book can only act as a touch point for further scholarship on these compelling and important women.

The biographical accounts of Empress Shōken and Empress Teimei tell us much about Japanese queenship. The exercise of their roles established the very idea of the modern empress in Asia, pivoting from the secret, hidden world of the pre-Meiji imperial household to a court that was visible and influential in the public sphere, modeling proper comportment and behaviors in a variety of media. In line with, and reacting to, contemporary global monarchies in Asia and Europe, Shōken and Teimei had an outsized impact on Japanese women's social, economic, and political behaviors in the Meiji and Taishō eras, showing that their position as the premier woman at the head of the realm was central to Japan's project of modernity.

As images of the Japanese royals transitioned from fantasy woodblock prints to lithographs of lineage, mass media photographs to filmed documentaries, and from formal to familiar, sacred to symbolic, the visual monarchy responded to social and political concerns in domestic and international spheres. This book has shown the flexibility of the institution and the centrality of women to the Japanese monarchy, uncovering how the illusion of parasocial relationships maintained the celebrity status of the empresses through visual culture over time. The imperial institution may seem unstable, but through the power of the visual monarchy, they have endured innumerable crises through the modern period and will likely react to future predicaments with perseverance and flexibility.

Note

1 For more on the evolution of the imperial family photograph, see: Kitahara Megumi, "Gantan shimen ni miru tennō ikkazō no keisei," in *"Sei" no bunkatsusen: kin-gendai Nihon no jendā to shintai*, ed. Ogino Miho (Tokyo: Sekiyusha, 2009).

APPENDIX

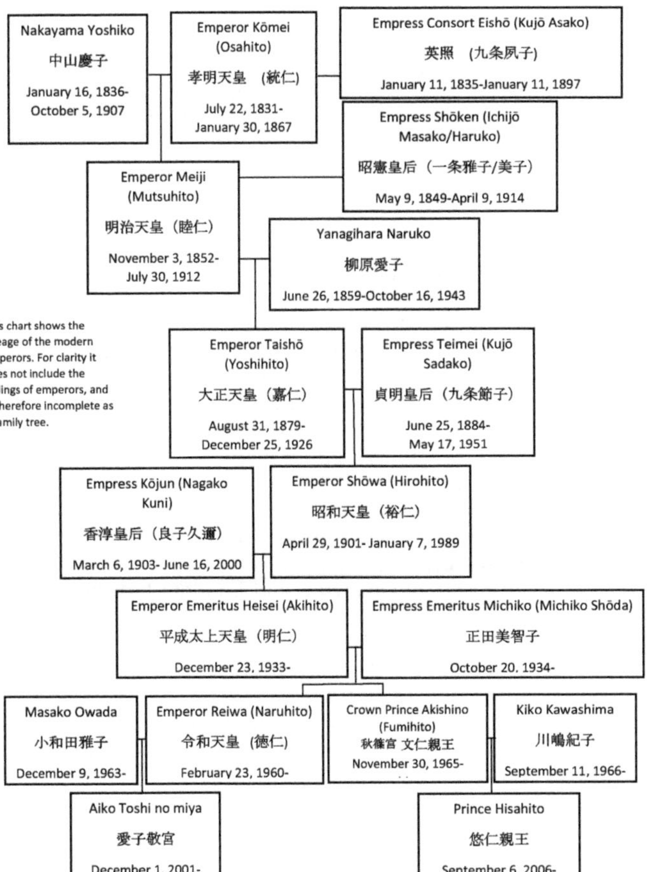

This chart shows the lineage of the modern emperors. For clarity it does not include the siblings of emperors, and is therefore incomplete as a family tree.

BIBLIOGRAPHY

Agency for Cultural Affairs. "Kunishite bunkazai tō dētabēsu." https://kunishitei.bunka.go.jp/bsys/index_pc.asp.

Ajioka, Chiaki. *Modern Boy, Modern Girl: Modernity in Japanese Art, 1910–35*. Sydney: Art Gallery of New South Wales, 1998.

Anderson, Marnie. *A Place in Public: Women's Rights in Meiji Japan*. Cambridge, MA: Harvard University Asia Center, 2010.

Aoki, Junko. "Zasshi 'Kōzoku gahō' ni miru kindai kōzoku fuasshon no imeji: gunpuku to doresu." *Contentsu Bunkashi Kenkyū* 8 (2013): 69–87.

Aoki, Shōji. "Goshinei chokugo tōhon 'hōan' no jissō: Yamagataken no jirei." *Yamagataken hakubutsukan kenkyū hōkoku* 26 (2006): 13–38.

Asahi shinbun. "Gosei." May 11, 1900.

Asahi shinbun. "Gyōkōkei o agite Tokyoshi tentosai." May 10, 1919.

Asahi shinbun. "Gunjijō yori mita fusen." March 29, 1923.

Asahi shinbun. "Mausoleum, Cremation Plans Revealed for Emperor, Empress." November 15, 2013. http://ajw.asahi.com/article/behind_news/social_affairs/AJ201311150060.

Baelz, Toku, ed. *Awakening Japan: The Diary of a German Doctor, Erwin Baelz*. Bloomington and London: Indiana University Press, 1974.

Bardsley, Jan. "Japanese Feminism, Nationalism and the Royal Wedding of Summer '93." *The Journal of Popular Culture* 31, no. 2 (Fall 1997): 189–205.

Batten, Bruce. *To the Ends of Japan: Premodern Frontiers, Boundaries, and Interactions*. Honolulu: University of Hawai'i Press, 2003.

Bennett, Terry. *Photography in Japan, 1853–1912*. Tokyo: Tuttle Publishing, 2006.

Bernstein, Andrew. *Modern Passings: Death Rites, Politics, and Social Change in Imperial Japan*. Honolulu: University of Hawai'i Press, 2006.

Bix, Herbert P. "Inventing the 'Symbol Monarchy' in Japan, 1945–1952." *Journal of Japanese Studies* 21 (Summer 1995): 319–363.

Bix, Herbert P. *Hirohito and the Making of Modern Japan*. New York: Harper Collins, 2000.

Blacker, Carmen. *The Catalpa Bow: A Study of Shamanistic Practices in Japan*. London: George Allen and Unwin, 1975.

Breen, John. "Ornamental Diplomacy: Emperor Meiji and the Monarchs of the Modern World." In *The Meiji Restoration: Japan as a Global Nation*, edited by Robert Hellyer and Harald Fuess, 232–248. Cambridge: Cambridge University Press, 2020.

Breen, John and Mark Teeuwen. *A New History of Shinto*. West Sussex: Wiley-Blackwell, 2010.

Breen, John and Mark Teeuwen. *A Social History of the Ise Shrines: Divine Capital*. London: Bloomsbury Shinto Studies, 2017.

Bunka gakuen fukushoku hakubutsukan. *Meiji, Taishō, Shōwa senzenki no kyūteifuku—yōsō to shōzoku*. Tokyo: Bunka gakuen fukushoku hakubutsukan, 2013.

Burns, Susan L. and Barbara J. Brooks, eds., *Gender and Law in the Japanese Imperium*. Honolulu: University of Hawai'i Press, 2014.

Chandler, Daniel and Rod Munday. *A Dictionary of Media and Communication*. Oxford: Oxford University Press, 2011. www.oxfordreference.com/view/10.1093/oi/authority.20110803100305809.

Chiba-shi bijutsukan. *Bunmei kaika no nishikie shinbun: Tōkyō nichinichi shinbun, yūbin hōchi shinbun zen sakuhin*. Tokyo: Kokusho kankōkai, 2008.

Clancey, Gregory. *Earthquake Nation: The Cultural Politics of Japanese Seismicity, 1868–1930*. Berkeley: University of California Press, 2006.

Coats, Bruce A. *Chikanobu: Modernity and Nostalgia in Japanese Prints*. Leiden: Brill, 2006.

Como, Michael. *Weaving and Binding: Immigrant Gods and Female Immortals in Ancient Japan*. Honolulu: University of Hawai'i Press, 2009.

Copeland, Rebecca. "Fashioning the Feminine: Images of the Modern Girl Student in Meiji Japan." *U.S.-Japan Women's Journal*, no. 30/31 (2006): 13–35.

Croissant, Doris. "Icons of Femininity: Japanese National Painting and the Paradox of Modernity." In *Gender and Power in the Japanese Visual Field*, edited by Joshua S. Mostow, Norman Bryson and Maribeth Graybill, 119–140. Honolulu: University of Hawai'i Press, 2003.

Croissant, Doris. "In Quest of the Real: Portrayal and Photography in Japanese Painting Theory." In *Challenging Past and Present: The Metamorphosis of Nineteenth-Century Japanese Art*, edited by Ellen P. Conant, 153–176. Honolulu: University of Hawai'i Press, 2006.

Curtis, Paula. "Japan's Once and Future Female Emperors." *Nursing Clio*. April 30, 2019. https://nursingclio.org/2019/04/30/japans-once-and-future-female-emperors/.

Dalby, Liza. *Kimono: Fashioning Culture*. New Haven: Yale University Press, 1993.

Denney, Colleen. *Representing Diana, Princess of Wales: Cultural Memory and Fairy Tales Revisited*. Madison, NJ: Fairleigh Dickinson University Press, 2005.

De Spiegeller, Christoph. " 'Her Death Is as Saintly as Her Life'. Media Representations of Royal Deathbeds in Belgium, 1850–1910." *Mortality* 24, no. 4 (2019): 450–466.

Dobson, Sebastian. "Frederick William Sutton, 1832–1883: Photographer of the Last Shogun." In *Britain and Japan: Biographical Portraits*, vol. 4, edited by Hugh Cortazzi. London: Japan Society, 1994.

Dunscomb, Paul E. *Japan's Siberian Intervention, 1918–1922*. Lanham, MD: Rowman & Littlefield Publishers, 2011.

Earenfight, Theresa. "Without the Persona of the Prince: Kings, Queens and the Idea of Monarchy in Late Medieval Europe." *Gender and History* 19, no. 1 (2007): 1–21.

Earenfight, Theresa. "Highly Visible Often Obscured: The Difficulty of Seeing Queens and Noble Women." *Medieval Feminist Forum: A Journal of Gender and Sexuality* 44, no. 1 (2008): 86–90.

Earenfight, Theresa. *The King's Other Body: Maria of Castile and the Crown of Aragon*. Philadelphia: University of Pennsylvania Press, 2009.

Edwards, Walter. *Modern Japan Through Its Weddings: Gender, Person, and Society in Ritual Portrayal*. Stanford: Stanford University Press, 1989.

Empress Shōken Fund. "Empress Shōken Fund." http://shokenfund.org/.

Evans, Jessica and David Hesmondhalgh, eds. *Understanding Media: Inside Celebrity*. Berkshire: Open University Press, 2005.

Ewing, Elizabeth and Alice Mackrell. *History of 20th Century Fashion*. London: B.T. Batsford, 1997.

Falero, Alfonso. "Origuchi Shinobu's *Marebitoron* in Global Perspective: A Preliminary Study." In *Classical Japanese Philosophy*, edited by J.W. Heisig and R. Raud, 274–302. Nagoya: Nanzan Institute for Religion and Culture, 2010.

Felski, Rita. *The Gender of Modernity*. Cambridge, MA: Harvard University Press, 1995.

Fleiner, Carey and Elena Woodacre, eds. *Virtuous or Villainess? The Image of the Royal Mother from the Early Medieval to the Early Modern Era*. New York: Palgrave Macmillan, 2016.

Foucault, Michel. *Discipline and Punish: The Birth of the Prison*. Translated by Alan Sheridan. New York: Vintage, 1977.

Fraser, Karen. "Beauty Battle: Politics and Portraiture in Late Meiji Japan." In *Visualizing Beauty: Gender and Ideology in Modern East Asia*, edited by Aida Yuen Wong. Hong Kong: Hong Kong University Press, 2012.

Frederick, Sarah. *Turning Pages: Reading and Writing Women's Magazines in Interwar Japan*. Honolulu: University of Hawai'i Press, 2006.

Freedman, Alisa, Laura Miller and Christine R. Yano. "You Go, Girl! Cultural Meanings of Gender, Mobility, and Labor." In *Modern Girls on the Go: Gender, Mobility, and Labor in Japan*, edited by Alisa Freedman, Laura Miller and Christine R. Yano, 1–20. Stanford: Stanford University Press, 2013.

Fuchs, Rachel G. and Victoria E. Thompson. *Women in Nineteenth-Century Europe*. New York: Palgrave Macmillan, 2005.

Fujimura-Fanselow, Kumiko. "The Japanese Ideology of 'Good Wives and Wise Mothers': Trends in Contemporary Research." *Gender and History* 3, no. 3 (1991): 345–349.

Fujin gahō. www.fujingaho.jp/.

Fujin gahō. "Fujin Gahō Media Kit." www.hearst.co.jp/brands/fujingaho/media_kit_print.

Fujitani, Takashi. *Splendid Monarchy: Power and Pageantry in Modern Japan*. Berkeley: University of California Press, 1996.

Fukuoka, Maki. *The Premise of Fidelity: Science, Visuality, and Representing the Real in Nineteenth-Century Japan*. Stanford: Stanford University Press, 2012.

Funke, Manuel, Moritz Schularick, and Christoph Trebesch. *Going to Extremes: Politics after Financial Crises, 1870–2014* (October 2015). CEPR Discussion Paper No. DP10884. CEPR Press, Paris and London. https://cepr.org/publications/dp10884

Furukawa, Takahisa. "Taishō tennō tōmeganejiken: naze fūsetsu ga umaretanoka." *Rekishi tokuhon* 55, no. 8 (2010): 132–137.

Garon, Sheldon. *Molding Japanese Minds: The State in Everyday Life*. Princeton: Princeton University Press, 1997.

Gartlan, Luke. "A Chronology of Baron Raimund von Stillfried-Ratenicz." In *Japanese Exchanges in Art 1850s–1930s*, edited by John Clark, 121–188. Sydney: Power Publications, 2001.

Gartlan, Luke. *A Career of Japan: Baron Raimund von Stillfried and Early Yokohama Photography*. Leiden: Brill, 2016.

Getty Art and Architecture Thesaurus. "Portraits." www.getty.edu/vow/AATFullDisplay?find=portrait&logic=AND&note=&english=N&prev_page=1&subjectid=300223022.

Gilday, Edmund T. "Bodies of Evidence: Imperial Funeral Rites and the Meiji Restoration." *Japanese Journal of Religious Studies* 27, no. 3/4 (2000): 273–296.

Gluck, Carol. *Japan's Modern Myths: Ideology in the Late Meiji Period*. Princeton: Princeton University Press, 1985.

Gluck, Carol. "The Invention of Edo." In *Mirror of Modernity: Invented Traditions of Modern Japan*, edited by Stephen Vlastos, 262–284. Berkeley: University of California Press, 1998.

Gomes, M. da Mota, Lucio Lage Goncalves, et al. "King George III of England and Queen Maria I of Portugal: Bipolar Disorder and Prince Regents as Common Features of Their Reigns." *Trends in Psychiatry and Psychotherapy* (March 19, 2023). https://doi.org/10.47626/2237-6089-2021-0315.

Gordon, Andrew. *A Modern History of Japan*. New York: Oxford University Press, 2009.

Griffis, William Elliot. *The Mikado: Institution and Person*. Princeton: Princeton University Press, 1915.

Guth, Christine. "Memorial Portraits of Kabuki Actors: Fanfare in the Floating World." *Impressions*, no. 27 (2005): 22–41.

Hämmerle, Christa, Oswald Überegger and Birgitta Bader Zaar. *Gender and the First World War*. Basingstoke, Hampshire: Palgrave Macmillan, 2014.

Hara, Takeshi. *Taishō tennō*. Tokyo: Asahi shinbunsha, 2000.

Hara, Takeshi. "Emperor Taishō—Image vs. Reality." *Japan Quarterly* 48, no. 2 (2001): 56–63.

Hara, Takeshi. "'Kokutai' no shikakuka—Taishō·Shōwa shoki ni okeru tennōsei no saihen." In *Ō o meguru shisen*, edited by Yoshihiko Amino, 135–159. Vol. 10 of *Tennō to ōken o kangaeru*. Tokyo: Iwanami shoten, 2002.

Hara, Takeshi. "Taishō: An Enigmatic Emperor and His Influential Wife." In *The Emperors of Modern Japan*, edited by Ben-Ami Shillony, 211–225. Leiden: Brill, 2007.

Hara, Takeshi. *Kōgōkō*. Tokyo: Kodansha, 2015.

Hardacre, Helen. *Shinto and the State, 1868–1988*. Princeton: Princeton University Press, 1989.
Hardacre, Helen. *Shinto: A History*. Oxford: Oxford University Press, 2017.
Hastings, Sally A. "Empress Nagako and the Family State." In *The Emperors of Modern Japan*, edited by Ben-Ami Shillony, 241–269. Leiden: Brill, 2008.
Hayakawa, Noriyo. *Kindai tennōsei to kokumin kokka*. Tokyo: Aoki shoten, 2005.
Hayakawa, Noriyo. "The Formation of Modern Imperial Japan from the Perspective of Gender." Translated by Leonie Stickland and Urlike Wöhr. In *Gender, Nation and State in Modern Japan*, edited by Andrea Germer, Vera Mackie and Ulrike Wöhr, 25–47. London: Routledge, 2014.
Hellyer, Robert and Harald Fuess, eds. *The Meiji Restoration: Japan as a Global Nation*. Cambridge: Cambridge University Press, 2020.
Hinsch, Bret. *Chinese Empresses: The Nature of Female Power*. Lanham: Rowman & Littlefield, 2024.
Hirai, Atsuko. *Government by Mourning: Death and Political Integration in Japan, 1603–1912*. Cambridge, MA: Harvard University Asia Center, 2014.
Hirase, Reita. *"Shōzō" bunkakō*. Tokyo: Shunjusha, 2014.
Hirayama, Mikiko. "The Emperor's New Clothes: Japanese Visuality and Imperial Portrait Photography." *History of Photography* 33, no. 2 (2009): 165–184.
Hogge, David. "Alice in Asia: The 1905 Taft Mission to Asia." *Freer Sackler Galleries, Smithsonian Institution*. www.asia.si.edu/research/archives/alice/.
Homans, Margaret. *Royal Representations: Queen Victoria and British Culture, 1837–1876*. Chicago: University of Chicago Press, 1998.
Honjo, Shigeru. *Emperor Hirohito and His Chief Aide-de-Camp: The Honjo Diary, 1933–1936*. Translated by Mikiso Hane. Tokyo: University of Tokyo Press, 1967.
Hori, Hikari. *Promiscuous Media: Film and Visual Culture in Imperial Japan, 1926–1945*. Cornell: Cornell University Press, 2017.
Hosoi, Wakizō. *Jokō Aishi*. Tokyo: Iwanami Shoten, 2009. Reprint 1925.
Howarth, David. *Images of Rule: Art and Politics in the English Renaissance, 1485–1689*. Berkeley: University of California Press, 1997.
Howe, Sondra Wieland. "Women Music Educators in Japan During the Meiji Period." *Bulletin of the Council for Research in*

Music Education 119. The 14th International Society for Music Education: ISME Research Seminar (Winter 1993/1994): 101–109.

Howe, Sondra Wieland. "The Role of Women in the Introduction of Western Music in Japan." *The Bulletin of Historical Research in Music Education* 16, no. 2 (January 1995): 81–97.

Huffman, James L. *Creating a Public: People and Press in Meiji Japan*. Honolulu: University of Hawai'i Press, 1997.

Hvass, Svend M. *Ise: Japan's Ise Shrines, Ancient Yet New*. Holte, Denmark: Aristo, 1999.

Ichiro, Kikuchi. "Hansen's Disease in Japan: A Brief History." *International Journal of Dermatology* 36 (1997): 629–633.

Igarashi, Yoshikuni. *Bodies of Memory: Narratives of War in Postwar Japanese Culture, 1945–1970*. Princeton: Princeton University Press, 2000.

Ikeda, Shinobu. "The Allure of a 'Woman in Chinese Dress': Representation of the Other in Imperial Japan." In *Performing "Nation": Gender Politics in Literature, Theater, and the Visual Arts of China and Japan, 1880–1940*, edited by Doris Croissant, Catherine Vance Yeh and Joshua S. Mostow, 347–382. Leiden: Brill, 2008.

Imaizumi, Yoshiko. "The Making of a Mnemonic Space: Meiji Shrine Memorial Art Gallery 1912–1936." *Japan Review* 23 (2011): 143–176.

Imaizumi, Yoshiko. *Sacred Space in the Modern City: The Fractured Pasts of Meiji Shrine, 1912–1958*. Leiden: Brill, 2013.

Imatani, Akira. "The Strange Survival and Its Modern Significance." In *The Emperors of Modern Japan*, edited by Ben-Ami Shillony, 15–22. Leiden: Brill, 2007.

International Federation of the Red Cross and Red Crescent. "Empress Shoken Fund: Supporting Red Cross Red Crescent Work For 100 Years." www.ifrc.org/en/news-and-media/news-stories/asia-pacific/japan/empress-shoken-fund-supporting-red-cross-red-crescent-work-for-100-years/.

Isao, Toroko. *Kōi keishō no arikata: "josei, boeki tennō" wa kanō ka*. Tokyo: PHP, 2006.

Itō, Kimio. "The Invention of Wa and the Transformation of the Image of Prince Shōtoku in Modern Japan." In *Mirror of Modernity*, edited by Stephen Vlastos, 37–47. Berkeley: University of California Press, 1998.

Ivy, Marilyn. *Discourses of the Vanishing: Modernity, Phantasm, Japan*. Chicago: University of Chicago Press, 1995.

Iwamoto, Tsutomu. *Goshinei ni junijita kyōshitachi*. Tokyo: Ōtsuki shoten, 1989.

Izao, Tomio. "Shinbun no naka no Shiberia shuppei." *Yamaguchi kenritsu daigaku kokusai bunka gakubu kiyō* 12 (2006): 1–12.

Jacob, Frank. "Queen Min, Foreign Policy and the Role of Female Leadership in Late Nineteenth-Century Korea." In *The Routledge History of Monarchy*, edited by Elena Woodacre, Lucinda H.S. Dean, et al., 700–717. London: Routledge, 2019.

Jansen, Marius. "Monarchy and Modernization in Japan." *Journal of Asian Studies* 36 (August 1977): 611–622.

Japanese Architecture and Art Net Users System. "Nise-e." www.aisf.or.jp/~jaanus/deta/n/nisee.htm.

Japanese Red Cross Society. "History." www.jrc.or.jp/english/about/history/.

Japan Times. "Lawsuit Filed Against Japan's State-Funded Ceremonies to Mark Imperial Enthronement." December 11, 2018. www.japantimes.co.jp/news/2018/12/11/national/crime-legal/lawsuit-filed-japans-state-funded-ceremonies-marking-imperial-enthronement/.

Japan Times. "Nearly 80% in Japan Support Having Women on the Throne and 82% Feel Affection for New Emperor." May 2, 2019.

Jaundrill, D. Colin. *Samurai to Soldier: Remaking Military Service in Nineteenth-Century Japan*. Cornell: Cornell University Press, 2016.

Jiang, Hua. "Kōtō jogakkō ni okeru ryōsai kenbo kyōiku no jissai ni kansuru kōsatsu—kōchō nado no kunwa, kōkun, seitokokoroe, ryō seikatsu nado no bunseki o chūshin ni shite." *Waseda daigaku daigakuin kyōikugaku kenkyūka* 19 (2011): 81–91.

Josephson, Jason Ānanda. *The Invention of Religion in Japan*. Chicago: University of Chicago Press, 2012.

Kadoya, Atsushi. "Myths, Rites, and Icons: Three Views of a Secret." In *The Culture of Secrecy in Japanese Religion*, edited by Bernhard Scheid and Mark Teeuwen, 269–283. New York: Routledge, 2006.

Kanagawa kenritsu hakubutsukan. *Oke no shōzō: Meiji kōshitsu arubamu no hajimari*. Yokohama: Kanagawa kenritsu rekishi hakubutsukan, 2001.

Kanō, Mikiyo, ed. *Josei to tennōsei*. "'Omigokoro' to 'hahagokoro': 'Yasukuni no haha' o umidasu mono." In *Josei to tennōsei*, edited by Kanō Mkiyo, 64–81. Tokyo: Shisō no kagakusha, 1979.

Kanō, Mikiyo. *Tennōsei to gendā*. Tokyo: Inpakuto shupansha, 2002.

Kantorowicz, Ernst H. *The King's Two Bodies: A Study in Medieval Political Theology*. Princeton: Princeton University Press, 1998.

Karatani, Kojin. "The Discursive Space of Modern Japan." Translated by Seiji M. Lippit. In *Kojin Karatani: History and Repetition*, edited by Seiji M. Lippit, 47–86. New York: Columbia University Press, 2004.

Karatani, Kojin and Seiji M. Lippit. "The Discursive Space of Modern Japan." *boundary* 2, no. 18 (1991): 203–204.

Karlin, Jason G. *Gender and Nation in Meiji Japan: Modernity, Loss, and the Doing of History*. Honolulu: University of Hawai'i Press, 2014.

Kamiya, Makiko. "Saishoki no 'Kōshitsu eiga' ni kansuru kōsatsu: Kakusareru/sarasareru 'karada'." *Eizōgaku* 100 (2018): 32–52.

Kamiya, Masako. "Is the Japanese Monarchy in Crisis Due to Its Gender Bias?" *Royal Studies Journal* 7, no. 2 (2020): 117–132.

Kasza, Gregory J. *The State and Mass Media in Japan, 1918–1945*. Berkeley: University of California Press, 1988.

Katano, Masako. *Kōgō no kindai*. Tokyo: Kodansha, 2003.

Kato, Shūichi. "Taishō Democracy as the Pre-Stage for Japanese Militarism." In *Japan in Crisis: Essays on Taishō Democracy*, edited by Bernard S. Silberman and H.D. Harootunian, 217–236. Princeton: Princeton University Press, 1970.

Kawaguchi, Yukiya. "Portraits of the Self: Characteristics and Development of Asian Portraits." In *Self and Other: Portraits from Asia and Europe*, edited by Kenji Yoshida and Brian Durrans. Tokyo: Asahi Shinbun, 2008.

Kawahara, Toshiaki. *Higeki no kōjo: Mikasanomiya futagosetsu no shinsō*. Tokyo: Dainamiku-sarazu, 1984.

Kawahara, Toshiaki. *Hirohito and His Times*. Tokyo: Kōdansha International, 1990.

Kawamoto, Aya. "Chōsen to Nihon ni okeru ryōsai kenbo shisō ni kansuru hikaku kenkyū: Kaikokuki kara 1940 nendai zenhan o chūshin ni." *Osaka shiritsu daigaku shakaigaku kenkyūkai* 11 (2010): 51–66.

Kawamura, Kunimitsu. "Tennōke no konin to shussan." In *Ō o meguru shisen*, edited by Yoshihiko Amino, 161–182. Vol. 10 of *Tennō to ōken o kangaeru*. Tokyo: Iwanami shoten, 2002.

Kawanishi, Hideya. *Kindai tennōsei kara shōchō tennōsei e: "Shōchō" e no dōtei*. Tokyo: Yoshida shoten, 2018.

Kawase, Hiroyuki. *Teimei kōgō: kokō no kokubo shirarezaru "Shōwa tennō no haha,"* Tokyo: Ushioshoshobo kojinshinsha, 2020.

Keene, Donald. "Portraits of Emperor Meiji." *Impressions* 21 (1999).

Keene, Donald. *Emperor of Japan: Meiji and His World, 1852–1912*. New York: Columbia University Press, 2002.

Kent, Susan Kingsley. *Queen Victoria: Gender and Empire*. Oxford: Oxford University Press, 2016.

Kim, Gyewon. "Tracing the Emperor: Photography, Famous Places, and the Imperial Progresses in Prewar Japan." *Representations* 120 (Fall 2012): 115–150.

Kitahara, Megumi. "Gantan shimen ni miru tennō ikkazō no keisei." In *"Sei" no bunkatsusen: kin-gendai Nihon no jendā to shintai*, edited by Ogino Miho, 19–56. Tokyo: Sekiyusha, 2009.

Kitahara, Michio. "Douglas MacArthur as a Father Figure in Occupied Japan After World War II." *International Social Science Review* 64, no. 1 (Winter 1989): 20–28.

Kitamura, Tōkoku. *Kokumin to shisō*. Tokyo: Aozora Bunko, 1893. Reprinted 2004.

Kitano, Masako. "Kindai kōgōron." In *Jendā to sabetsu*, edited by Yoshihiko Amino, 79–103. Vol. 7 of *Tennō to ōken o kangaeru*. Tokyo: Iwanami shoten, 2002.

Kobayashi, Shigeyoshi. *Meiji no Tokyo seikatsu: josei no kaita Meiji no nikki*. Tokyo: Kadokawa shoten, 1991.

Kogakuin University. "Meiji setsu." *Encyclopedia of Shinto*. http://eos.kokugakuin.ac.jp/modules/xwords/entry.php?entryID=894.

Kōgō no doresu no nazu. NHK. Aired March 18, 2023. www.nhk.jp/p/ts/98L4Y9JJ62/episode/te/6678RN8VNV/.

Kōjiki. Translated by Donald L. Phillipi. Princeton: Princeton University Press, 1969.

Kojima, Kaoru. "The Image of Woman as a National Icon in Modern Japanese Art: 1890s–1930s." PhD Thesis. University of the Arts London, 2006.

"Kokutai no hongi." 1937. In *Sources of Japanese Tradition*, edited by W. Theodore deBary, Carol Gluck and Arthur L. Tiedemann, 968–973. New York: Columbia University Press, 2005.

Koscak, Stephanie E. *Monarchy, Print Culture, and Reverence in Early Modern England: Picturing Royal Subjects*. New York: Routledge Studies in Eighteenth-Century Cultures and Societies, 2021.

Kōshitsu tenpan. https://elaws.e-gov.go.jp/document?law_unique_id=322AC0000000003.

Koyama, Itoko. *Nagako: Empress of Japan*. New York: John Day Co., 1958.

Koyama, Noboru. *Japanese Students at Cambridge University in the Meiji Era, 1868–1912: Pioneers for the Modernization of Japan*. Translated by Ian Ruxton. Raleigh, NC: Lulu, 2004.

Koyama, Shizuko. "Domestic Roles and the Incorporation of Women into the Nation-State: The Emergence and Development of the 'Good Wife, Wise Mother' Ideology." Translated by Vera Mackie. In *Gender, Nation and State in Modern Japan*, edited by Andrea Germer, Vera Mackie and Ulrike Wöhr, 85–100. London: Routledge, 2014.

Kudō, Miyoko. *Hahamiya Teimei kōgō to sono jidai: Mikasa nomiya ryōdenka ga kataru omoide*. Tokyo: Chuokoron shinsha, 2010.

Kunaichō. "Emperor Shōwa and Empress Kōjun." www.kunaicho.go.jp/e-about/history/history11.html.

Kunaichō. "Genealogy of the Emperors of Japan." www.kunaicho.go.jp/e-about/genealogy/img/keizu-e.pdf.

Kunaichō. "Imperial Funerals, Accession to the Throne, Weddings, and other Events." www.kunaicho.go.jp/e-about/seido/seido10.html.

Kunaichō. "Imperial Sericulture of Her Majesty the Empress," DVD. Mainichieiga Co Ltd., 2013. www.youtube.com/watch?v=Md0UErOni4U.

Kunaichō. *Meiji tennō ki*. Tokyo: Yoshikawa kōbunkan, 1968–1977.

Kunaichō. "Organizations and Functions of the Imperial Household Agency." www.kunaicho.go.jp/e-kunaicho/soshiki.html.

Kunaichō. *Shōken kōtaigō jitsuroku*. Tokyo: Kunaichō, 2014.

Kunaichō. *Shōwa tennō jitsuroku*. Tokyo: Tokyo Shoseki, 2014–2017.

Kunaichō sannomaru shōzōkan. *Meiji jūninen Meiji Tennō gokamei "jinbutsu shashinchō": 4500-yomei no shōzō*. Tokyo: Kunaichō, 2013.

Kuramochi, Motoi. "Meiji tennō shashin hiroku." *Rekishi yomihon* 54, no. 3 (2009): 26–36.

Kurazumi, Yuko. "Kindai joshi dōtoku kyōiku no rekishi: Ryōsai kenbo to joshi tokuseiron to iu futatsu no isō." *Tokyo daigaku dagakuin kyōikugaku kenkyūka kyōikugaku kenkyūshitsu* 34 (2008): 49–57.

Kuroda, Hideo. "Kinsei no tennō to shōgun no shozōga." In *Ō no shintai ō no shōzō*. Tokyo: Heibonsha, 1993.

Kushner, Barak. *The Thought War: Japanese Imperial Propaganda*. Honolulu: University of Hawai'i Press, 2006.

Kyoto kokuritsu kindai bijutsukan. *Kōshitsu no meihin: kindai Nihon bijutsu no iki*. Kyoto: Kyoto kokuritsu kindai bijutsukan, 2013.

Lachaud, Frédérique and Michael Penman. *Absentee Authority across Medieval Europe*. Rochester, NY: Boydell & Brewer, 2017.

Langley, William. "Japanese Empress Who Dreams of Being Invisible." *Telegraph*, May 20, 2007. www.telegraph.co.uk/comment/personal-view/3639999/Japanese-Empress-who-dreams-of-being-invisible.html.

Lanman, Charles. *The Japanese in America*. New York: University Publishing Company, 1872.

Large, Stephen S. *Emperor Hirohito and Shōwa Japan: A Political Biography*. London: Routledge Japanese Studies, 1996.

Large, Stephen S. *Emperors of the Rising Sun: Three Biographies*. Tokyo: Kodansha International, 1997.

Lebra, Takie Sugiyama. *Above the Clouds: Status Culture of the Modern Japanese Nobility*. Berkeley: University of California Press, 1993.

Lee, Woo-young. "The Making of a Joseon Queen: Exhibition Highlights Queens and Concubines of Joseon." *The Korea Herald*, July 13, 2015.

Li, Vivian, ed. *The Kimono in Print: 300 Years of Japanese Design*. Worcester: Worcester Museum of Art, 2021.

Life Magazine. "Japanese Bury Their Dowager Empress." July 9, 1951.

Linhart, Sepp. "The Japanese Emperors as Seen on Japanese and Western Postcards, 1900–1945." In *Nihon bunka no chū no tennō—tennō to wa?* Tokyo: Kokusai nihongaku kenkyū sōsho, 2008.

Lokowandt, Ernst. "The Imperial House Law and Its Meaning for the Position of the Tennō in the Meiji State." In *Leaders and Leadership in Japan*, edited by Ian Nery, 128–146. Surrey: Japan Library, 1996.

Low, Morris. *Japan on Display: Photography and the Emperor*. New York: Routledge, 2006.

Lowy, Dina. *The Japanese "New Woman" Images of Gender and Modernity*. Rutgers: Rutgers University Press, 2007.

Lucken, Michael. "Classical Greece in Japan. Why It Matters. A Postcolonial Perspective." In *The Visual Culture of Meiji Japan: Negotiating the Transition to Modernity*, edited by Ayelet Zohar and Alison J. Miller, 46–57. New York: Routledge, 2021.

Lyden, Anne M., ed. *A Royal Passion: Queen Victoria and Photography*. Los Angeles: J. Paul Getty Museum, 2014.

MacWilliams Mark W. and Okuyama Michiaki. *Defining Shinto: A Reader*. New York: Routledge, 2020.

Mae, Michiko. "The Nexus of Nation, Culture and Gender in Modern Japan: The Resistance of Kanno Sugako and Kaneko Fumiko." Translated by Leonie Stickland. In *Gender, Nation and State in Modern Japan*, edited by Andrea Germer, Vera Mackie and Ulrike Wöhr, 68–84. London: Routledge, 2014.

Mainichi shinbunsha. *Tennō yondai no shōzō: Meiji Taishō Shōwa Heisei*. Tokyo: Mainichi shinbunsha, 1999.

Makibayashi, Kōji. "Hihyō no seisei: 'Kokumin to shisō' tameshikō." *Nihon bungaku* 40, no. 11 (1991).

Marcus, Sharon. *The Drama of Celebrity*. Princeton: Princeton University Press, 2019.

Marshall, Amy Bliss. *Magazines and the Making of Mass Culture in Japan*. Toronto: University of Toronto Press, 2019.

Martin, Peter. *The Chrysanthemum Throne: A History of the Emperors of Japan*. Honolulu: University of Hawai'i Press, 1997.

Masato, Miyachi. *Tokugawa Yoshinobu, Akitake, Yoshikatsu shashinshū: Shogun tonosama ga totta Bakumatsu Meiji*. Tokyo: Shin jinbutsu ōraisha, 1996.

Mashino, Keiko. "Meiji tennō imeji no hensen nitsuite: sekihanga ni miidaseru tennōzō." *Bijutsushi kenkyū* 38 (2000).

Maxey, Trent E. *The 'Greatest Problem': Religion and State Formation in Meiji Japan*. Cambridge, MA: Harvard University Asia Center, 2014.

Mayer, Adrian C. "The Funeral of the Emperor of Japan." *Anthropology Today* 5, no. 3 (June 1989): 3–6.

Mayer, Adrian C. "Recent Succession Ceremonies of the Emperor of Japan." *Japan Review* 2 (1991): 35–61.

McCormick, Melissa. *The Tale of Genji: A Visual Companion*. Princeton: Princeton University Press, 2018.

McNeill, David and Herbert P. Bix. "Trouble at the Top: Japan's Imperial Family in Crisis." *Asia-Pacific Journal: Japan Focus* 2 (2004): n.p.

McPherson, Heather. *Art and Celebrity in the Age of Reynolds and Siddons*. University Park, PA: Penn State University Press, 2017.

Meech-Pekarik, Julia. *The World of the Meiji Print: Impressions of a New Civilization*. New York: Weatherhill, 1986.

Meiji jingū. *Nisei Goseda Hōryū to kindai yoga no keifu: kindai no rekishiga no kaitakusha: Meiji Jingū kyōgaku kenkyū sentā*. Tokyo: Meiji jingu, 2006.

Meiji jingū. *Meiji no kōgō: Meiji tennō to ayumareta Shōken kōtaigō*. Tokyo: Meiji jingū, 2014.

Meiji jingū. "Facts About Meiji jingu." www.meijijingu.or.jp/english/about/1.html.

Meiji jingū gaien. *Seitokukinen kaigakan hekiga, Meiji jingū*. Tokyo: Meiji jingu gaien, 2009.

Migita, Hiroki. "'Kōshitsu gurabia' to 'goshinei': senzenki shinbun zasshi ni okeru kōshitsu shashin no tsūjiteki bunseki." *Kyōtō shakaigaku nenpō* (2001): 93–114.

Miller, Alison J. "Coronation of Emperor Taishō." In *Divine Inspiration in Japanese Prints*, Spencer Museum of Art, 2012. www.spencerart.ku.edu/exhibitions/divine-inspiration/miller-taisho.shtml.

Miller, Alison J. "Imperial Images: The Japanese Empress Teimei in Early Twentieth-Century Newspaper Photography." *Trans Asia Photography* 7, no. 1 (October 1, 2016): n.p. https://doi.org/10.1215/215820251_7-1-103

Miller, Alison J. "Imaging Industry: Woodblock Prints, Factory Women, and Sericulture in Meiji Japan." In *The Visual Culture of Meiji Japan: Negotiating the Transition to Modernity*, edited by Ayelet Zohar and Alison J. Miller, 92–110. New York: Routledge, 2021.

Mitchell, Richard H. *Thought Control in Prewar Japan*. Ithaca: Cornell University Press, 1976.

Mitchell, Richard H. *Censorship in Imperial Japan*. Princeton: Princeton University Press, 1983.

Miyajima, Shinichi. *Shōzōga*. Tokyo: Yoshikawa Kōbunkan, 1994.

Miyajima, Shinichi. *Shōzōga no shisen*. Tokyo: Yoshikawa kōbunkan, 1996.

Morishima, Yuki. "Political and Ritual Usages of Portraits of Japanese Emperors in Eighteenth and Nineteenth Centuries." PhD Dissertation. University of Pittsburgh, 2014.

Mosley, Leonard. *Hirohito: Emperor of Japan*. London: Weidenfeld and Nicolson, 1966.

Murakami, Shigeyoshi. *Kokka Shintō*. Tokyo: Iwanami shinsho, 1970.

Nakagawa, Keiichiro and Henry Rosovsky. "The Case of the Dying Kimono: The Influence of Changing Fashions on the Development of the Japanese Woolen Industry." *Business History Review* 37, no. 1&2 (1963): 59–78.

Nakano, Masashi. *Josei tennōron: shōchō tennōron to Nippon no mirai*. Tokyo: Asahi shinbunsha, 2004.

Nakata, Ayako and Narasaki Takashi. "Kōi keishō nennai ni ronten seiri e yūshikisha kaigi ga giron sutāto." *Asahi Shinbun Digital*, March 23, 2021.

Nakazawa, Shin'ichi. *Kodai kara kuta miraijin: Origuchi Shinobu*. Tokyo: Chikuma Primer Shinsho, 2008.

Naruse, Fujio. *Nihon shōzōgashi*. Tokyo: Chūōkōron bijutsu shuppan, 2005.

Nelson-Davis, Julie. *Utamaro and the Spectacle of Beauty*. Honolulu: University of Hawai'i Press, 2008.

New York Times. "Japanese Bury Dowager in Pomp." June 23, 1951.

Nihongi 697. Translated by W.G. Aston. London: Japan Society, 1896.

Nihon shoki. Translated by Hideo Yamada. Tokyo: Kyōikusha, 1979.

Nolte, Sharon H. and Sally Ann Hastings. "The Meiji State's Policy Toward Women, 1890–1910." In *Recreating Japanese Women, 1600–1945*, edited by Gail Lee Bernstein, 151–174. Berkeley: University of California Press, 1991.

The Official Website of the British Monarchy. "Order of the Garter." www.royal.gov.uk/monarchUK/honours/Orderofthegarter/orderofthegarter.aspx.

Ōhara, Yasuo. "Shinto shirei [The Shinto Directive]." *Encyclopedia of Shinto*. Kokugakuin University. http://k-amc.kokugakuin.ac.jp/DM/dbTop.do?class_name=col_eos.

Olick, Jeffrey K. and Joyce Robbins. "Social Memory Studies: From 'Collective Memory' to the Historical Sociology of Mnemonic Practices." *Annual Review of Sociology* 24 (1998): 105–140.

Ono, Masaaki. "Taishō tennō no goshinei kafu to sono 'bōgo' keitai no mosaku: Miyazakiken ni yoru Kyūshū, Okinawa chihō kakuken no goshinei 'bōgo' jittaichōsa no imi." *Kyōiku shigakkai kiyō* 48 (2005): 28–38.

Ono, Masaaki. "Tennō no shōzō shashin (goshinei) to gakkō to no kankeishi kenkyū." PhD Dissertation. Nihon daigaku, 2011.

Orbach, Danny. *Curse on This Country: The Rebellious Army of Imperial Japan*. Cornell: Cornell University Press, 2017.

Origuchi, Shinobu. *Origuchi Shinobu zenshū*. Tokyo: Chūō kōronsha, 1966.

Otabe, Yūji. *Kōzoku*. Tokyo: Chūōkōron shinsha, 2009.

Otabe, Yūji. *Shōken kōtaigō Teimei kōgō: hitosuji ni makoto o mochite tsukaenaba*. Kyoto: Mineruva Nihon hyōdensen, 2010.

Ozawa, Asae. *Meiji no kōshitsu kenchiku: kokka ga motometa "wafū" zō*. Tokyo: Yoshikawa kōbunkan, 2008.

Parsons, John Carmi. " 'Never Was a Body Buried in England with Such Solemnity and Honour': The Burials and Posthumous Commemorations of English Queens to 1500." In *Queens and Queenship in Medieval Europe*, edited by Anne J. Duggan, 317–337. Suffolk: Boydell Press, 1995.

Patessio, Mara. *Women and Public Life in Early Meiji Japan: The Development of the Feminist Movement*. Ann Arbor: Michigan Monograph Series in Japanese Studies, 2011.

Peat, Rachel, ed. *Japan Courts and Culture*. London: Royal Collection Trust, 2020.

Peleggi, Maurizio. *Lords of Things: The Fashioning of the Siamese Monarchy's Modern Image*. Honolulu: University of Hawai'i Press, 2002.

Peng, Ying-chen. *Artful Subversion: Empress Dowager Cixi's Image Making*. New Haven: Yale University Press, 2023.

Perelman, Elisheva A. "The Japanese Way of Silence and Seclusion: Memes of Imperial Women." *Asia-Pacific Journal* 12, no. 41 (October 13, 2014): n.p.

Piggott, Joan R. *The Emergence of Japanese Kingship*. Stanford: Stanford University Press, 1997.

Piggott, Juliet. *Queen Alexandra's Royal Army Nursing Corps*. London: Leo Cooper Ltd., 1975.

Ponce de Leon, Charles L. *Self-Exposure: Human-Interest Journalism and the Emergence of Celebrity in America, 1890–1940*. Chapel Hill: University of North Carolina Press, 2002.

Redfern, Mary. "Dinner Table Negotiations: Tableware and the presentation of Japan at the Enryōkan." In *The Visual Culture of Meiji Japan: Negotiating the Transition to Modernity*, edited by Ayelet Zohar and Alison J. Miller, 75–91. New York: Routledge, 2021.

Reid, T.R. "The Empress Speaks." *The Washington Post*, December 13, 1993.

Rich, Motoko. "As a New Emperor Is Enthroned in Japan, His Wife Won't Be Allowed to Watch." *New York Times*, April 29, 2019.

Roces, Mina and Louise Edwards. "Transnational Flows and the Politics of Dress in Asia and the Americas." In *The Politics of Dress in Asia and the Americas*, edited by Mina Roces and Louise Edwards, 1–18. Eastbourne: Sussex Academic Press, 2007.

Ruckston, Ian. "Suematsu Kenchō, 1855–1920: Statesman, Bureaucrat, Diplomat, Journalist, Poet and Scholar." In *Britain and Japan: Biographical Portraits*. Vol. 5, edited by Hugh Cortazzi, n/p. Folkestone: Global Oriental, 2005.

Ruoff, Kenneth J. *The People's Emperor: Democracy and the Japanese Monarchy, 1945–1995*. Cambridge, MA: Harvard East Asia Monographs, 2001.

Ruoff, Kenneth J. *Imperial Japan at Its Zenith: The Wartime Celebration of the Empire's 2,600th Anniversary*. Ithaca: Cornell University Press, 2010.

Saaler, Sven. *Men in Metal: A Topography of Public Bronze Statuary in Modern Japan*. Leiden: Brill, 2020.

Sand, Jordan. *House and Home in Modern Japan*. Cambridge, MA: Harvard University Press, 2004.

Sannomaru Shōzōkan. *Kōgō heika no goyōsan to Shōsōin-gire no fukugen: Kōgō heika koki kinen tokubetsuten*. Tokyo: Kunaichō, 2005.

Sasaki, Suguru. "Kindai tennō no imeji to zuzō." In *Hyōchō to geinō*, edited by Ōtsuka Shinichi, 139–163. Vol. 6 of *Tennō to ōken o kangaeru*. Tokyo: Iwanami shoten, 2002.

Sasamoto-Collins, Hiromi. "The Emperor's Sovereign Status and the Legal Construction of Gender in Early Meiji Japan." *The Journal of Japanese Studies* 43, no. 2 (Summer 2017): 257–288.

Sato, Barbara. *The New Japanese Woman: Modernity, Media, and Women in Interwar Japan*. Durham: Duke University Press, 2003.

Sato, Barbara. "Commodifying and Engendering Morality: Self-Cultivation and the Construction of the 'Ideal Woman' in 1920s Mass Women's Magazines." In *Gendering Modern Japanese History*, edited by Barbara Molony and Kathleen Uno, 99–132. Cambridge, MA: Harvard University Asia Center, 2005.

Schencking, J. Charles. *Making Waves: Politics, Propaganda, and the Emergence of the Imperial Japanese Navy, 1868–1912*. Stanford: Stanford University Press, 2005.

Scott, Gregory Adam Scott. "Finding Aid for Daikokumin Records." *The Burke Library Archives*. Columbia University Libraries, Union Theological Seminary, New York, 2009, updated 2014. http://library.columbia.edu/content/dam/libraryweb/locations/burke/fa/mrl/ldpd_4492622.pdf

Scott, Jennifer. *The Royal Portrait: Image and Impact*. London: The Royal Collection Trust, 2010.

Screech, Timon. "Shōgun no zuzō o utsusu." Translated by Takayama Hiroshi. In *Edo no kirikuchi*, edited by Takayama Hiroshi, 259–273. Tokyo: Maruzen, 1994.

Screech, Timon. *The Shogun's Painted Culture: Fear and Creativity in the Japanese States, 1760–1829*. London: Reaktion, 2000.

Seagrave, Sterling and Peggy Seagrave. *The Yamato Dynasty: The Secret History of Japan's Imperial Family*. New York: Broadway Books, 1999.

Segi, Shinichi, ed. *Tsukioka Yoshitoshi gashū*. Tokyo: Kōdansha, 1978.

Seigle, Cecilia Segawa and Linda H. Chance. *Ōoku: The Secret World of the Shogun's Women*. Amherst, NY: Cambria Press, 2014.

Sekiguchi, Sumiko and Michael Burtscher. "Gender in the Meiji Renovation: Confucian 'Lessons for Women' and the Making of Modern Japan." *Social Science Japan Journal* 11, no. 2 (2008): 201–221.

Sensu, Tadashi. *Nishikie ga kataru tenno no sugata*. Tokyo: Yushikan, 2009.

Shillony, Ben-Ami. "'Restoration,' 'Emperor,' 'Diet,' 'Prefecture,' or: How Japanese Concepts Were Mistranslated into Western Languages." In *Ben-Ami Shillony—Collected Writings*. Abingdon: Routledge, 2004.

Shillony, Ben-Ami. *Enigma of the Emperors: Sacred Subservience in Japanese History*. Kent: Global Oriental, 2005.

Shillony, Ben-Ami. *The Emperors of Japan*. Leiden: Brill, 2008.

Shimamori, Michiko. *Kōkoku no naka no onnatachi*. Tokyo: Daiwa shobō, 1984.

Shimazono, Susumu. "State Shinto in the Lives of the People: The Establishment of Emperor Worship, Modern Nationalism, and Shrine Shinto in Late Meiji." *Japanese Journal of Religious Studies* 36, no. 1 (2009).

Shimazono, Susumu. *Kokka Shintō to Nihonjin*. Tokyo: Iwanami shoten, 2010.

Shin jinbutsu ōraisha. *Rekidai kōgō jinbustsu keifu sōran*. Tokyo: Shin jinbutsu ōraisha, 2002.

Shizume, Masato. "The Japanese Economy During the Interwar Period: Instability in the Financial System and the Impact of the World Depression." *Institute for Monetary and Economic Studies*, May 2009. www.boj.or.jp/en/research/wps_rev/rev_2009/data/rev09e02.pdf.

Shōken, Empress Consort of the Meiji Emperor of Japan. *Kenshō kōtaigō gyoka*. Tokyo: Meiji jingū shamusho, 1980.

Shufu no tomo. *Teimei kōgō*. Tokyo: Shufu no tomo, 1971.

Sievers, Sharon. *Flowers in Salt: The Beginnings of Feminist Consciousness in Modern Japan*. Stanford: Stanford University Press, 1983.

Silberman, Bernard S. "Conclusion: Taishō Japan and the Crisis of Secularism." In *Japan in Crisis: Essays on Taishō Democracy*, edited by Bernard S. Silberman and H.D. Harootunian, 411–426. Princeton: Princeton University Press, 1970.

Silverberg, Miriam. "The Modern Girl as Militant." In *Recreating Japanese Women, 1600–1945*, edited by Gail Lee Bernstein, 239–266. Berkeley: University of California Press, 1991.

Silverberg, Miriam. *Erotic, Grotesque Nonsense: The Mass Culture of Japanese Modern Times*. Berkeley: University of California Press, 2006.

Sin, Myung-ho. *Joseon Royal Court Culture: Ceremonial and Daily Life*. Translated by Timothy V. Atkinson. Gyeonggi-do: Dolbegae Publishers, 2004.

Skov, Lise and Brian Moeran. "Introduction: Hiding in the Light: From Oshin to Yoshimoto Banana." In *Women, Media and Consumption in Japan*, edited by Lise Skov and Brian Moeran, 1–74. Honolulu: University of Hawai'i Press, 1995.

Slade, Toby. *Japanese Fashion: A Cultural History*. Oxford: Berg Publishing, 2009.

Smith, Robert J. "Wedding and Funeral Ritual: Analyzing a Moving Target." In *Ceremony and Ritual in Japan: Religious Practices in an Industrialized Society*, edited by Jan van Bremen and D.P Martinez, n.p. New York: Routledge, 2005.

Sōseki, Natsume. *Kokoro*. Tokyo: Kadokawa, 1952.

Strasdin, Kate. *Inside the Royal Wardrobe: A Dress History of Queen Alexandra*. London: Bloomsbury Academic, 2017.

Suematsu, Kenchō. "Eikoku teishitsu shorei kansatsu hōkoku." no. 1, 1881. Shoryōbu, Imperial Household Agency, Tokyo.

Suzuki, Mamiko C. *Gendered Power: Educated Women of the Meiji Empress' Court*. Ann Arbor: University of Michigan Press, 2019.

Taishō tennō godaisōgi kiroku. Tokyo: Keishichō, 1928.

Taishō tennō goshashinchō. Tokyo: Taishō tennō goshashinchō kankōkai, 1927.

Taishō tennō gotaisō shashinchchō. Tokyo: Dai Nihon kokumin kyōikukai, 1927.

Takagi, Hiroshi. "The Buddhist Faith of the Japanese Imperial Family after the Meiji Restoration." *Japan Review*, no. 25 (2013): 21–32.

Takemura, Tamio. *Taishō bunka teikoku no yūtopia: sekaishi no tenkanki to taishū shōshakai no keisei*. Tokyo: Sangensha, 2010.

Taki, Kōji. *Tennō no shōzō*. Tokyo: Iwanami, 2002.

Tanaka, Stefan. *Japan's Orient: Rendering Pasts into History*. Berkeley: University of California Press, 1995.

Tanida, Etsuji. *Nihon fukushokushi*. Tokyo: Koseikan, 1989.

Tano, Yasunori and Kawada Akihisa. *Imēji no naka no sensō: Nisshin nichiro kara reisen made*. Tokyo: Iwanami shoten, 1996.

Taro, Sakamoto. *Nihon shoki*. Tokyo: Iwanami shoten, 1967.

Teeuwen, Mark and Fabio Rambelli. "Introduction: Combinatory Religion and the *honji-suijaku* Paradigm in Pre-Modern Japan." In *Buddhas and Kami in Japan: Honji Suijaku as a Combinatory Paradigm*, edited by Mark Teeuwen and Fabio Rambelli, 1–53. London: Routledge, 2003.

Teikoku gunjin kyōikukai. *Meiji Jingū oshashinchō: fu gozōeikiroku*. Tokyo: Teikoku gunjin kyōikukai shuppanbu, 1920.

Thernstrom, Amy McCreedy, ed. *Japanese Women: Lineage and Legacies*. Washington, DC: Woodrow Wilson International Center for Scholars, 2005.

Thompson, John B. *The Media and Modernity: A Social Theory of the Media*. Stanford: Stanford University Press, 1995.

Thompson, Sarah E. and H.D. Harootunian. *Undercurrents in the Floating World: Censorship and Japanese Prints*. New York: The Asia Society Galleries, 1991.

Titus, David Ansun. *Palace and Politics in Prewar Japan*. New York: Columbia University Press, 1974.

Tokuza, Akiko. *The Rise of the Feminist Movement in Japan*. Tokyo: Keio University Press, 1999.

Tokyo Kokuritsu Hakubutsukan. *Nihon no shōzōga*. Tokyo: Asahi Shinbun, 1991.

Tonomura, Hitomi. "Royal Roles, Wider Changes: Understanding Japan's Gender Relations from a Historical Perspective." In *Japanese Women: Lineage and Legacies*, edited by Amy McCreedy Thernstrom. Washington, DC: Woodrow Wilson International Center for Scholars, 2005.

Tōyama, Shigeki, ed. *Nihon kindai shisōshi taikei: Tennō to kazoku*. Tokyo: Iwanami shoten, 1988.

Tōyama, Shigeki, ed. *Tennō to kazoku, nihon kindai-shisō taikei*. Vol. 2. Tokyo: Iwanami, 1989.

Toyoda, Maho. "State, Sterilization, and Reproductive Rights: Japan as Occupier and Occupied." In *Japan as the Occupier and Occupied*, edited by Christine de Matos and Mark E. Caprio, 45–64. New York: Palgrave MacMillan, 2015.

Trede, Melanie. "Banknote Design as a Battlefield of Gender Politics and National Representation in Meiji Japan." In *Performing "Nation": Gender Politics in Literature, Theater, and the Visual Arts of China and Japan, 1880–1940*, edited by Doris Croissant, Catherine Vance Yeh and Joshua Mostow, 55–104. Leiden: Brill, 2008.

Tseng, Alice Y. "Imperial Portraiture and Popular Print Media in Early Twentieth Century Japan." *Journal of Japanese Studies* 46, no. 2 (2020).

Tsunoda, Ryusaku and L.C. Goodrich, eds. *Japan in the Chinese Dynastic Histories*. Pasadena: P.D. and Ione Perkins, 1951.

Tsuyoshi, Kaizuka, ed. *Egakareta Chaina doresu: Fujishima Takeji kara Umehara Ryūzaburō made: tēma tenji*. Tokyo: Bridgestone Museum of Art, 2014.

Ueda, Atsuko. *Concealment of Politics, Politics of Concealment: The Production of "Literature" in Meiji Japan*. Stanford: Stanford University Press, 2007.

Ueno, Chizuko. "In the Feminine Guise: A Trap of Reverse Orientalism." In *Contemporary Japanese Thought*, edited by Richard F. Calichman, 3–25. New York: Columbia University Press, 2005.

Uno, Kathleen. "Womanhood, War, and Empire: Transmutations of 'Good Wife, Wise Mother' before 1931." In *Gendering Modern Japanese History*, edited by Barbara Molony and

Kathleen Uno, 492–519. Cambridge, MA: Harvard University Asia Center, 2005.
Van Asche, Annie. "Japanese Kimono Fashion of the Early Twentieth Century." *Textile Society of America Symposium Proceedings*, Paper 799 (2000). http://digitalcommons.unl.edu/cgi/viewcontent.cgi?article=1800&context=tsaconf
Wakabayashi, Bob Tadashi. "In Name Only: Imperial Sovereignty in Early Modern Japan." *Journal of Japanese Studies* 17, no. 1 (Winter 1991): 25–57.
Wakakuwa, Midori. *Kōgō no shōzō: Shōken kōtaigō no kyōshō to josei no kokuminka*. Tokyo: Chikuma shobō, 2001.
Wakita, Haruko, Anne Bouchy and Ueno Chizuko, eds. *Gender and Japanese History: Religion and Customs/The Body and Sexuality*. Vol. 1. Osaka: Osaka University Press, 1999.
Walthall, Anne. "Hiding the Shoguns." In *The Culture of Secrecy in Japanese Religion*, edited by Bernhard Scheid and Mark Teeuwen, 331–356. New York: Routledge, 2006.
Walthall, Anne, ed. *Servants of the Dynasty: Palace Women in World History*. Berkeley: University of California Press, 2008.
Weisenfeld, Gennifer. *Imaging Disaster: Tokyo and the Visual Culture of Japan's Great Earthquake of 1923*. Berkeley: University of California Press, 2012.
Wilson, Sandra. "Enthroning Hirohito: Culture and Nation in 1920s Japan." *The Journal of Japanese Studies* 37, no. 2 (Summer 2011): 289–323.
Woodacre, Elena. "Understanding the Mechanisms of Monarchy." In *The Routledge History of Monarchy*, edited by Elena Woodacre, et al., 1–20. London: Routledge, 2019.
Woodacre, Elena. *Queens and Queenship*. Leeds: Arc Humanities Press, 2021.
Woodacre, Elena and Carey Fleiner, eds. *Royal Mothers and Their Ruling Children: Wielding Political Authority from Antiquity to the Early Modern Era*. New York: Palgrave Macmillan, 2015.
Woodacre, Elena and Cathleen Sarti. "What Is Royal Studies?" *Royal Studies Journal* 2 (2015): 13–20.
Wright, Harold. *Meiji as Composed in Elegant Verse: 100 Poems by Empress Shōken*. Tokyo: Chuo Koron Shinsha, 2024.
Yamada, Shunji. *Taishū shinbun ga tsukuru Meiji no "Nihon"*. Tokyo: Nihon hōsō shuppan kyōkai, 2002.
Yamamoto, Yōko. "Tennō o egaku koto o habakaru hyōgen no shūen." *Myōjyō daigaku kenkyū kiyō* 9 (2001): 21–35.

Yamato Bunkakan. *Nihon no shōzōga*. Nara: Yamato Bunkakan, 1991.

Yamazaki, Masukichi. "Shōken kōtaigo to Tomioka seishijo no ētosu." *Sangyō kenkyū* 47, no. 1 (2011): 27–44.

Yi, Jo-lan. "Gender and Sericulture Ritual Practice in Sixteenth-Century China." *Journal of Asian History* 48, no. 2 (2014): 281–302.

Yokohama bijutsukan. *Fuasshon to āto uruwashi tōzai kōryū*. Yokohama: Yokohama bijutsukan and Kyoto fukushoku bunka kenkyū zaidan, 2017.

Yomiuri Shinbun. "Jingū kōgō o dai 15dai on-rekidai ni kuwae." May 30, 1924.

Yomiuri Shinbun. "Taishō tennō jitsuroku no kuroneri ōhaba kaijo, menkaisha nado kōkai." June 30, 2015. Tokyo Morning Edition, 13.

Yoneda, Sayoko. "Hiratsuka Raichō's Idea of Society: Nature, Cooperation and Self-Government," Translated by Hiroko Tomida. In *Japanese Women: Emerging from Subservience, 1868–1945*, edited by Hiroko Tomida and Gordon Daniels. Kent: Global Oriental, 2005.

Yoshimi, Shunya. *Karuchuaru tān bunka no seijigaku e*. Kyoto: Jinbun shoin, 2003.

Yoshimoto, Hiroko. "Taishō shoki no shinbun ni miru kazoku shashin: *Yomiuri shinbun*, Tokyo *Asahi shinbun* o jirei toshite." *Matsuyama shinonome jyoshi daigaku jinbunkagaku bukiyo* 10 (2002–2003): 91–101.

Yutaka, Yokō. *Rekidai Tennō to Kōgōtachi*. Tokyo: Kashiwa Shobō, 1987.

INDEX

For Product Safety Concerns and Information please contact our EU representative GPSR@taylorandfrancis.com
Taylor & Francis Verlag GmbH, Kaufingerstraße 24, 80331 München, Germany

www.ingramcontent.com/pod-product-compliance
Ingram Content Group UK Ltd.
Pitfield, Milton Keynes, MK11 3LW, UK
UKHW020039090825
461685UK00018B/1044
9781032452371